AFTER CUSTER

Also by Paul L. Hedren

First Scalp for Custer: The Skirmish at Warbonnet Creek, Nebraska, July 17, 1876 (Glendale, 1980)

With Crook in the Black Hills: Stanley J. Morrow's 1876 Photographic Legacy (Boulder, 1985)

Fort Laramie in 1876: Chronicle of a Frontier Post at War (Lincoln, 1988)

(ed.) *The Great Sioux War 1876–77: The Best from* Montana The Magazine of Western History (Helena, 1991)

(ed.) *Campaigning With King: Charles King, Chronicler of the Old Army* (Lincoln, 1991)

Traveler's Guide to the Great Sioux War: The Battlefields, Forts, and Related Sites of America's Greatest Indian War (Helena, 1996)

We Trailed the Sioux: Enlisted Men Speak on Custer, Crook, and the Great Sioux War (Mechanicsburg, 2003)

Great Sioux War Orders of Battle: How the United States Army Waged War on the Northern Plains, 1876–1877 (Norman, 2011)

AFTER CUSTER

LOSS AND TRANSFORMATION IN SIOUX COUNTRY

Paul L. Hedren

University of Oklahoma Press : Norman

Library of Congress Cataloging-in-Publication Data

Hedren, Paul L.
  After Custer : loss and transformation in Sioux country / Paul L. Hedren
    p.   cm.
  Includes bibliographical references and index.
  ISBN 978-0-8061-4216-6 (hardcover : alk. paper)
    1. Dakota Indians—History—19th century. 2. Cheyenne Indians—History—
  19th century. 3. Dakota Indians—Wars, 1876—Influence. 4. Cheyenne
  Indians—Wars, 1876—Influence. 5. United States. Army. Cavalry—History—
  19th century. 6. United States. Army. Infantry—History—19th century. 7. Dakota
  Indians—Government relations. 8. Cheyenne Indians— Government relations.
  9. Great Plains—Historical geography. I. Title.
    E99.D1H44 2011
    978.004'975243—dc22

                                                                2011007486

The paper in this book meets the guidelines for permanence and durability of the Committee on Production Guidelines for Book Longevity of the Council on Library Resources, Inc.∞

1 2 3 4 5 6 7 8 9 10

To my daughters, Ethne and Whitney,
who are grown now and married
but continue to make this father very proud

Contents

Maps

Preface

I began work on *After Custer: Loss and Transformation in Sioux Country* many years ago while still gainfully employed by the National Park Service. I had moved from North Dakota to a small town in Nebraska and mostly devoted my time and energy to the needs of two new, politically charged Wild and Scenic River units assigned to the park service for management. It was serious business and left little time for research and writing Indian wars history, an avocational pursuit that I have enjoyed throughout my entire career. Early in this assignment, I developed a special interest in the historical geography of the Great Sioux War, spawned by the close exploration of the northern plains undertaken a few years earlier for my book *Traveler's Guide to the Great Sioux War*. I had been introduced to the precepts of historical geography by a fine old scholar in the Geography Department at Saint Cloud State College in Minnesota, where I graduated with a degree in geography in 1972. I could see that writing a Great Sioux War epilogue, a complex story grounded in the geography of the past and with an array of significant and nearly independent themes, was certain to be a long-term project. I felt gratified if I produced a single chapter each winter, and I often undertook other small writing projects instead.

When I retired in October 2007 after nearly thirty-seven years with the park service, I presumed that I would pick up the epilogue project and complete it. By then five chapters were finished, along with the research on what remained. A different project took hold, however, becoming the book *Great Sioux War Orders of Battle*. I thoroughly enjoyed the diversion and saw that effort through from start to finish. But the time had come to complete this particular writing project, lest my attention be diverted again.

The more I learned of the cultural and environmental history of the northern Great Plains in the late nineteenth century and of the Great Sioux War itself, the more I saw an intertwined and largely untold story. Some individual facets were reasonably well known but not necessarily swaddled in the context I imagined. In the spirited debate on the origins of this Sioux war in *Montana The Magazine of Western History* in 1961–62 and again in 1992, the esteemed scholars Mark Brown, Harry Anderson, and Robert Utley argued the war's roots. They focused on undergirding and precipitating issues, including treaty terms and violations, the opening of the Black Hills, the prospects of a northern transcontinental railroad, cattle on the Montana prairie, and final control of the Sioux people and the landscape they called home. Brown and Anderson advanced cases that one variable or another was more important. Utley argued that government policy and bureaucratic maneuvering were equally relevant.[1] In fact, as I saw it, every one of those points was pertinent. The Great Sioux War was all about entry into and gold in the Black Hills, firm control of the Lakotas and their homeland (especially as manifested in the 1868 Fort Laramie Treaty), completion of the Northern Pacific Railroad, and a great deal more. It mattered less in my estimation which variable was somehow weightiest, as espoused in the arguments. In thinking through that debate and in my own studies and travels, I came to appreciate all the more the interconnectedness of what Brown, Anderson, and Utley so energetically put forth. And I saw consequences.

The Great Sioux War in and of itself brought irreversible change to the northern plains. Foremost, the Sioux Country of old no longer existed, except in a largely imaginary and emotional sense. And the war indeed provided unfettered access to an irresistible and undeniably valuable quarter of the American West. With access, the Northern Pacific Railroad finally extended itself through Sioux Country to a completion in western Montana in 1883. With access and that railroad, hide hunters took aim at the millions of buffalo still roaming the newly wrested countryside. And with access and a prairie without buffalo, cattle ranchers filled Sioux Country—or, in their lingo, portions of the Open Range—to a state of overflowing.

For the protagonists of the Great Sioux War, I saw different consequences. For the Lakotas and Northern Cheyennes, their surrenders at the agencies following eighteen months of vicious warfare (whether in 1877, 1880, or 1881) proved merely to be the next step, albeit a monstrous one, on a long and excruciating road that led to devastations of another sort and for some provided even more stress and calamity than they had already suffered in the war itself. The victors were faced with a different array of challenges, including maintaining hard-fought gains and providing security for those railroaders, hide hunters, and cattlemen. And certainly both sides had to contend with the figurative and sometimes literal price paid in waging this war, measured not just in blood but in the stigmas of war that emerged almost from the start.

I have attempted to tell all this and more in *After Custer: Loss and Transformation in Sioux Country*. At its most basic, this book is a historical geography of the northern Great Plains—Sioux Country—and the story of the consequences of one climactic Indian war in 1876–77 that set the stage for all that came next in the late 1870s and 1880s. I have attempted to expose the interconnectedness of it all: a war, the generals who came west in 1877 to bask in the accomplishments of their army, the forts they built to lock up a countryside and people, a new transcontinental railroad, the demise of the massive northern buffalo herd, the saga of the dynamic Beef Bonanza, the tribulations of the Lakotas and Northern Cheyennes, and the army's substantial effort at memorialization. I have attempted to write good narrative history, drawing from an abundance of pertinent primary sources on the conflict and its associated and subordinate themes. Where possible I have interjected the voices of those who were there and witnessed firsthand events such as burying George Armstrong Custer, building a railroad, or taking a good stand downwind of hundreds of buffalo, because the vibrancy and pathos of those observations is sometimes astounding.

I have also taken complete advantage of an ever-expanding body of secondary source material on this remarkable war and its trailing themes. For instance, I have unhesitatingly drawn from new works on the Little Big Horn Battle and its aftermath, critical campaign studies and administrative histories, northern borderlands histories, the story of the Lakota Ghost Dance, and a spate of exceptional new biographies, especially of important Indian leaders. The sophistication of this scholarship deserves nothing but the highest praise and belies the notion held in some quarters that this history already has been told well enough.

Several historians have developed the case that what occurred in Sioux Country in the late nineteenth century was patently American colonialism or empire-building: the expansion of the United States through conquest, displacement, and domineering rule. This premise has some merit. The nation's external boundaries were established in an earlier day, but many of those lands within the defined bounds had not been filled. The process of in-filling or settling largely occurred hand in hand with the westward movement that had characterized American history from the eighteenth century onward. But the premise of colonialism, like that of Manifest Destiny, is dynamic and value laden and perhaps suggests greater overt premeditation than existed, as opposed to the consequences of happenstance. In *After Custer* I have worked to acknowledge change without espousing any particular ideology.[2]

In my writings, I do hold to a handful of biases. I call the great monarchs of the plains buffalo, not bison. Historians do not call elk and wolves *Cervus canadensis* and *Canis lupus* in their writings. The same, I say, should hold for buffalo. I dislike the spelling "Bighorn" because the greater and lesser rivers, the range of mountains, and the Montana battlefield were all historically named "Big Horn." I use "Custer's Battlefield" and "Custer Battlefield" often and with ease, because that is what the place was called in the decades following the battle. And I use "Little Bighorn Battlefield" with equal ease in context, because this place has come to represent a great deal more in our time. I avoid the use of brevet ranks in introducing and discussing army officers. The army's brevet system was a noteworthy form of recognition but meant little in the actual day-to-day functioning of the Indian-fighting army and has no place in modern-day scholarship.

Acknowledgments

As always, a host of friends and individuals provided help, access to source material, and insight as I undertook, momentarily put aside, and returned again to the "epilogue project." My warmest thanks to Riva Dean, Arizona Historical Society; Jack Lepley, Fort Benton, Montana; Scott Forsyth, National Archives, Chicago; Rick Collin, State Historical Society of North Dakota, Bismarck; Sandra Lowry, Fort Laramie National Historic Site; John Lubetkin, McLean, Virginia; Pam Beckstrom and Christy Goll, Montana Historical Society, Helena; Jack McDermott, Rapid City, South Dakota; Debbie Vandenberg, Havre, Montana; Michael Tate, University of Nebraska at Omaha; James Brust, San Pedro, California; John Doerner, Little Bighorn Battlefield National Monument; Randy Kane, Williston, North Dakota; George Kush, Monarch, Alberta; and Marc Abrams, Brooklyn, New York.

Some friends simply watched and encouraged this project through the years. I recall many kind words from Laurie Wise and Tim Herchenroether, now of Yankton, South Dakota; and Marv and Joyce Kaiser, of Prescott, Arizona. Marv is an especially faithful booster: he has avidly followed my work for many years, acquired my books, and actually read them but often reminded me that what he really wanted to read was the "epilogue book." Marv, I hope you are not disappointed.

I owe Robert M. Utley of Scottsdale, Arizona, warm thanks for allowing me to use two maps from his book *The Indian Frontier of the American West, 1846–1890*, and for his continued encouragement of my work.

Along the way, I unblushingly pestered friends to read portions or all of this work in manuscript form and am exceedingly grateful to Willy Dobak, Gaithersburg, Maryland, who sharpened my understanding of buffalo on the northern plains; and Tom Buecker, Fort Robinson Museum, Crawford, Nebraska; Jerry Greene, Arvada, Colorado; Doug McChristian, Tucson, Arizona; and Eli Paul, Kansas City, Missouri, who chased details and offered constructive criticism and continued encouragement throughout the course of the project.

My friends at the University of Oklahoma Press deserve special recognition as well. Charles "Chuck" Rankin, associate director and editor-in-chief, read several chapters early on and kept telling me: "Give me more." His continued support and sage counsel over the years were always appreciated. The ever genial Alice Stanton, special projects editor at the Press, kept the manuscript on a timely schedule, conceded to several special requests (the important ones), and stood firm on certain matters of style, much to the manuscript's betterment. And my copy editor, Kathy Burford Lewis, demonstrated again her extraordinary wordsmithing gift while always respecting the language of military history and such verve as this author could muster. I very much enjoyed working with her.

Thank you all very much.

I most want to acknowledge my wife, Connie, the tolerant one in our house and a most excellent traveler who only rarely cringed when I laid on the next version of "I need to see the Stronghold, and that trail, again, dear."

AFTER CUSTER

1

A Good Year to Die?

Custer was dead, and Crazy Horse, Sitting Bull, and Morning Star were desperate. In the six months after Sioux and Northern Cheyenne warriors unleashed devastation on the Seventh Cavalry in the Battle of the Little Big Horn, the army's senior department and field commanders, guided by Lieutenant General Philip Henry Sheridan, resolutely poured fresh troops and limitless war matériel onto the northern plains and irreversibly altered the course of the Great Sioux War. From Tongue River Cantonment (located where the Tongue and Yellowstone rivers join in southeastern Montana), Colonel Nelson A. Miles led his Fifth Infantry against a succession of Indian bands still residing in that untrammeled, buffalo-rich locale; never once did that fiercely determined, veteran campaigner allow his foe to recuperate or resupply. Similarly, in late November 1876 Colonel Ranald S. Mackenzie led cavalry troops in the horrible destruction of a Northern Cheyenne village located in the southern Big Horn Mountains. As the nation's centennial year closed, he reunited with Brigadier General George Crook's sizable, well-outfitted column and scoured the Powder River countryside for others.

What began for the United States Army nearly a year earlier as a simply imagined, three-pronged campaign (focused on the Yellowstone and Powder River countryside and aimed at forcing

3

scattered, independent Sioux bands back to their assigned agencies on the Great Sioux Reservation) had opened ominously. Fearsome late winter weather hindered the initial movements of columns from western Montana, Wyoming, and Dakota, and the army had not yet reckoned with the elusiveness and resolve of its foe. The first significant engagement of this Sioux War occurred on March 17, 1876, when six companies of cavalry led by Colonel Joseph J. Reynolds were defeated by Old Bear's Cheyennes on the Powder River, just north of the Wyoming line. Reynolds commanded a superior force but chanced onto warriors who were fighting to protect families and homes. At month's end the so-called Big Horn Expedition, of which Reynolds's movement was a part, returned in failure to Fort Fetterman, Wyoming, and disbanded. Crook returned to the field a second time in May, leading a significantly enlarged column now christened the Big Horn and Yellowstone Expedition. By then Colonel John Gibbon was inching a small column of infantry and cavalry east along the Yellowstone River from posts in western Montana, and Brigadier General Alfred H. Terry and Lieutenant Colonel George A. Custer led nearly one thousand combatants, including all twelve companies of the heralded Seventh Cavalry, west from Fort Abraham Lincoln on the Missouri River in northern Dakota. By early June the segments of Sheridan's straightforward campaign were finally in place, with troops presumably positioned to drive increasingly headstrong tribesmen eastward into government control.

But still nothing went right for Sheridan's Army. Crook personally led troops in the Battle of Rosebud Creek, Montana, on June 17, in what proved to be the war's largest engagement. In a bucolic setting in the midst of the Wolf Mountains—ironically, the landscapes of the Great Sioux War were all bucolic—soldiers clashed with nearly one thousand Sioux and Cheyenne warriors in an encounter filled with fierce thrusts and parries on a battlefield of sweeping proportions. At battle's end, Crook held the vast Rosebud field and rightly claimed victory. But the notion of merely holding ground was meaningless to his foe, who also claimed victory at Rosebud Creek: the Sioux and Cheyenne had lost few combatants and their village, located some twenty miles away on a tributary of the Little Big Horn River, remained secure. In any case, Crook's unceremonious withdrawal to his staging area in northern Wyoming signaled the battle's true victors and intensified the warriors' resolve and sense of invincibility against these soldiers and the other troops maneuvering against them.

Eight days later, Custer's attack on an enlarged village now located on the Little Big Horn some eighteen miles above its confluence with the Big Horn River completely surprised the inhabitants. But the outcome was far less uncertain than at Rosebud. The Indian encampment had swelled substantially by then as agency Indians (summer roamers as they were known to the agents and army) joined fellow tribesmen to hunt and—this season—fight. The villagers' resolve was powerful too, strengthened by their phenomenal numbers. Moreover, their great prophet Sitting Bull had prophesied this success. Already these roamers had twice defeated soldiers coming from the south; while not unaware of troop movements north along the Yellowstone, they felt no particular threat from that quarter. For the flamboyant and self-assured Custer, the element of surprise at Little Big Horn was his sole earthly reward on June 25: his defeat was swift, sure, and, for the U.S. Army and nation, utterly imponderable.

Ever since that time Custer's actions preceding and during the Little Big Horn battle have been scrutinized exhaustively, and faults loom large. Custer refused Terry's proffered four-company Second Cavalry battalion and pair of Gatling guns. He divided his twelve companies into small, widely separated battalions well before learning of the size and specific position of his opponent, and many in his officer corps abandoned him. But reversing any or all of these considerations might have mattered little on that hot June Sunday. Almost assuredly, a cavalry force twice the size of Custer's led by any other of Sheridan's pet commanders would have fared just as poorly against this momentarily invincible league of Sioux and Northern Cheyenne warriors.

But the extraordinary Indian coalition at Little Big Horn was a fleeting phenomenon that unraveled almost immediately after the final shots were fired on Custer's doomed battalion. The sheer numbers of people and animals in that Indian village exhausted immediate sources of game, wood, and grass and obliged them to move or separate. More importantly, the Seventh Cavalry's survivors, well entrenched on a high bank overlooking the Little Big Horn River and dust clouds on the distant northern horizon foreshadowing Terry's and Gibbon's approaching infantry and cavalry, threatened a resumption of the battle and perhaps a different outcome. Late on the afternoon of June 26 the villagers disbanded and fled upstream.

The victorious Sioux and Cheyenne tribesmen as well as the U.S. Army and federal government were unaware that the Indians' fate, visible only through a historian's crystal-perfect lens, had been sealed the very moment they abandoned the Little Big Horn village. Their resolve and sheer numbers had affirmed their invincibility against the soldiers in the opening engagements of this profound war, but the glory-filled season waned. Midsummer was the time to hunt buffalo and prepare for the inevitable winter, not wage a continuous and increasingly costly war. This season soldiers hounded the splintered bands relentlessly: when Crook's, Terry's, and Gibbon's summer troops wearied, on came reinforcements led by Wesley Merritt, Mackenzie, Elwell Otis, and Miles. Each commanded fresh cavalry, infantry, and even regular dismounted artillery, all well supplied and fiercely determined to avenge Custer's death and enforce the government's will. Crazy Horse, Sitting Bull, Gall, Morning Star, and the others knew no such luxuries as reinforcement and resupply and instead faced the ominous alternatives of submission at an agency, flight to Canada, or death on a battlefield.[1]

The Indian war of 1876–77 was known from the earliest times as the Great Sioux War, a descriptive name harmonious with other contemporary references such as Great Sioux Nation and Great Sioux Reservation. Historians and others quickly embraced the name and used it to distinguish this Indian war from other conflicts with the Sioux occurring along the North Platte River in the 1850s and 1860s, in Minnesota and Dakota in 1862 and 1863, along the Bozeman Trail in Wyoming and Montana in the middle and late 1860s, and associated with the Ghost Dance in 1890.[2] Like other American Indian wars, this one had its root in the possession and development of tribal land by an ever-expanding American culture. But this time the contest was not confined to the outer margins of what was recognized as Sioux Country, as in most of the other conflicts; instead it was waged to attain irrefutable control of the entire vast Sioux homeland that spanned the northern Great Plains. Moreover, this war was aimed at firm control over the Sioux people on their designated reservation.

For most Americans, the vastness and unsettled nature of Sioux Country remained an unfamiliar phenomenon in the mid-1870s. The occurrence of conflict there during the nation's centennial year spoke more to the helter-skelter nature of American settlement in the West than to any initial government wish to control these particular Indians and that landscape, at least until it became a crisis. Settlement interests west of the Missouri River always had been focused elsewhere—agriculturally rich Oregon, the religious haven in the Great Basin, and the gold country of California and then Colorado. The roads feeding those destinations had only skirted Sioux Country. When gold was discovered in Montana in 1862, the Bozeman Trail sliced through the western margins of Sioux Country. Red Cloud and his followers fought a vicious war and successfully closed the road, however, and forced the abandonment of its three army garrisons. But after 1869 Montana-bound argonauts had access to the Union Pacific and Central Pacific railroads to Corinne, Utah, and the Montana Trail north from Corinne to the goldfields. The Bozeman Trail had been rendered unnecessary.[3]

Into the 1870s much of the landscape lying north of the overland trails and between the Missouri River and western mountains was not particularly well known to whites or coveted by them. Government surveying expeditions had crossed these northern plains from time to time, and fur-trading companies encamped on its margins had captured a hearty business from its core. But this vast untrammeled prairie was recognized by one and all as Sioux Country, home of the Teton or Lakota Sioux Indians and not open to invasion. The seven distinct Teton bands—Oglala, Brulé, Two Kettle, Miniconjou, Sans Arc, Blackfeet, and Hunkpapa—numbered some 15,500 people in the 1870s. These Indians were relative newcomers to this particular landscape too, having captured it from other tribes late in the preceding century. Friends of the Lakotas like the Northern Cheyennes and Arapahos also resided there. Interlopers like the Crows, Assiniboines, Shoshones, Crees, and Arikaras, the possessors of these plains in earlier times, still invaded from the margins, especially to hunt buffalo.[4]

From the 1850s onward, the respective Teton bands were generally recognized as occupying discrete subsections of Sioux Country. These traditional or favored homelands later figured in the allotment of agencies according to the Fort Laramie Treaty of 1868 and later still in the proceedings of the Great Sioux War. The middle Missouri River region of today's western South Dakota, for instance, was recognized as the homeland of the Two Kettle Sioux, while the Hunkpapa and Blackfeet Sioux lived farther north in the Upper Missouri country of today's western North Dakota and eastern Montana. The Miniconjou Sioux generally resided north and east of the Black Hills, and the Sans Arcs customarily inhabited lands west and southwest of the Black Hills in today's eastern Wyoming. The North Platte River basin of Wyoming and Nebraska was the favored homeland of the Oglalas, while the Brulés occupied the White River and Pine Ridge country of Nebraska and Dakota. Across this vast landscape, these preferred homelands had flexible, nearly imperceptible margins. As the Sioux met and conquered Indian enemies, their holdings continually expanded westward and northward.[5]

While band affiliation in Sioux society was a matter of birth, allegiances were flexible. An Oglala could live among and marry a Sans Arc; the Brulés freely hunted in the favored haunts of the Hunkpapas; and a young Miniconjou or Blackfeet man might share a common vista with a Cheyenne male during a vision quest atop Bear Butte. The Teton Sioux were united by language and tradition. People from the seven bands counseled together each summer, typically in June at a predetermined location: they renewed friendships, forged alliances, and conducted the sun dance ceremony. Nearly all the Tetons distrusted the whites; but into the 1860s they focused greater enmity on common enemies like the Crows, Assiniboines, and other tribes who challenged for their homeland and the rich hunting grounds.[6]

Perhaps the greatest difficulty confronting government commissioners charged with brokering the 1868 Fort Laramie Treaty (which brought closure to Red Cloud's Bozeman Trail War) lay in defining and imposing what was in effect a reimagined and severely diminished Sioux homeland. In accordance with the government's plan to gain greater control over the Sioux and eventually transform them from nomadic hunters into Christian farmers, the treaty proposed confining them to one-third, maybe barely one-quarter, of their former well-established territory. As prescribed in article 2, the new Great Sioux Reservation encompassed the southwestern quarter of the extant Dakota Territory or what is generally South Dakota west of the Missouri River today. Before this imposition, Sioux Country was substantially larger, spanning the entire western half of the Dakota Territory, all of eastern Montana and Wyoming, and all of central and western Nebraska.[7]

Government commissioners were also challenged when establishing agencies for the Sioux bands that accommodated preferred homelands and also provided for ease and efficiency of administration. The government preferred that the Sioux agencies be located somewhere along the Missouri River, where steamboats could transport annuities and stocks more economically than by overland trails. The treaty stipulated that a single central agency would serve the reservation. In reality, the government yielded to the preferential homelands and diverse character of the Sioux people, as evidenced by the eventual array of agencies established along the Missouri River and in western Nebraska.

Recognizing the continuing importance of buffalo hunting to the tribesmen, the Fort Laramie Treaty wisely conceded two vast landscapes for that select purpose. The Oglalas and Brulés living in western Nebraska and eastern Wyoming hunted south of their preferred homeland as often as they did north of it, so the treaty allowed the chase to continue in the Republican River country of southern Nebraska and northern Kansas as long as buffalo ranged there. Of course, these bands often looked to the Powder and Yellowstone River country for hunting opportunities, as did every other Sioux band and northern plains tribe. This was also conceded by the treaty for a Wyoming landscape generally bounded by the North Platte River to the south, the new reservation to the east, and the summits of the Big Horn Mountains to the west. The commissioners generally envisioned that the Sioux would only absent themselves from their agencies seasonally and no longer reside permanently in these hunting lands. The Nebraska hunting lands were given no specific name, but the treaty labeled the Wyoming tract the "unceded Indian territory." It was silent on whether the unceded territory stretched northward across the Yellowstone River into Montana's Big Open, a matter that was later contested. Clearly the Big Open, that great flat-iron shaped landscape bounded by the Musselshell, Yellowstone, and Missouri rivers, was as much a favorite haunt for Sitting Bull's and Gall's Hunkpapa followers as Nebraska's Pine Ridge and Republican River countryside was for Red Cloud's Oglalas and Spotted Tail's Brulés.[8]

The breadth and diversity of Sioux Country had other attributes as well. Viewing these northern Great Plains simply as a vast sea of grass perfect for sustaining immense buffalo herds hit the mark in general but missed the subtleties characterizing and enhancing its diverse subsections. While the lush, short- and mixed-grass prairies of western Nebraska and eastern and northeastern Wyoming certainly offered perfect grazing for large ungulates like deer, pronghorns, and buffalo, scattered topographic anomalies dramatically enriched the faunal diversity and other life-sustaining resources available to the Sioux and other tribes. The character of these northern Great Plains, as a topographic and ecological whole, both accommodated the Indians' nomadic and cyclic lifeways and had virtually dictated those cultural roots.

Nebraska's Pine Ridge illustrates the point. Best remembered for lending its name to today's vast Oglala Sioux reservation in southwestern South Dakota, the Pine Ridge is a sinewy, pine-timbered escarpment rising in eastern Wyoming's Hat Creek Breaks, stretching east through northwestern Nebraska and into South Dakota and across today's Pine Ridge Reservation. The escarpment's width varies from a mile or two in Wyoming to as many as twenty miles in Nebraska, and elevations change dramatically wherever the ridge is crossed. When coming to the Pine Ridge, Black Hills–bound prospectors and freighters traveling northward in 1875 and 1876, whether on the Sidney–Black Hills or Cheyenne–Black Hills roads, invariably noticed the long, treacherous descents over white chalky breaks. Southbound trips through the Pine Ridge were all the more arduous, becoming long, taxing pulls for stagecoaches and freight wagons.

For the Sioux, the Pine Ridge offered tantalizing hunting diversity with a wondrous array of fowl and mammals. This was comfortable country to live in, blending tall sheltering pines and hardwoods with open glades of luxuriant grasses, with plentiful water in seeps, springs, perennial creeks, and small rivers. The Fort Laramie Treaty commissioners conceded agencies near and eventually in the Pine Ridge country, which was recognized as the homeland of the Oglalas and Brulés. But they also established protectorate military garrisons, Camps Robinson and Sheridan. Both the agencies and the camps were located in northwestern Nebraska along the White River and were highly visible fixtures on the 1870s public stage.

In eastern Wyoming lay another geographic anomaly that helped frame Sioux Country. West of Fort Laramie and south of the North Platte River stretched the Laramie Mountains (a subsection of the Rocky Mountains), a gently curving, generally north-south running range. For Overland Trail pioneers, a glimpse of the 10,272-foot-tall Laramie Peak in the heart of the range was a dramatic first sighting of the long-anticipated Rockies. The Laramie Range was the pinery for the Fort Laramie garrison (located some fifty miles east) and for Fort Fetterman (located to the north). It was a favorite hunting ground of the Oglalas, Brulés, and Sans Arcs, on a mountainscape where prairie ungulates and game birds mixed with elk, black bear, and mountain lions.

The vast Wyoming prairie lying north of the North Platte River and east of the Big Horn Mountains was known as the Powder River Country to the 1870s campaigners and cattlemen who soon followed. The three principal forks of the Powder River and its main stem watered a vast expanse of Wyoming east of the Big Horns before the river exited north into Montana and eventually merged with the Yellowstone. The Powder was a reliable river fed by abundant melting snows from the Big Horns, notwithstanding the pioneer lament that it, like other plains streams, was a proverbial mile wide and inch deep. For the Sioux, the Powder provided a welcome summer haven. Large buffalo herds grazed in the region. Majestic cottonwood groves along the Powder's winding banks checked the summer's intense heat and provided good camping. The Montana-bound Bozeman Trail bisected the Powder River Country in the 1860s, and the ferocity of Red Cloud's War is testimony in part to its favor among all the Sioux people.

North of the Montana border Wyoming's prairies transformed into pinched valleys and divides marking the courses of a half-dozen parallel streams flowing north to the Yellowstone. The Big Horn, Little Big Horn, Tongue, and Powder rivers gained their waters from the Big Horn Mountains, while the Rosebud, Pumpkin, Little Powder, and O'Fallon were fed by groundwater and seasonal moisture. The valleys also featured good grazing and sheltering belts of cotton-woods but were unlike the rolling Wyoming prairies. The divides between these Montana streams were high and typically pine studded, and the landscape overall was much more irregular and broken. Game was richly abundant here too, but the disjointed character of the landscape afforded rather substantial protection. Views of the valley floors from the heights at the divides were rare, and the lateral vistas in the valleys hardly ever extended beyond the next bend in the river. Because of the abundance of game, the greater distances from established military posts, and the heightened protection offered by these knurled landscapes, more Great Sioux War battles were fought in southeastern Montana than in any other sector of Sioux Country.

Even more remote was Montana's Big Open. Except for the Musselshell River that watered its western margins and the Yellow-stone and Missouri rivers to the south and north, this was hard country with limited water and hard grazing. Perhaps because of its perceived uninviting qualities and extreme remoteness, this was the last buffalo stronghold in America and a favored haunt of the Sioux, Crows, Assiniboines, and other tribes. The Hunkpapas in particular ranged the Big Open, having done so for generations and continuing to the very moment of capitulation.

Before the Great Sioux War, the nation's "civilizing" forces had barely touched eastern Montana. Fur traders had established Fort Union in 1828 near the confluence of the Yellowstone and Missouri rivers and occasionally dispatched seasonal trading caravans into the region, but the basin was never occupied permanently. A feeble incursion occurred in 1875 when businessmen from Bozeman established Fort Pease near the confluence of the Big Horn and Yellowstone rivers, hoping to capture trade with the Crow Indians and hunt wolves. But incessant harassment from the Sioux forced the closure of Fort Pease in February 1876; the enterprise was a decided failure. The army, meanwhile, established Fort Buford in 1866 near Fort Union. These soldiers had even less reason to venture into the buffalo country, focusing their primary effort instead on safeguarding Missouri River steamboat traffic bound for Fort Benton and the Montana goldfields.[9]

Similarly, until the early 1880s pioneers paid scant attention to the Little Missouri River country of today's western North Dakota, which was steadfast Hunkpapa homeland until the close of the war. Generally, the Little Missouri flowed northward, paralleling the North Dakota–Montana border, and carried seasonal and spring waters through a distinct, highly eroded landscape later characterized as a badlands. Yet that unique, harsh valley offered inviting cottonwoods, reliable grazing, and an amazing diversity of wildlife, including elk and buffalo.

East and south of the Little Missouri drainage rolled grasslands quite different from those of Wyoming and Nebraska, largely due to the landscape's openness and aridity. East-flowing rivers like the Heart, Cannonball, Grand, and Moreau were dependent on groundwater and precipitation and carried less reliable flows to the Missouri than other rivers in Sioux Country. These streams and valleys were not particularly well wooded until they neared the Missouri and as such were not especially desirable for long-term occupation. The Cheyenne River also coursed eastward to the Missouri but drained waters from the Black Hills and was similar to the Tongue and Powder rivers in Montana in terms of flow and cover. Several of the Sioux agencies authorized by the Fort Laramie Treaty were

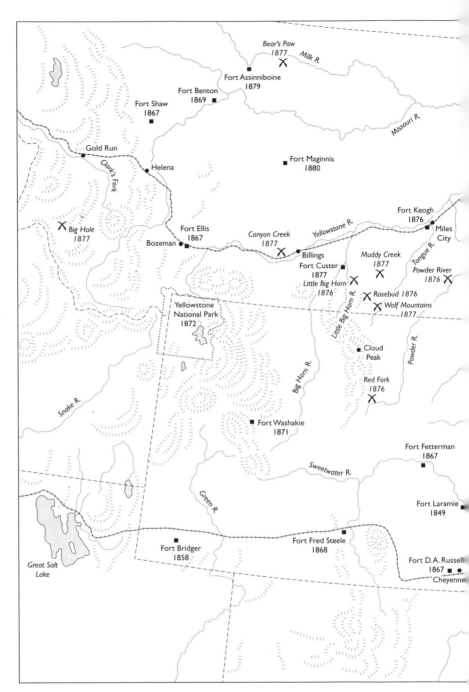

The Northern Plains, 1868–1890. Adapted from Robert M. Utley, *The Indian Frontier of the American West, 1846–1890* (Albuquerque: University of New Mexico Press, 1984), 152–53.

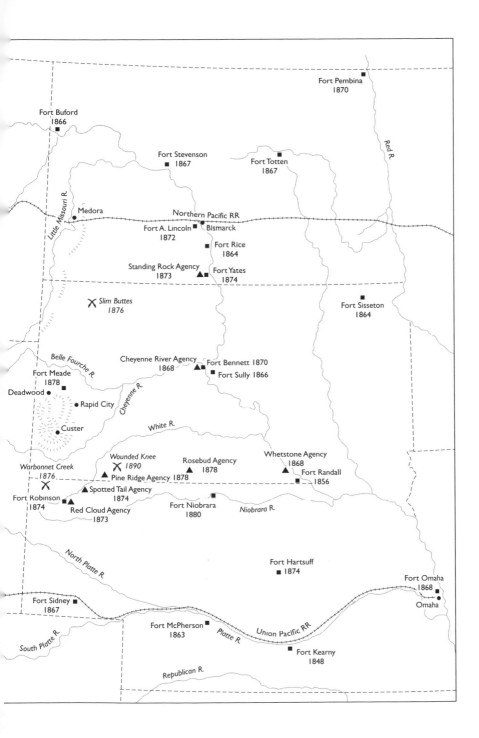

Fort Pembina
1870

Fort Buford
1866

Red R.

Fort Stevenson
■ 1867

Fort Totten
1867

Little Missouri R.

Medora

Northern Pacific RR

Fort A. Lincoln ■ Bismarck
1872

Fort Rice
1864

Standing Rock Agency
1873

Fort Yates
1874

Fort Sisseton
1864

✗ Slim Buttes
1876

Belle Fourche R.

Cheyenne River Agency
1868

Fort Bennett 1870

Fort Sully 1866

Fort Meade
1878

Deadwood ●

● Rapid City

Cheyenne R.

White R.

● Custer

Wounded Knee
✗ 1890

Rosebud Agency
▲ 1878

Whetstone Agency
1868

Warbonnet Creek
1876

▲ Pine Ridge Agency 1878

▲ Fort Randall
1856

✗

Fort Robinson
1874

▲ Spotted Tail Agency
1874

Fort Niobrara
1880

Niobrara R.

Red Cloud Agency
1873

North Platte R.

Fort Hartsuff
■ 1874

Fort Omaha
1868

Fort Sidney ■
1867

Omaha

South Platte R.

Fort McPherson
1863

Platte R.

Union Pacific RR

Fort Kearny
1848

Republican R.

located along the Missouri River on this eastern margin of Sioux Country, later called the West River Country by others. But for the tribesmen in the 1870s buffalo and other large ungulates were not particularly plentiful here. Moreover, army garrisons along the Missouri were menacingly close. For most, this was land to be crossed en route to Wyoming's and Montana's bountiful hunting and seclusion.

The Lakotas measured the material wealth of the vast Sioux Country in grass, freedom from interference from whites and other tribes, winter and summer protection from the cold and heat, and the richness of hunting. But comparisons of worth paled when the Black Hills were added to the mix. Lying in the southwestern quarter of Dakota Territory, lapping into northeastern Wyoming and within sight from Nebraska, the Black Hills then as now constituted *the* anomaly on the northern Great Plains. Elliptically shaped and spanning at their widest points some 125 miles north to south and 65 miles east to west, the Black Hills were a revered treasure to the Sioux, most other contemporary and earlier plains tribes, and eventually the whole of late nineteenth-century America.[10]

The natural history of the Black Hills is extraordinary. Embraced as a forested island in a grassland sea, the Black Hills are a mountainous uplift densely covered with pines and spruces and interspersed with fertile grassy valleys, laced throughout with reliable mountain water. The name "black" derives from the ponderosa pine forests, which appeared dark or black on the horizon as travelers approached from any direction. Black Hills elevations generally range from 3,000 to 4,000 feet above the surrounding plains, crowned by Harney Peak, reaching 7,242 feet above sea level. This peak is rightly heralded as the highest mountain between the American Rockies and European Alps, but it had company in the interior, where other peaks also topped 7,000 feet. In the main the Black Hills were very well watered by streams that ran cool and clear before miners arrived. The area also featured abundant wildlife of virtually every sort recorded on the northern plains, though by the mid-1870s buffalo and grizzly bear were rare there.[11]

Although the region was long thought to have been unoccupied in prehistory, modern-day archaeological surveys have discovered an incredibly rich and diverse prehistoric record dating to ten thousand years before the present. The Black Hills archaeological register speaks to both hunting and occupational episodes in prehistory and to a rich cultural fluorescence following the introduction of the horse and gun to the Plains tribes. Crows, Plains Apaches, Poncas, Comanches, Kiowas, Kiowa-Apaches, Arapahos, and Cheyennes lived and hunted in or near the Black Hills before being forced away by the powerful oncoming Sioux, beginning about 1770. By the turn of the nineteenth century the Sioux were well established across the Black Hills region and throughout the northern plains. They allied with Northern Cheyennes for mutual defense, moving with the seasons on a landscape that offered a richness of biotic diversity, seemingly limitless resources, and a unique spirituality.[12]

It was not the clean water, lofty Harney Peak, or the dense black pines that lured America's pioneering forces to the Black Hills in the mid-1870s but the widely heralded discoveries of gold there. Gold in the Black Hills had been the topic of campfire chatter well before Custer's Expedition confirmed its presence in 1874. As early as the 1840s, Catholic missionary Father Pierre-Jean De Smet supposedly counseled Indians to conceal gold that they were picking from the streams (or taking from errant miners). Some Indians evidently heeded De Smet's advice; but others, particularly in the 1860s and later, freely exchanged Black Hills placer gold for food-stuffs and trade goods at Fort Laramie and Fort Pierre. As miners scoured the Black Hills during the great boom they found abundant evidence of early prospecting, but no rush ensued in the 1850s or 1860s.[13]

Interest in the Black Hills and its golden riches was dramatically magnified by the nation's desperate economic plight in the early 1870s, even though the area had been included in the Great Sioux Reservation and thus, for all intents and purposes, excluded from white exploitation and settlement. Inflationary cycles following the Civil War brought on bankruptcies, bank failures, and a near-total national economic collapse in 1873, in a depression characterized as one of the most or the most devastating in American history. Unlike the situation in later decades, federal and state governments refused to provide relief, believing that the depression was a "natural process" that should run its course until all unsound economic activities were eliminated. Meanwhile, for unemployed and hungry Americans, no greater elixir existed than the prospects of riches in the next western El Dorado.[14]

With rumors of gold lingering in the Black Hills for decades and now a depression-driven clamor to exploit any potential, Sheridan ordered a scientific exploration to survey the mineral wealth of the region and determine a location for a new military post. Sherman and Sheridan believed that such a post would surely be needed to buffer eventual mining communities from the Sioux, if gold was discovered in paying quantities. Contrary to assertions by later apologists, government surveys of the sort were permitted under article 11 of the Fort Laramie Treaty.

At Sheridan's direction, Custer led an expedition from Fort Abraham Lincoln, Dakota Territory, to the Black Hills in 1874. Practical miners in his group indeed found evidence of gold common enough to create quite a stir. Custer's miners never fully measured its worth, however, and news reports dispatched from the expedition were vague and conflicting. Gold was seemingly downplayed in favor of the agricultural attributes of the Black Hills, which were themselves considerable. But Americans fixated on gold, not farming or timber. They commenced a great rush to the area in the fall of 1874, long before the consequences of treaty obligations had been fully considered by the administration of Ulysses S. Grant. Initially, President Grant's only recourse was to enforce the terms of the Fort Laramie Treaty. That fall and winter he ordered troops from Wyoming, Nebraska, and Dakota to intercept invading miners and escort them from the diggings. This was fruitless labor, and Grant eventually acquiesced to the invasion pressure. Perhaps instead, he reasoned, the Black Hills could be purchased from the Sioux.[15]

In hindsight, the frustrating haggling with Sioux leaders in the summer of 1875 in the government's attempt to purchase the Black Hills seems strikingly reminiscent of Fort Laramie Treaty negotiations in 1868. But this time the commissioner's overtures were rebuffed repeatedly, despite the willingness of some Indian leaders to agree to the sale if a price could be determined. Negotiations failed, however, and Grant and his generals next reasoned that the government's will should be achieved by force. Thus dawned the Great Sioux War of 1876–77.

The desire to exploit Black Hills gold was not the sole justification for the launch of this extraordinary Indian war. Though the Yellowstone River country of eastern Montana was as yet uninhabited by whites, railroad surveying parties had penetrated the region in 1871, 1872, and 1873, plotting a rail connection linking Bismarck, Dakota, with Bozeman, Montana, and points beyond. The surveyors met fierce Sioux resistance each summer, as did occasional civilian traders like those who established Fort Pease. The traders' lack of safe access to eastern Montana to engage peaceful Indians like the Crows was especially irritating to western Montanans, who clamored loudly through political channels and in their newspapers for military intervention and protection. Those cries were heard by the Grant administration. The "Sioux Problem," as the collective situation came to be labeled, was thus rooted in Black Hills gold, the advance of the Northern Pacific Railroad, and the government's desire to gain permanent control of the Sioux people and all of Sioux Country.

Ultimately, the options open to the Lakotas and Northern Cheyennes at war's end spoke to the resolve of Sheridan's Army to finish the Great Sioux War on endless battlefields if it could not attain acquiescence by the tribesmen at the various agencies. Each adult Indian faced this unthinkable individual choice. At best, counsel from tribal leaders was mixed. Reconciled chiefs like Red Cloud and Spotted Tail offered pragmatic views. Although Red Cloud had masterminded the Bozeman Trail War a decade earlier, he had visited the East several times since then and knew well of America's burgeoning population and industrial energy. He counseled now that the old world could not be restored and that the time had come to accept change. Red Cloud's message was accepted by many Sioux. By the spring of 1877, after nearly a year of fighting, hundreds of Indians reported to the agencies, some drifting in quietly and simply appearing at the next census or ration call and others surrendering with great pageantry.

Camp Robinson, Nebraska, adjacent to the Red Cloud Agency (the largest of those servicing the Sioux), bore the brunt of the submissions. In March and April 1877 numerous bands of one hundred or two hundred people each relinquished firearms and horses and were duly counted by the agents. One of the largest early surrenders at Red Cloud occurred on April 21 when Morning Star and Standing Elk led more than five hundred Northern Cheyenne followers into the agency. Other Cheyennes led by Dirty Moccasins, Little Wolf, and Old Bear followed. These erstwhile Sioux allies were particularly destitute, because their winter camp and provisions had been destroyed by Mackenzie's troops in the fierce late November fight on the Red Fork of the Powder River.[16]

The nearby Spotted Tail Agency witnessed significant surrenders as well, including the arrival of some one thousand Sioux on April 14: Miniconjous under Touch the Clouds and Roman Nose and Sans Arcs under Red Bear and High Bear. The casual manner in which the Indians allied with these agencies speaks more to the nature of friendships and kin allegiances in Indian society than to any comprehension of preordained governmental order or desire. While this probably startled some observers, it was perfectly natural for Cheyennes to submit at the Oglala agency (their agency home thus far in accordance with the Fort Laramie Treaty) and Miniconjous and Sans Arcs to appear at the Brulé agency. Assignments and accountability would be straightened out later, much to the surprise and anger of some Indians.[17]

Along the Yellowstone, meanwhile, Colonel Miles orchestrated several significant surrenders at his Tongue River Cantonment. Emissaries from his outpost had established regular contact with Crazy Horse's followers and Morning Star's Cheyennes following a rugged winter battle in the Wolf Mountains on January 8. Most of the Cheyennes preferred to surrender at Red Cloud Agency, but the followers of Two Moon, Crazy Head, and Old Wolf were convinced that they would receive fairer treatment from Miles. In March and April they trickled in and relinquished weapons and ponies to him. So too did Hump and many Miniconjou Sioux followers on April 20.[18]

Despite these notable surrenders, by mid-spring thousands of Sioux were still unaccounted for. The submission of Crazy Horse in particular and hundreds of his followers became the object of considerable government effort. In the late winter both Spotted Tail and Red Cloud personally visited Crazy Horse's camp to persuade him to surrender. These visits netted the return of other Indians, but not Crazy Horse or his immediate followers. Continued intercession by Miles's emissaries on the Yellowstone and Crook's agents from Nebraska eventually broke Crazy Horse's resolve, however, and on May 6 he, Little Big Man, and He Dog led 889 men, women, and children into Red Cloud Agency. This surrender was the most distinguished of them all. The tribesmen were bedecked in their best finery, and their entrance procession stretched for more than two miles. These Oglalas relinquished some 2,200 horses and dozens of firearms. In the eyes of many, Crazy Horse's surrender marked the end of the Great Sioux War. But that was not exactly the case.[19]

Sitting Bull had counseled with Crazy Horse after the Wolf Mountains battle on January 8. The Hunkpapas did not participate in that fight but, like the Oglalas and Cheyennes, were wearying of the continuing war. Sitting Bull found his followers badly divided on the issue of war or peace, and many in the camps had come to favor the overtures of the peace faction. Sitting Bull argued for the war faction but knew that sustaining a successful resistance was growing increasingly impossible. Finding buffalo to nourish their families was challenge enough without the even greater trial of having to elude the soldiers. Sitting Bull's Hunkpapas had spent much of the winter in the Big Open, although some, he announced, were already bound for Canada. He did indeed urge that Canada should be the destination in the Oglala camp, but he was speaking mostly to Pine Ridge people whose kin and territorial allegiances were in the southernmost reaches of Sioux Country. Sitting Bull, in contrast, knew much about Canada, because it bordered the traditional Hunkpapa homeland. Through the years he had crossed the great Medicine Line often to hunt and engage with British traders.[20]

Sitting Bull's eventual flight to Canada was more a casual meander than a straight, harried run. He and his Hunkpapas spent most of March in the Big Open, hunting buffalo and eluding soldiers scouting from the Yellowstone or ranging from the army garrison at Fort Peck, the Assiniboine Indian agency on the Missouri. The growing flight of American Sioux across the international border into Canada, however, astounded Canadian agents as numbers grew from dozens to hundreds to thousands. Black Moon and fifty-four Hunkpapa lodges were among the first, having crossed the boundary to Wood Mountain in the North-West Territories as early as December 1876. By March several thousand Indians from all the Sioux bands in the United States were counted in Canada, and the number grew steadily. Sitting Bull and his followers lingered in the Big Open and along the Missouri until the first week of May 1877, when they too finally crossed the Medicine Line. The patriarchal warrior knew that Miles could not pursue him there, but these Sioux also quickly came to realize that life in Canada was not a particularly restful solution.[21]

The last battle of the Great Sioux War was fought on May 7, 1877, on Muddy Creek, a small tributary of Rosebud Creek, in Montana. Ironically, this was the day after Crazy Horse's surrender at Camp Robinson and the same week when Sitting Bull appeared in Canada. The battle was commonly called the Lame Deer fight owing to the presence and leadership of the Miniconjou chief Lame Deer. The Indian camp contained his followers and many other small groups of disaffected Sioux and Northern Cheyennes who wanted to resist in the hunting country as long as possible. Miles knew of Lame Deer's presence within seventy miles of his Tongue River Cantonment but delayed a movement against him until he received fresh provisions and grain from the railhead at Bismarck by way of steamboats on the Missouri and Yellowstone. Once resupplied at the end of April, Miles moved with the same vigor and determination that had marked his campaigning the previous winter.[22]

In the fight Miles commanded some 470 men of the Fifth and Twenty-second Infantry and Second Cavalry. Lame Deer's village numbered 61 lodges, perhaps 488 people. As had often been the case during the Great Sioux War, except notably at the Little Big Horn, the troops approached the village under cover of darkness and attacked at daybreak while most of the occupants slept. The Indian pony herd was captured and driven off at the onset of the fight, and initial resistance was light.

As the villagers scrambled from their tipis, Lame Deer was spotted and hailed by one of Miles's interpreters. Hoping to gain

Lame Deer's surrender and end the fight, Miles approached him cautiously and evidently even shook his hand. It was quickly apparent, however, that the chief was not inclined to yield. Warriors hovered nervously around Lame Deer, and Miles was closely shielded by a throng of officers and Indian scouts. A tussle ensued between White Bull (a recently surrendered Cheyenne now scouting for Miles) and Iron Star (one of Lame Deer's lieutenants), and shots were fired. Lame Deer, having laid his Spencer carbine at his feet as he began talking with Miles, grabbed the weapon, leveled it at the colonel, and fired. Miles, who had not dismounted during this meeting, spurred his horse aside. Lame Deer's bullet narrowly missed Miles but struck his orderly, killing him instantly.[23]

Pandemonium erupted, and several soldiers shot at the chief. Lame Deer eluded fire for several hundred yards before being cut down by a rifle fusillade from one of the companies. As the fighting intensified, the campaign-hardened infantrymen laid down a withering fire that proved devastating to the tribesmen, who scrambled for protection on the steep hillsides west of Muddy Creek. By 9 A.M. the shooting ended. The troops counted fourteen Indian fatalities, including Lame Deer and Iron Star, and themselves sustained four killed and nine wounded. They captured 450 ponies and destroyed Lame Deer's village. The troops did not pursue the villagers, who scattered and eventually surrendered that summer and fall.[24]

As the springtime sun continued to warm Sioux Country and transform the prairie into a radiant green, the successes of Crook's fall campaign and Miles's dogged winter war became increasingly evident. Except for the Lame Deer battle, news of Sioux Indians in the region's and nation's newspapers centered on the dilemma of British agents in Canada who were forced to reckon with so many American Indians seeking haven there and the continuing surrenders and attendant bustle at the Sioux agencies. Sheridan, Crook, and Terry did not believe that the landscape had been swept permanently clean of the Sioux and knew that troops surely would again have to reckon with defections from the agencies, if only small groups pursuing a good hunt in the buffalo country. Across Sioux Country, Sheridan prepared for another season of war.[25]

Meanwhile, in the Black Hills region during the first months of 1877 troops from Camp Robinson repeatedly chased small bands of Indian raiders preying on livestock herds and hay cutters. The harassment was so annoying and occasionally deadly that in July Crook dispatched additional companies of the Third Cavalry from Fort Laramie and Camp Robinson to the countryside north of Deadwood to police the region more efficiently. Some of the trouble was blamed on survivors of Lame Deer's Miniconjous, who perhaps had chosen to revisit their old homeland before eventually surrendering at Spotted Tail Agency in September. Crook also recognized that some of the lawlessness in the northern Black Hills was the fault of non-Indian outlaws skulking in the region and was among the first to call for proper civil control in the mining communities.[26]

Elsewhere in his Department of the Platte, Crook dispatched five companies of Fifth Cavalry from Fort D. A. Russell at Cheyenne in late May to the Powder River Country. Since the previous November four infantry companies had been hutted on the Powder in an unpretentious outpost known as Cantonment Reno, named for nearby Fort Reno, the abandoned Bozeman Trail post. With smug satisfaction, the *Cheyenne Daily Leader* intoned that these infantry and cavalry troops would ensure that "the whole country along the base of the Big Horn Mountains would be kept clear of Indians."[27]

Similarly, in Terry's Department of Dakota, even larger numbers of troops flooded the Yellowstone Valley and points east and north. A command of infantry and cavalry from Miles's Tongue River Cantonment, for instance, scouted the Little Missouri countryside in June, partly to keep a watchful eye out for Indians venturing into the area and partly to assess the potential for a wagon road to the Black Hills. This command, led by Major Henry M. Lazelle of the First Infantry, chanced upon several recently deserted Indian villages, one evidently belonging to Lame Deer's survivors and another to Fast Bull's Northern Cheyennes. His scouts exchanged shots with a few of the Indians near Sentinel Butte, Dakota, on July 3, but the tribesmen escaped.[28]

A separate command of Second Cavalry and mounted Fifth Infantry led by Major James Brisbin of the Second Cavalry made a sweeping, largely uneventful scout eastward from the Yellowstone to the Little Missouri River. It united briefly with Lazelle's column, then trailed southwestward across the Little Powder and Powder rivers and into Wyoming before returning to the Tongue River Cantonment at the end of August. Miles, meanwhile, led a seventeen-company command of Seventh and Second Cavalry and mounted Fifth Infantry into the Big Open in July, partly to explore a countryside that he had otherwise only seen during its wintry worst and partly to interpose himself between remnants of the Lame Deer band and Sitting Bull's growing refugee alliance in Canada. Miles's sortie lasted only twelve days, however. The colonel learned that General Sherman was en route to Tongue River Cantonment and hurried to meet his commander's steamboat.[29]

The human and financial toll of the Great Sioux War was astounding. In December 1877 the Senate asked General Sherman for information on the costs of this lengthy war with the Sioux. Sherman reported that the army had spent $2,312,531 waging the war and that in twenty-two battles and skirmishes 16 officers and 267 enlisted men had been killed and 125 wounded. He did not estimate the toll among scouts and packers. More recent scholarship has refined those figures and now counts 16 officers killed and 7 wounded and 275 enlisted men, scouts, and packers killed and 133 wounded. Sherman did not estimate the human and cultural toll on the Sioux and Northern Cheyennes. The Senate had not asked for such details. Even today they are difficult to assess, but tallies derived from army battle reports and continuing scholarship on the matter suggest that some 162 Indians were killed and 236 wounded.[30]

The lapse of years has provided a much firmer understanding of the Indians' cultural devastation, however. In the attacks on the villages at Powder River, Slim Buttes, Cedar Creek, Red Fork of the Powder, and Muddy Creek Indian possessions were destroyed in toto, including daily apparel, utensils, and foodstuffs, prized personal and family belongings, and religious and cultural finery. In appraising the devastation in Morning Star's village on November 26, 1876, alone, one historian concluded that Northern Cheyenne material culture never again reached the heights of richness and splendor that the people knew before that bitter day in the Big Horns.[31] But more importantly to some and central to the administration's very objectives in waging the Great Sioux War, Sioux Country had changed hands. Sheridan and Sherman were coming west to inspect this freshly claimed if costly and blood-soaked landscape. For both Indians and whites, a new day had arrived on the northern plains.

2

SHERIDAN AND SHERMAN EXPLORE SIOUX COUNTRY

As commander of the army's Military Division of the Missouri, an administrative region spanning the nation's heartland and all of Sioux Country, forty-six-year-old Philip Henry Sheridan was a pugnacious, hands-on chief who delighted in shaping virtually every critical decision affecting his realm. During the long course of the Great Sioux War, Sheridan participated in the private but decisive White House conference on November 3, 1875, where President Grant chose to open the Black Hills to mining interests and unleash the army to resolve the so-called Sioux Problem. Sheridan frequently orchestrated strategy sessions with his senior department and field commanders tasked with waging this Indian war and systematically deployed troops from the farthest reaches of the Division of the Missouri and beyond to support the campaign. Twice at critical stages of the war, Sheridan traveled from his headquarters in Chicago to Sioux Country: in June to investigate matters at Fort Laramie, Camp Robinson, and Red Cloud Agency; and in September to Fort Laramie to confer with Crook and Mackenzie on matters related to the closure of Crook's summer campaign and the formation of a new wintertime movement. Sheridan did not micromanage the affairs in his division but was diligent, superbly assertive, and riveted on success.[1]

It was logical and completely in keeping with Sheridan's manner that he should seize an opportunity at the evident close of the fighting to inspect the newly wrested Sioux Country. That his friend and the army's commanding general, William Tecumseh Sherman, should do so as well speaks to the encompassing national significance of the Great Sioux War and the generals' unequivocal commitment to success. Though he hardly needed one, Sheridan's public motive for a western survey in 1877 was an understated desire to understand and appreciate the lands whereon the army was establishing new military posts in order to estimate the garrisons required there more precisely.[2]

These new forts in Sioux Country were the culmination of a campaign of persuasion that the generals had waged with Congress since 1870, when interest in a northern transcontinental railroad had gained momentum. Sheridan rightly pointed to a strong cordon of military posts buffering Sioux Country on its east and south but saw only Fort Buford, at the confluence of the Yellowstone and Missouri rivers, guarding an increasingly critical northern border, and nothing to the west. Sheridan certainly appreciated that the existing forts in western Montana distinctly served the mountainous mining communities but were inconsequential to the settlement prospects of Montana's eastern plains. Members of Congress at first repeatedly balked at the generals' overtures for new northern plains forts, but their resolve melted in the wake of the Custer disaster. Funds were hurriedly appropriated in July 1876 for two major Yellowstone River garrisons.[3]

Sheridan's and Sherman's 1877 western itineraries were purposefully different, but they envisioned their paths intersecting at the new but yet unnamed Big Horn River post on or about July 25. As he planned his western survey, Sheridan particularly sought to examine the Wind and Big Horn River countryside in central Wyoming and the expansive Big Horn Mountains before descending to the Big Horn and Yellowstone rivers and new posts. At that very time, his brother Michael was policing Custer's Battlefield and its piteous, animal-ravaged graves and removing certain officer remains for reburial in eastern cemeteries (see chapter 8). General Sheridan clearly wished to explore that intriguing field when opportunity allowed. In addition, he sought to determine the region's agricultural worth, assess its physical characteristics, and investigate rumors of gold in the Big Horn Mountains. Sherman's declared agenda, meanwhile, was decidedly less ambitious. He also desired to inspect the new military posts in Sioux Country and travel newly established routes on the Yellowstone and in Montana. Thereafter, he would extend "his examination to such points as the interests of the frontier may suggest."[4]

Sheridan departed Chicago on June 25, perhaps not coincidentally on the first anniversary of the Little Big Horn Battle. Among his small entourage were Colonel Delos B. Sacket, the division's inspector general; Lieutenant Colonel James W. Forsyth, Sheridan's military secretary and a midsummer participant in the previous year's campaigning on the Yellowstone with Brigadier General Terry; Major George A. Forsyth, hero of the Beecher Island fight in 1868 and long one of Sheridan's trusted aides-de-camp; and First Lieutenant William L. Carpenter, Ninth Infantry, a self-trained botanist who accompanied the party to report on the natural history of the Big Horn Mountains. Brigadier General Crook joined Sheridan's entourage in Omaha as they continued to the Union Pacific's Green River station in southwestern Wyoming. Sheridan's party traveled northeast from Green River on a Sweetwater Stage through the storied South Pass to Camp Stambaugh, continued across the southern Wind River Mountains to Lander City, and arrived at nearby Camp Brown, the announced rendezvous, on June 30.[5]

Awaiting Sheridan at Camp Brown were two of Crook's aides, First Lieutenants Walter S. Schuyler and John G. Bourke, who had traveled ahead to make local arrangements. Also present was the assistant surgeon, Julius H. Patzki, detailed from Fort D. A. Russell at Cheyenne as the survey's medical officer. Company L, Fifth Cavalry, from Fort D. A. Russell, commanded that season by First Lieutenant Charles H. Rockwell, and Company C, Second Cavalry, from Camp Brown, commanded by Captain Thomas J. Gregg, served as the armed escort. The party included seven Indian guides, ironically all recently surrendered Sioux warriors from Camp Robinson,

led by Frank Grouard and Baptiste "Bat" Pourier. Crook's friend
and veteran packer Thomas Moore handled the baggage and a
mule train. Diarists among the party included Sacket, Bourke, and
George Forsyth.[6]

On July 1 the 97-man cavalcade departed Camp Brown, a small,
two-company post situated in the eastern foothills of the Wind River
Mountains. Sheridan's party generally ambled north by northeast
through the Wind River and Big Horn basins en route to the western
foothills of the Big Horn Mountains. Though this colorful and tum-
bling landscape west of the Big Horns lay beyond the bounds of
Sioux Country, national sentiment and General Sheridan agreed
that it too would eventually be tamed by cattlemen and farmers.
In accordance with one of Sheridan's survey objectives, his diary
keepers paid particular heed to the land cover, soil types, and fitness
for cultivation of this landscape and all the others crossed. Each
day's estimations varied; but from start to finish the country that
the party passed through was deemed luxuriant enough to sustain
profitable ranching and agriculture. As in the case of other Sheridan-
Crook jaunts, of which there were many in the 1870s and 1880s,
the generals fished and hunted extravagantly, often from sunup to
sundown, and their successes fed the officers' mess for the duration
of the survey.[7]

On the third day Sheridan's party reached the Big Horn River,
where the Wind and Little Wind rivers join. From that confluence the
Big Horn coursed northward, bisecting the Owl Creek Mountains
in a picturesque, rugged canyon and emerging in a broad fertile
valley carpeted with luxuriant grass and flowers. Sheridan estimated
that it could sustain cattle by the thousands. His party did not typically orient itself to easygoing valley floors, however, but maintained
a direct course northeastward over rough, dry ridges and through
small, narrow, but typically well-watered canyons and valleys.[8]

For several days the journey was uneventful. On July 4 George
Forsyth noted that the party was now sunburned and taking on the
character of plainsmen. In camp that evening Sheridan gathered his
officers to toast the anniversary of the nation, indulging them from
his private cache of French Mumm champagne. After listening to a
few appropriate remarks from Sheridan, Bourke noted that the men

passed a pleasant hour of conversation, storytelling, and song before retiring for the evening.[9]

On July 5 Sheridan's party gained its first sight of Cloud Peak, the 13,165-foot pinnacle of the Big Horns. The soldiers were equally impressed by an immense buffalo herd that they encountered on the hillsides east of Bridger's Creek. In his diary, Bourke used the words "countless" and "thousands." Pandemonium reigned as Indian guides fell on the shaggy beasts, firing wildly and splitting the herd into many smaller bunches. Even Bourke joined the frenzy and proudly killed a "lordly bull." In all, he estimated that about a dozen animals were killed in this spontaneous hunt, providing the entire column with an evening feast of fresh liver and roasted tongue and hump. Sheridan was curiously circumspect about these buffalo in his report, and so was Sacket. Later that evening some of the still agitated herd turned on the camp and spooked many of the army's horses and mules. It was well past dark before the domestic stock was again securely hobbled.[10]

For the next several days Sheridan's party worked its way north on a route in the lower foothills that roughly paralleled the snow-covered peaks of the Big Horns. Game was not especially plentiful, but the soldiers could nearly always see buffalo to the west. After angling east on Painted Rock Creek and then north on Medicine Lodge Creek, the party finally commenced its formal ascent of the mountains on July 10. Gregg's Second Cavalry company departed at noon that day for Camp Brown. Sheridan's exploration had been safe and effortless thus far, and additional troops awaited him across the divide in the eastern foothills.[11]

The picturesqueness of the landscape intensified as the column gained elevation. Bourke thought it all delightful, with abundant wood and water and grass and wildflowers in seasonal splendor. Buffalo were seen in the higher range too, in singles, pairs, and small groups. Camp on July 11 was on the shore of a bucolic lake at the foot of Cloud Peak. That afternoon Carpenter, Schuyler, four enlisted men, and two packers cut from the column for an ascent of the mountain, expecting to be absent from two to four days. They returned on the fifteenth, having failed in their attempt to gain the craggy summit. The command, meanwhile, spent the remainder of the day and all of the twelfth fishing and hunting in the shadows of the peak. For some enlisted men, fishing amounted to discharging weapons into small pools and collecting percussion-stunned trout as they floated to the surface. Again faithful to his purpose, Sheridan extolled the nutritious grasses, bountiful wildflowers, and abundant elk, deer, sheep, buffalo, and trout enriching the summit environment.[12]

Sheridan's journey resumed on July 13. For the next several days the troops angled northward over a faint, rocky, and often snow-covered trail. Of growing interest to Sheridan and his officers were the scattered prospector trails increasingly scoring the landscape in the eastern half of the range. Trailing the column were several small parties of miners who maintained a sufficient separation to avert direct contact but kept close enough to fall within its mantle of protection. The potential of gold or other precious metals in the Big Horns had not yet been scientifically ascertained, but newspapers like the *Cheyenne Daily Leader* had trumpeted those prospects for months. Sheridan, Carpenter, and the other officers made no mention of gold in their respective reports or communications, and in the end the prospect of it proved to be terribly overblown.[13]

Sheridan's party maintained its high-country course through the alpine meadows and forests of the Big Horns. It reached the North Fork of the Tongue River on July 16 and then commenced a slow, sometimes challenging descent of the mountains, generally following the cascading Tongue. The route that day passed the scene of Second Lieutenant Frederick W. Sibley's brisk fight on July 7, 1876, between his small command of scouts from General Crook's Big Horn and Yellowstone Expedition and several hundred pressing Sioux and Cheyenne warriors. Sibley eventually eluded his attackers and returned to Crook's camp on Goose Creek with the alarming report that the Tongue and Little Big Horn headwaters were alive with Indians.[14] Thus far on Sheridan's survey one year later, the party had seen no Sioux or Cheyenne tribesmen anywhere. Instead, the explorers came upon miners recently arrived from Deadwood who were prospecting the Tongue at its mountain-prairie juncture.[15]

The Tongue River flowed generally eastward from its frothy mountain emergence, roughly paralleling the Wyoming-Montana border for some twenty-five miles before coursing north to the Yellowstone. Having finally reached Sioux Country, Sheridan's party lingered in the foothills for two days. On the seventeenth it united with four companies of Fifth Cavalry commanded by Major Verling K. Hart. Five companies of that regiment had been dispatched from Fort D. A. Russell in May; Company L separated from that column at Fort Fetterman, detailed to Camp Brown to await and escort Sheridan. Until now Hart's companies had been engaged in a continuous reconnaissance of the eastern foothills of the Big Horns. That day Sheridan's party passed another half-dozen camps of miners anxiously prospecting the Big Horns. Bourke quipped sardonically in his diary that these miners would never find gold there any richer than the green grass waving at their feet.[16]

Elsewhere in his diary, Bourke extolled the untapped agricultural richness of the mountainscape that he, Sheridan, and Crook had just crossed and the front range where they now lingered. "Everywhere, our column files through nutritious grasses," he noted. "It ought, inside of two years, to be filled with a population of herders and graziers, superintending hundreds of thousands of fat cattle. Mowing machines can be used here and thousands of tons of hay, of the most superior quality, gathered every year." Sheridan also belabored the point in his formal report in September. Of the foothills east of the Big Horns, he wrote that "the grass is much better than in Colorado, Kansas, or Texas" and the "climate is so dry that the grass makes hay without being cut."[17]

Sheridan's party resumed its march on July 19. From the foothills, the route cut north to Montana and into the valley of the Little Big Horn River. Hart and three companies of the Fifth Cavalry battalion accompanied Sheridan, while two companies remained encamped on the Tongue River. One was immediately dispatched to Fort Laramie, carrying a sizable cargo of mail. The column followed the well-scored Bozeman Trail to its Little Big Horn crossing and then for two days proceeded downstream in that valley until mid-morning of July 21, when it reached the scene of Custer's fight.[18]

Custer's Battlefield was intriguing new ground for the white men traveling with Sheridan and probably only an odd memory for the Sioux scouts. Some of them perhaps had fought Custer. Crook,

Bourke, Patzki, Moore, and some of the Fifth Cavalrymen had passed within thirty miles of the sprawling field in late summer 1876 as they closed on General Terry's command, but their attention then was riveted on the war and not this calamitous landscape. Portions of the battlefield were impossible to miss, however. Upon reaching the site of the immense Sioux and Northern Cheyenne village attacked on June 25, 1876, Bourke recorded seeing erect tipi poles and pots, pans, kettles, cups, and dishes strewn everywhere. But the scattered debris marking the Indian encampment was far less arresting to the soldiers than the hillsides directly east of the village and across the river where Custer and five companies engaged and perished and the bluff tops to the southeast where Major Marcus Reno, Captain Frederick Benteen, and seven other Seventh Cavalry companies entrenched, fought hard, and survived the fight.[19]

This was especially emotional ground for Sheridan. Custer, though capable of outlandish indiscretions, was an intimate friend and favorite officer. Sheridan still struggled to comprehend his destruction. Barely two weeks earlier, his brother Michael had policed the field, partly to exhume officers' remains (including Custer's) for reburial elsewhere and partly to tidy it for the pending inspections by the army's top generals. Sheridan spent the remainder of July 21 combing the sprawling battleground, sizing up its nuances, and speculating on the ebb and flow of the fighting. Since learning details of the battle in the previous months, Sheridan had harbored the conviction that Custer might have defeated these Indians if he had not divided his regiment. Now, as he poked about the swales and ridges of the vast grass and sage-covered field, he affirmed that belief. In Sheridan's mind this was a horrible sacrifice; but knowing the war's outcome, exploring the diversity and worth of Sioux Country, and appreciating the civilizing forces about to be unleashed across the northern plains, he knew that Custer's death would be atoned.[20]

Sheridan was dismayed, however, by the unkempt nature of the battlefield. The 260-odd soldier casualties received only cursory burials on June 28, 1876, as the survivors and Terry's and Gibbon's relief force ushered wounded soldiers to medical care and pressed the campaign onward. While his brother Michael's cleanup effort three weeks earlier had left many graves nicely mounded, the weather had already disturbed too much. Sheridan ordered Major Forsyth to organize the Fifth Cavalry escort for yet another policing of the field. The available troopers in Hart's three companies scoured the hills minutely for human remains. Forsyth noted that seventeen skeletons were found, including ten that had not been previously buried. Several officers also seized opportunities to collect souvenirs. Bourke and Second Lieutenant Homer W. Wheeler of the Fifth Cavalry cut the hooves from the horse supposedly ridden by Custer. Bourke's pair eventually became inkstands, but Wheeler's were lost before he returned to Fort D. A. Russell.[21]

Forsyth's policing of the battlefield carried into the evening and might have continued on July 22 had Sheridan not received a courier from Lieutenant Colonel George P. Buell, Eleventh Infantry, who was commanding troops constructing the new Big Horn Post eighteen miles away. Buell knew of Sheridan's proximity and was also anticipating the arrival of General Sherman, then en route on one of the many steamboats ascending the Big Horn River.[22]

Sheridan resumed his travel on July 22. After advancing north a few miles he came upon soldiers cutting hay from lush valley meadows and felling cottonwood trees to be slabbed at the new steam-powered Big Horn sawmill for dimensional lumber at the post. While still some eight miles off, Sheridan's party spotted wagons, tents, and other evidence of military industry on the high bluff overlooking the confluence of the Big Horn and Little Big Horn rivers. Four companies of Eleventh Infantry and nearly two hundred civilian tradesmen from Minnesota were engaged in constructing Big Horn Post.

Lieutenant Colonel Buell and his wife, Rochie, welcomed Sheridan, Crook, and the officers of the Wyoming party when they arrived at mid-morning on July 22. The lanky, sandy-haired Buell had commanded the army garrison at Cheyenne River Agency, Dakota, before being transferred to Montana and was a veteran of the Red River War before coming to the northern plains.[23] The generals, Buell, and others jointly discussed Sheridan's Big Horn Mountain crossing, expressed opinions about the Custer Battlefield, and groused about the weather. As is typical for Montana in late summer, daily temperatures soared. The recorded high that afternoon was 108 degrees. Sherman had not yet arrived, so the members of Sheridan's party established camp in a cottonwood grove along the Big Horn next to the Eleventh Infantry's camp. They welcomed a few guests from the garrison that afternoon, freshened themselves in the Little Big Horn, and explored the fledgling post that evening.[24]

Though Sheridan's diarists found little to say about Big Horn Post, the bustle both at river's edge and on the imposing bluff towering in the west bespoke a frenetic effort to complete principal quarters and storage for a large garrison before the onset of winter. Heavily laden steamboats were still safely navigating the Big Horn River as far as the post, and the banks of the Big Horn west of the Little Big Horn were piled high with the stocks necessary to sustain a permanent garrison plus bricks, glass, finishing wood, tin, iron, and other wares needed during construction. Before departing, Sheridan and his entourage explored the bluff top. Only one building was complete, but the frameworks of a half-dozen more and precisely arrayed surveyor's stakes defined dozens yet to come. In Sheridan's view, the setting and layout were perfect. During the visit he, Sacket, Crook, Buell, and others proposed names for the new post. "Camp Custer" was favored from the onset, while "Camp Keogh" was suggested for the new Tongue River post. The name "Fort Custer" was announced in orders soon thereafter.[25]

That evening the steamboats *Western*, *Big Horn*, and *Silver City* arrived at the Big Horn landing and discharged cargo. Sherman's party was still en route aboard the *Rosebud* and was reportedly hours behind. Anxious to resume travel, at noon on July 23 Sheridan and his Chicago entourage plus Crook, Patzki, and the Omaha party bade good-bye to the officers of the Big Horn Post and Fifth Cavalry escort, scouts, and packers and boarded the *Silver City* for conveyance to the Yellowstone and new Tongue River post downstream.[26]

Bourke called the Big Horn River passage tedious and difficult. For most of the run to the Yellowstone (some thirty miles directly and more than fifty by water) the channel was narrow and the current swift. On the curves of the tight, twisting river the boat repeatedly butted against points of land, which unnerved the passengers but apparently did not cause any harm to the craft or any delay. About three miles from their start, the *Silver City* passed the steamer

General Sherman, whose engineers were repairing a blown cylinder head, and, eight miles down, the *Rankin*. Both boats were bound for Big Horn Post. Two miles beyond the *Rankin*, the *Silver City* met the *Rosebud*, captained that season by Grant Marsh, hero of last summer's dramatic evacuation of wounded Seventh Cavalrymen from the Little Big Horn Battlefield to Fort Abraham Lincoln below Bismarck. Aboard were General Sherman and a bevy of officers traveling with him from Washington and Saint Paul.[27]

Thus far Sherman's survey of Sioux Country was not as hurried as Sheridan's. After attending personal business in Saint Louis, his preferred home and occasional headquarters since the close of the Civil War, Sherman embarked by rail on July 4 for Chicago with his young son, Thomas. They reached Saint Paul on the sixth. There the lanky fifty-seven-year-old was joined by his Washington aides, colonels Orlando M. Poe and John M. Bacon, as well as Brigadier General Terry, commander of the Department of Dakota. Accompanying Terry were his department quartermaster, Major Benjamin C. Card, and an aide-de-camp, Captain Edward W. Smith. From Saint Paul, Sherman's entourage traveled north to Duluth in a Northern Pacific Railroad business car lent by the company. In Duluth, the private car was attached to the next regularly scheduled Northern Pacific train bound for Bismarck, the end of track. Sherman penned a series of well-distributed letters to the secretary of war, George W. McCrary, detailing these western travels in 1877. Poe also maintained an informative diary of their ultimately far-ranging survey.[28]

Sherman reached Bismarck on the evening of July 8 and promptly secured transportation to the Yellowstone. Several steamboats were then loading freight for the new military posts, and he selected the *Rosebud*. This new, small, strong craft was more likely than others to reach the Big Horn Post as waters receded in the waning boating season. It was piloted by Grant Marsh, veteran Missouri and Yellowstone River captain, which was surely important too. The *Rosebud* was scheduled to depart when loading was finished later on the ninth, so that morning Sherman, Terry, and their aides ferried across the Missouri for a tour of Fort Abraham Lincoln. Major Joseph G. Tilford, Seventh Cavalry, commanded the nearly deserted post. At that time its resident Seventh Cavalry garrison was mostly deployed to the Yellowstone River valley, scouting for Lame Deer's elusive followers and the few other Indians still resisting surrender. Sherman found Lincoln to be a satisfying and well-built fort, supporting a firm mission of safeguarding a prosperous frontier community at a vital rail and river intersection.[29]

The fully loaded *Rosebud* reached Fort Lincoln, four miles below Bismarck, at about 4 P.M. on July 9, loaded the officers, and commenced its push to the Yellowstone. Poe's only comment about Fort Lincoln concerned mosquitoes interfering with lunch at Tilford's quarters. Mosquitoes plagued the Upper Missouri when Meriwether Lewis and William Clark passed in 1805 and 1806, troubled Sherman's party repeatedly in 1877, and continue to torment North Dakota's river residents mercilessly to this day. The journey to the mouth of the Yellowstone was tedious anyway: because of the Missouri's swift current, it took nearly seventy-four hours to cover the 303 river miles from Bismarck to Fort Buford. The *Rosebud* did not travel at night; otherwise it paused only to take on wood and at Fort Stevenson on July 10 to discharge freight. Marsh nosed the *Rosebud* into the Fort Buford landing, one of Sherman's intermediate stops, as the sun set on July 12. Ironically, among the downriver boats passed en route was the *John G. Fletcher*, bearing Lieutenant Colonel Michael Sheridan and the boxed remains of George Armstrong Custer and ten other casualties of the Little Big Horn Battle.[30]

It was important that Sherman and Sheridan gain a well-rounded appreciation of the evolved Upper Missouri and Yellowstone transportation corridor. Steamboating to the Upper Missouri's fur trading posts and western Montana's goldfields was a well-established enterprise by the 1860s. Although the boating season was short (typically from mid-April to late summer), the steamboats played a highly significant role as the northern Great Plains continued to develop. Though they were competitive in obvious ways, a symbiotic relationship existed between the entrenched Missouri River steamboat industry and the advancing transcontinental railroad network. When the Northern Pacific reached Bismarck in 1873, for instance, it immediately halved long-haul river traffic between Sioux City, Iowa, and Yankton, Dakota, and distant Fort Benton, Montana. All commerce bound for Montana and the prairie country of southern Canada now came from Bismarck rather than the downriver ports. Moreover, the end of the Great Sioux War brought prospects of new markets in the Yellowstone Basin. At first they were based on the needs of the new military posts, but these were bolstered and eventually supplanted by ranching and agricultural output to northern urban markets, particularly via the looming northern transcontinental railroad.[31]

Awaiting Sherman at Fort Buford was Colonel William B. Hazen, the irascible forty-six-year-old commander of the Sixth Infantry. Hazen had long espoused the view that the northern plains—Sioux Country—had no particular agricultural worth, except perhaps for grazing. He had openly feuded with Custer and others in newspapers like the *New York Tribune* and *Minneapolis Tribune* over assertions by Northern Pacific Railroad promoters that the northern plains were a "Fruitful Garden." Privately, Sherman tended to agree with Hazen; but Sherman and Sheridan also appreciated the necessity of railroad expansion across Sioux Country if the transforming forces of land settlement, community growth, and market development were to succeed. That evening, Hazen conducted Sherman, Terry, Poe, and others on a tour of the well-built and sizable Fort Buford. Hazen had not taken a particularly large role in the Great Sioux War, but his regiment had. Fort Buford also had played a critical role in the war as a pivotal staging and supply post for Terry's and Miles's field operations and as a protector of Montana-bound river commerce.[32]

The *Rosebud* pulled away from Fort Buford early on July 13 and promptly turned onto the Yellowstone and into the very heart of Sioux Country. In addition to the Sherman-Terry entourage, a ten-man Sixth Infantry escort commanded by First Lieutenant Charles G. Penney, the Sixth's quartermaster, was on board. Late on the afternoon of the fourteenth the boat paused at Glendive Cantonment, a small supply depot maintained where the overland trail from Fort Abraham Lincoln reached the Yellowstone River.

Second Lieutenant Edward J. McClernand, Second Cavalry, commanded the small detachment of Second and Seventh Cavalry at Glendive. Scattered about McClernand's dugout and tent camp were imposing stockpiles of foodstuffs, munitions, and forage for Major Henry Lazelle's and Major James Brisbin's ongoing expeditions into the Little Missouri countryside. Sherman learned from McClernand that Colonel Miles was on the river and anxious to join him. Miles and Sherman were family by marriage: Miles had married Sherman's niece.[33]

Early on July 14 the *Rosebud* overtook the steamer *Key West* with Colonel Miles aboard, also bound for Tongue River Cantonment. The indefatigable Miles joined Sherman and Terry as Grant Marsh's boat continued upriver. Upon reaching Wolf Rapids, an occasional obstacle on the river just below the mouth of Powder River, the boat paused long enough to receive a report from First Lieutenant Edward Maguire of the Corps of Engineers and chief engineer for the Department of Dakota. Maguire and a dozen civilian tradesmen from Saint Paul had been working since late June to obliterate this river obstruction.[34] They soon passed the Powder River and then Buffalo Rapids. By 6 P.M. on July 16 the *Rosebud* had reached Miles's Tongue River Cantonment.[35]

Miles had established Tongue River Cantonment the previous August when Sheridan ordered the Fifth Infantry Regiment from Kansas to support General Terry's flagging Sioux campaign. From there his troops aggressively ranged against Sioux and Northern Cheyennes in all directions. The troops closed on the Indians in a number of large and small engagements that disrupted their ability to sustain a free-roaming life and led directly to surrenders or, for some, flight to Canada. The post itself was an unpretentious assembly of sod-roofed, cottonwood log buildings tucked into the southwest angle of the Tongue and Yellowstone confluence. Despite its colorlessness, that evening the garrison warmly received the Sherman-Terry entourage. The Fifth Infantry band struck up a martial air at the riverbank and escorted the generals and their party to the post. On hand in addition to the dignitaries from Washington and Saint Paul were Miles's wife, Mary, daughter Cecelia, and niece

Elizabeth Sherman. Along with other wives and family members, they had just arrived from Fort Leavenworth, Kansas, the previous headquarters of the regiment.[36]

The next morning Sherman, Terry, Miles, and Poe visited the as yet unnamed "Post Number One," located on the south bank of the Yellowstone about two miles west of Tongue River Cantonment. Like Big Horn Post, or Post Number Two as it was often identified in initial records, the site was a whirl of activity, under the direction of Captain Charles S. Heintzelman of the Quartermaster Department. Construction of quarters and warehouses sufficient for eleven companies of infantry and cavalry had begun about a month later than at Big Horn Post and was advancing satisfactorily. As at Big Horn, the workforce of mechanics and laborers numbered nearly two hundred, mostly recruited from Minnesota.

Upon reflection, Sherman was greatly pleased by what he had observed thus far in the Yellowstone Valley and at Post Number One. The Yellowstone "affords lands capable of cultivation in wheat, oats, barley, and all garden vegetables," he wrote to Secretary of War McCrary, and has an "unlimited range for cattle, horses, [and] sheep." The troops at the new post would be comfortably quartered, he reported, and "the Indians cannot return." But "for some years," Sherman admonished, "we will be forced to keep here a pretty strong garrison, because, besides defending this point, detachments must go out to protect other threatened points, and to follow any small parties engaged in depredations."[37]

Sherman also shared thoughts with McCrary on the so-called Sioux Problem. That dilemma, he wrote, was "solved by the operations of General Miles last winter, and by the establishment of the two new posts on the Yellowstone now assured this summer. Boats come and go now where a year ago none would venture except with strong guards. Wood-yards are being established to facilitate navigation, and the great mass of hostiles have been forced to go to the agencies for food and protection, or have fled across the border into British territory."[38] Curiously, still encamped nearby under the close eye of Miles's Fifth Infantry were hundreds of Indians, mostly Northern Cheyennes under Two Moon and Miniconjou Sioux under Hump.

On the evening of July 17 Sherman formally received the officers and wives of the cantonment at Miles's quarters. In turn, on the eighteenth Terry received the same officers at his small cabin aboard the *Rosebud.* At 6:30 P.M. General Sherman formally reviewed the garrison at hand: the eight companies and band of the Fifth Infantry. Uniquely, four of the companies were mounted on surrendered Indian ponies. Poe thought they presented a motley appearance as cavalry but gave the impression of efficiency as skirmishers. During the review, Sherman awarded thirty-one enlisted men Medals of Honor for gallantry and exceptional bravery in the Fifth's many hard-fought engagements with the Sioux in the preceding year.[39]

Anxious to resume his voyage to the Big Horn and connect with General Sheridan, Sherman and his party, now including Miles, resumed their westbound travel as the sun set on July 18. Also aboard were two companies of the Eleventh Infantry commanded by Major Charles G. Bartlett, bound for the Big Horn Post. The *Rosebud* made only a few miles before tying up for the evening. The conversation the next day, according to Poe, centered on the campaigning in the area a year ago, especially as the boat passed the mouth of Rosebud Creek, where Custer and the Seventh Cavalry had departed from Terry on their fateful march to the Little Big Horn. The site of old Fort Pease was pointed out to Sherman as they passed that site on the twenty-first. This small traders' fort was operated by businessmen from Bozeman for several months in 1875 and 1876 and thereafter was a noted landmark during the course of the war. Hostilities there and the military relief expedition mounted from Fort Ellis in the early spring of 1876 for some marked the opening of the Great Sioux War. Now hardly anything remained at the site; its stockade and lofty flagpole had been cut up and consumed as fuel by passing steamboats.[40]

Two miles below the mouth of the Big Horn, the *Rosebud* passed Pease or Big Horn City, an unpretentious little burg best remembered according to Poe for its expansive vegetable garden filled with potatoes, corn, cabbages, and oats. By noon on July 21 Sherman's boat had entered the Big Horn River and progressed upstream eighteen miles before tying up for the evening. Travel that day was effortless, but on the twenty-second the *Rosebud* entered the river's constricted channel that Bourke had complained of soon after Sheridan's departure from Big Horn Post. Poe noted that navigation on the Big Horn became more difficult with every mile. He also observed that for two or three days the temperatures had been extreme, "especially today [July 22], when the heat was really distressing." That day the recorded temperature at Big Horn Post was 108 degrees.[41]

At 1 P.M. on July 23 the *Rosebud* and *Silver City* finally met and tied off on the riverbank. Sheridan, Crook, and their aides clambered aboard the *Rosebud* to confer with Sherman and Terry. It was "a long pow-wow to which we were all admitted without regard to rank," remembered Captain Erasmus C. Gilbreath, Eleventh Infantry. Captain Marsh's crew treated the generals, staffs, and onlookers to iced water and lager beer—a special kindness, according to Bourke, because ice was not yet available at Big Horn Post. During a conference that lasted two hours, the generals shared many observations and forecasts. Thus far no Indians had been seen either in the Big Horn country or on the Missouri or Yellowstone. "The principal end aimed at by the construction of these posts has already been reached," Sherman wrote, "and it is only to make this end permanent that we should persevere in their completion."[42]

Sheridan thought that the Big Horn Post was well situated and could be supplied with reasonable economy. Its garrison would soon have six companies of the Eleventh Infantry and four of Second Cavalry (the latter to be transferred from Crook's Department of the Platte), with Lieutenant Colonel Buell in command. Sherman likewise expressed his pleasures with the new post near Tongue River, soon to be the permanent home of Miles's Fifth Infantry. He noted that transportation was reliable there but predicted that a small depot would be needed at the mouth of the Big Horn River for freight relays to Post Number Two. The Big Horn was not viewed as particularly reliable for steamboats despite that season's considerable traffic. In terms of the economic prospects of the countryside, the generals agreed that they had both seen good country that would fill rapidly with emigrants. The cattle range east of the Big Horns was especially superb for hundreds of miles, Sheridan noted, and the broad valleys of the many rivers could easily

be cultivated. In the memories of former residents, this was the
revered Powder River Basin, still home to countless buffalo, prong-
horn, and deer.[43]

Sherman and Sheridan parted company late in the afternoon
of July 23: the *Rosebud* continued its tortured course to the Big
Horn Post, while the *Silver City* eased its way downriver. Soon
after departing, Sherman's boat came upon the steamer *Big Horn*,
descending the river with Lieutenant Colonel Buell aboard. Buell
transferred to the *Rosebud* and welcomed Sherman. The boat pushed
upstream to within five miles of the new fort before grounding in
shallow water. Buell had horses waiting there, however, and he and
Sherman continued to the Eleventh Infantry's tent camp and an
evening of hospitality. The *Rosebud*, meanwhile, partially unloaded
and reached the post the next morning.[44]

Sherman, Terry, Buell, and their innumerable aides spent July 24
exploring Big Horn Post. Their observations mirrored Sheridan's.
Buell had chosen the site well, and his construction plan would
yield substantial and comfortable quarters for the enlisted men,
officers, and families. Interestingly, neither Sherman nor Poe mentioned a side trip to Custer's Battlefield. The disturbing national
newspaper attention to its condition in the spring and summer
had prompted Michael Sheridan's policing action in the first days
of July. And surely General Sheridan spoke of his own recent minute
inspection there when he and Sherman conferenced aboard the
Rosebud. Terry no doubt detailed for his colleagues the horrors he
had witnessed there in the days following the battle, but Poe's
report only mentioned suffering the heat of another unbearable
afternoon. Did General Sherman visit the battlefield? Only
Captain Grant Marsh's biographer, who gained his story directly
from the aged pilot, says that he did. Such a trip would have
consumed eight or nine hours, including an hour or two for an
exploration of the field. An early morning departure after a look
at Big Horn Post's skeleton outline would have meant a late afternoon or early evening return. Sherman's and Poe's silence on the
matter is telling, despite the nation's solemn embrace of this remote,
hallowed ground.[45]

Sherman and Terry set out for the Yellowstone at daybreak on July 25, reaching there in six and a half hours. Their ascent to the Big Horn Post from the Yellowstone had taken three full days. On the descent, they reaffirmed their own belief that the Big Horn River was not particularly reliable for transportation; its current was much too swift and its channel too constricted for heavily laden steamboats. Determined to establish a freight depot at the mouth of the Big Horn, Terry and his quartermaster, Major Card, landed and reconnoitered the confluence area. The landscape was pinched, but the Yellowstone Valley opened on the south bank upriver from the Big Horn. The two men chose a site about three miles above the confluence. From there it was about thirty miles due south to the Big Horn Post over relatively easy terrain. Sherman concurred with the choice. Meanwhile, the *Rosebud* pushed to the newly selected site and landed Company H, Eleventh Infantry, commanded by Captain Gilbreath, which had been sent from Buell's command expressly to establish the new depot and guard the supplies anticipated there. In short order, Gilbreath gave the new camp the name "Terry's Landing."[46]

Terry and Card returned to the *Rosebud,* which nosed downstream to Pease City, the hamlet on the north bank of the Yellowstone some two miles below the Big Horn's mouth. There Sherman, Poe, Bacon, and young Thomas Sherman bade good-bye to Terry, his staff, and Grant Marsh and landed. They joined Captain Randolph Norwood and Company L, Second Cavalry, who were waiting to escort Sherman west to Fort Ellis at Bozeman.[47]

Sherman reached Fort Ellis on August 1. En route he paused to study Pompey's Pillar, a Yellowstone Valley landmark still emblazoned with William Clark's deeply etched signature from the passage of portions of the great Corps of Discovery in 1806. On July 28 the men chanced upon a large buffalo that they chased and killed. They saw several others, but nothing of the millions that Sherman knew still grazed throughout eastern Montana. On the twenty-ninth Sherman received an urgent dispatch via Fort Ellis, summoning him to Washington to assist President Rutherford B. Hayes in managing railroad labor strife then plaguing eastern cities. The president's summons had been countermanded by the time Sherman reached Fort Ellis, much to the general's relief. He was not comforted, however, by news of disaffected Nez Perce Indians battling soldiers in Oregon and Idaho and even having crossed the Bitterroot Mountains into Montana. A single small Seventh Infantry company garrisoned Fort Ellis; its other infantry and cavalry had already been dispatched to the Nez Perce emergency in the distant Bitterroot River valley.[48]

Sherman was nonplussed by the Nez Perce alarm and relieved that his summons east had been rescinded. He next intended to explore Yellowstone National Park, created in 1872 to protect a unique but still barely known geological wonderland. Sherman wrote McCrary with considerable satisfaction that owing to the new posts at Tongue River and Big Horn the Sioux could never again regain their country and would be forced to remain at their agencies or take refuge in the British possessions. Poe was equally sanguine. The new posts would surely exert a powerful influence in the region, he wrote, and "one cannot but think there will be little delay in occupying the magnificent agricultural lands in the vicinity."[49]

In Yellowstone National Park, Sherman learned of Colonel John Gibbon's fierce battle on August 9 with the Nez Perces in southwestern Montana's Big Hole, a picturesque high mountain valley ringed by the Pioneer and Beaverhead mountains. Sherman's trail in Montana then took him to Helena and Deer Lodge, where wounded Seventh Infantrymen were taken after the Big Hole fight. He consoled those soldiers before continuing west to Idaho, Oregon, and Washington, faithfully surveying the landscape en route, measuring the prosperity of the communities, and inspecting military posts. Sherman's western odyssey finally ended in San Francisco on October 6.[50]

After the *Silver City* pulled away from Sherman's *Rosebud* on July 23, Sheridan's descent of the Big Horn and Yellowstone rivers to Miles's Tongue River Cantonment was rapid and effortless. The boat arrived at the ramshackle post as the soldiers stood retreat on the evening of the twenty-fourth. Before the sun set completely, Sheridan, Crook, and their staffs were driven to the new post (soon to be called Fort Keogh) for a hurried inspection. The officers were immensely pleased. Back at the cantonment later that evening, Miles feted Sheridan's party and the officers of his garrison at an informal social. But by 10 P.M. the men had reboarded the steamer and pushed a few more miles downriver before tying off for the evening.[51]

As the *Silver City* passed landmarks like the mouth of the Powder River and Wolf Rapids on July 25, Lieutenant Bourke regaled Sheridan with recollections of episodes that had occurred there during the 1876 campaign, which he referred to several times in his diary as the "season of active operations." In 1876 Crook's Big Horn and Yellowstone Expedition had cut from its base camp in Wyoming with little more in the way of raiment and equipment than could be carried by individual soldiers and arrived on the Yellowstone in mid-August 1876 in ragged condition. Rations by then were deficient, yet Crook headed east into Dakota and into the throes of the not so warmly remembered and already legendary "Starvation March" to the Black Hills.[52]

A few miles above Glendive Creek Sheridan and Crook observed the steamer *Tiger* ferrying cavalry across the Yellowstone. These were Second Cavalrymen returning to the Tongue River Cantonment after their largely abortive expedition into the Little Missouri country, chasing Lame Deer's elusive followers. The Glendive Cantonment was abandoned now, its stockpiled supplies either fully distributed to Lazelle's or Brisbin's troops or advanced to the Tongue River Cantonment. Hay cutters and wood hawks occupied its assembly of unpretentious log huts.[53]

The *Silver City* reached Fort Buford at about 10:30 P.M. on July 25. Owing partly to the very late hour and partly to the plague of mosquitoes infesting the Yellowstone-Missouri confluence, Sheridan and Crook did not tour the post. Colonel Hazen had taken leave on July 18, just days after hosting Sherman and Terry. Major Orlando H. Moore, Sixth Infantry, a veteran of extended service against the Sioux the year before, now commanded. He and many of his officers visited the boat instead.[54]

Sheridan's river journey resumed at daybreak on July 26 and continued with few pauses until he reached Bismarck at 10:20 A.M.

on the twenty-seventh. There, evidently for the first time, Sheridan received news of the railroad labor strife consuming Chicago and other eastern cities and hastened to return to his headquarters after having been absent for more than one month. After dining at the Sheridan House, Bismarck's newest hotel, the officers secured passage on a special train placed at their disposal by the Northern Pacific Railroad and departed the city at 3 P.M. The train made only necessary fuel and water stops en route to Saint Paul, which it reached at midday on July 28. There the party transferred to the Chicago and Northwestern Railroad and continued the hurried run to Chicago, arriving just after sunup on the twenty-ninth. Sheridan promptly immersed himself in the unrest consuming the city and filed an official report on his survey of Sioux Country only months later. Meanwhile, to Crook's pleasant surprise, most of the troops ordered to Chicago to enforce calm among the rioters were from forts dotting the Union Pacific Railroad in Nebraska and Wyoming in his own Department of the Platte. Anxious to regain control of affairs in that department, Crook, Bourke, and Schuyler pushed on for Omaha, which they reached the next morning.[55]

Much more than Sherman, Sheridan brimmed with satisfaction over having swept the Sioux aside to open the northern Great Plains to settlement. Most Sioux and their Northern Cheyenne allies were now duly controlled at the various agencies on the Great Sioux Reservation. Even Sitting Bull and his followers were beyond Sheridan's immediate concern. They now constituted a problem for the British government in Canada, with Miles and the Fifth Infantry poised to keep it that way. Across Sioux Country, Sheridan had discovered fertile valleys and an extraordinary cattle range enriched by the finest grasses known on the plains. Miners, meanwhile, were spilling into the Big Horns from the Black Hills. Sheridan knew that the Northern Pacific Railroad would soon resume construction and one day bind the nation with yet another transcontinental rail line. And he saw other unfinished business in Sioux Country. Custer's Battlefield troubled him greatly. He would give it much attention in the coming months and years, perhaps shaping a memorial there to the army's sacrifices in opening Sioux Country. He would also press for a continually strengthened military presence across the newly wrested Sioux homeland, both to safeguard this former Indian hunting range as it opened to cattlemen and farmers and to secure the Indians' bondage to the Great Sioux Reservation.

3

NEW FORTS AND A
NEW MISSION

During the prolonged course of the Great Sioux War, Sheridan and his northern Great Plains department commanders, Terry and Crook, deployed troops from army posts scattered throughout their departments and beyond. Except for the newer agency garrisons like Camps Robinson and Sheridan (both founded in 1874 in the White River country of Nebraska) and the Standing Rock post (established in 1870 on the Missouri River), the existing forts in the Dakota and Platte departments had been founded for purposes generally unrelated to controlling the Sioux or their vast and now irresistibly beckoning landscape. Anticipating the inevitability of a decisive conflict, however, both Sheridan and Sherman pushed Congress hard in the 1870s for new forts on the Yellowstone River to serve various government purposes, including the waging of a foreseeable war with the Sioux and thereafter safeguarding presumed spoils. The outcome of the Great Sioux War had already been decided in part before garrisons were planted at Forts Keogh and Custer, but they did indeed protect the gains.

With Congress duly sensitized by the horror and shame of Custer's defeat at the Little Big Horn and the federal treasury opened for two forts, the generals vigorously pushed their advantage. They soon were rewarded by the establishment of an array of additional garrisons throughout Sioux Country, to enforce peace at the Sioux agencies and ensure the safety and success of the civilizing forces advancing on this new country. The generals indeed locked up Sioux Country through the establishment of Fort Robinson (1874), Fort Yates (1875), Fort Keogh (1876), Fort Custer (1877), Fort Meade (1878), Fort McKinney (1878), Fort Assinniboine (1879), Camp Poplar River (1880), Fort Niobrara (1880), and Fort Maginnis (1880), added to stalwart posts like Forts Fetterman, Sully, Abraham Lincoln, and Buford. They transformed the army's prewar presence from a paltry, scattered, and reactive constabulary into a sizable mobile force committed to safeguarding Indians and Indian agencies, a vast northern border, and the enterprise of settlement throughout the northern plains.

Before the onset of Great Sioux War the Regular Army troops deployed within the Platte and Dakota departments were arrayed chiefly to shield the nation's westbound transportation corridors that skirted but rarely penetrated Sioux Country. Fort Laramie, on the North Platte River in eastern Wyoming, is often seen as emblematic of these scattered prewar garrisons. Founded in 1849, Fort Laramie safeguarded Overland Trail traffic bound for Utah, Oregon, and California and later the Pony Express and transcontinental telegraph, which were also east-west enterprises. Completion of the transcontinental railroad at Promontory Summit, Utah, in May 1869 and the emergence of newer forts like D. A. Russell and Fred Steele along the rail line in Wyoming reduced the significance of old Fort Laramie. In the mid-1870s, however, that venerable fort found renewed purpose astride a northbound trail from Cheyenne that radiated from the post to the war's several fronts and also to the Black Hills goldfields in Dakota and the two Sioux agencies in Nebraska.[1]

Fort Fetterman on the North Platte River in central Wyoming (founded in 1867 during the late days of the Bozeman Trail) also experienced a renaissance during the Great Sioux War as the forward-most post supporting Crook's three successive campaigns into northern Wyoming and southern Montana. As at Fort Laramie, the flurry of activity at the small but bustling Fort Fetterman in 1876 and 1877 marked its zenith.[2]

Another critical post along the war's southern margins was Camp Robinson, Nebraska, founded in 1874 as the protectorate garrison for the adjacent and always turbulent Red Cloud Agency. During the war, its role expanded phenomenally due to its proximity to the Black Hills mining communities, its position on the Sidney–Black Hills stage and freight road, and the daunting Indian population tallied in its near proximity. Red Cloud Agency was the nominal home of the Oglala Sioux (the second largest of the Lakota bands, numbering nearly four thousand people) plus transient Brulés from nearby Spotted Tail Agency, a number of Arapaho bands, and virtually all of the Northern Cheyennes. It was by far the largest of the Sioux agencies.[3] Functionally related and located some forty miles east of Robinson was Camp Sheridan, the protectorate garrison for the adjacent Spotted Tail Agency. Although the Brulé population residing there was also substantial, the dominant atmosphere at this agency was markedly peaceable. Accordingly, Camp Sheridan's soldiers never shouldered the multiple wartime tasks engulfing the Laramie, Fetterman, and Robinson garrisons.[4]

Meanwhile, troops stationed behind the scenes, chiefly along the Union Pacific Railroad in southwestern Nebraska and southern Wyoming, actively supported Crook's front-line posts. Sidney Barracks, Fort D. A. Russell (and its adjacent quartermaster and commissary station, Cheyenne Depot), and Forts Sanders and Fred Steele were all founded in the late 1860s to protect the advance of the transcontinental railroad. Although these forts still played a vital part in this original role, Crook necessarily stripped them nearly clean of their infantry and cavalry garrisons in 1876 as he assembled and reinforced his varied campaigns. Meanwhile, remnant forces—sometimes numbering fewer than a dozen men commanded by a lone commissioned officer—safeguarded the movement of supplies from rail stations to the war zone and otherwise tended to the ordinary business of the posts.

In addition to this cordon of front-line garrisons and those with supporting roles on the southern and southwestern margins of Sioux Country, Crook commanded ten other posts in eastern Nebraska, western Wyoming, Utah, and southeastern Idaho. They surrendered elements of their garrisons to the campaigns but otherwise played no role in the conduct of the Great Sioux War.[5]

The posts in Alfred Terry's Department of Dakota fronted a broader span of Sioux Country. Like Crook's posts, they had been founded for reasons other than surrounding the Sioux. As scheduled steamboat navigation reached the middle and upper Missouri River, posts were established at strategic locations to protect the waning Middle and Upper Missouri fur trade and the increasingly important Montana-bound mining commerce. Such were the origins of Fort Randall, established in 1856, and Forts Sully, Rice, Stevenson, and Buford, all established in the 1860s.

The government's need to secure the Sioux agencies founded in accordance with the 1868 Fort Laramie Treaty led to the establishment of small army posts at the Lower Brule, Cheyenne River, and Standing Rock agencies on the Missouri River in 1870. Meanwhile, Terry's newest Missouri River post was Fort Abraham Lincoln, established in 1872 as Fort McKeen across the river from the Northern Pacific's temporary end of track at newly founded Bismarck. Camp Hancock, a crucially important military supply depot, was located in central Bismarck on the rail line.

In constituting and supporting his 1876 field campaign, Terry did not draw troops from the agency garrisons, all of which were infantry. But he did substantially drain troops from Forts Rice, Lincoln, Stevenson, and Buford as well as the seven other posts in his department located in eastern Dakota and Minnesota.[6] The only cavalry serving in the eastern half of the Dakota Department was the Seventh, commanded in that fateful year by its lieutenant colonel, George Custer. The Seventh was deployed in toto to the 1876 campaign, leaving no other mounted troops in Dakota Territory or Minnesota.

Terry's functional control actually spanned the eastern and western halves of a lanky administrative department stretching from the Mississippi River in Minnesota to the Rocky Mountains in Montana. Forts Ellis, Shaw, and Benton and Camp Baker were founded in the 1860s in western Montana during the gold rush and general settlement occurring there. Until the onset of the Great Sioux War, the mission of these mountain-bound posts was generally limited to buffering the mining communities from Indian country. Troops from Fort Ellis, however, were the first to deploy to a Sioux War–related incident, the relief of civilian Fort Pease on the Yellowstone River in February 1876.[7] Later that spring Terry's chief western Montana subordinate, Colonel John Gibbon, fully deployed what he could of the Seventh Infantry Regiment and the entire four-company Montana Battalion of Second Cavalry to the Sioux campaign, leaving behind only skeleton reserves at the Montana posts.

During the eighteen-month war, Sheridan, Terry, and Crook rotated available troops to five successive seasons of fighting and welcomed a continual array of new forces deployed to the conflict from beyond the Dakota and Platte departments. Along with the fresh troops came hints of permanent new garrisons in Sioux Country. In June 1876, for instance, Crook established single-company infantry outposts on the Cheyenne–Black Hills road north of Fort Laramie, exclusively to protect trail traffic between that post and the mining camps. Neither Camp on Sage Creek (later known as Camp Hat Creek) in Wyoming nor Camp Mouth of Red Cañon in Dakota survived beyond this Sioux War. But they proved the utility of troops shielding the Black Hills mining communities and in due course bolstered the generals' justifications for expanding Camp Robinson and establishing Fort Meade, Dakota.[8]

Similarly, in the fall of 1876 Crook seized the opportunity to locate a strong infantry garrison on the Powder River in north-central Wyoming. He envisioned continued campaigning against the Sioux in the spring and summer of 1877 and intended Cantonment Reno (named after Fort Reno, an abandoned Bozeman Trail post nearby) to function as a forward supply base during those presumed operations. Crook and Sheridan certainly appreciated the strategic importance of that garrison sited in the midst of the Indians' revered unceded hunting ground. In due course the temporary cantonment was succeeded by the formidable Fort McKinney.[9]

Colonel Nelson Miles's reassignment to the Yellowstone River countryside from Fort Leavenworth, Kansas, in mid-1876 coincided with congressional authorization for new posts on the Yellowstone. Miles established Tongue River Cantonment as home for his sizable

"Yellowstone Command." From this colorless and temporary cantonment, Miles mounted consecutive sorties that broke the resolve of the fighting Sioux, scattering them to the Dakota and Nebraska agencies or Canada. Unlike the other expedient garrisons of 1876, however, Miles's temporary outpost was clearly linked to Sherman's and Sheridan's vision of permanent new forts on the Yellowstone. When Congress relented, the generals replaced the Tongue River Cantonment with Fort Keogh and then founded the equally substantial Big Horn Post, soon called Fort Custer. At the same time they maintained a cordon of troops in the field to protect the Black Hills mining communities and Powder River buffalo country. Permanently housing those additional soldiers and others in effect became round two in the generals' broad scheme of establishing new order throughout Sioux Country.[10]

News of Congress's approval for construction of the Yellowstone River posts came in July 1876 during the crucial days of the Great Sioux War. Although Sheridan sought to begin construction of the newly authorized posts immediately, the lateness of the shipping season stymied immediate action. But it gave Major Benjamin Card, Terry's department quartermaster, time to secure and arrange shipment of some eight thousand tons of building matériel, provisions, and garrison equipage and to recruit two skilled civilian workforces, each several hundred men large, for the looming construction effort. News that hundreds of tradesmen would be needed in Montana unleashed a job-hunting frenzy in Minneapolis and Saint Paul, where Card's subordinates recruited the required carpenters, masons, plasterers, engineers, sawyers, laborers, cooks, and waiters. Unlike the situation in earlier years on the frontier, enlisted troops would not be the principal construction forces at these new forts.[11]

First Lieutenant George Ruhlen, an officer detached from the Seventeenth Infantry and detailed as an assistant to Card, organized Minnesotans bound for the Big Horn River as if orchestrating an Indian campaign. The civilian superintendent of the Big Horn project was Charles K. Poor of Sioux City, Iowa, an experienced military construction contractor who had previously overseen building projects at Forts Randall, Sully, and Benton.[12] The 197 foremen, tradesmen, and laborers enlisted in Minnesota boarded a Lake Superior & Mississippi train for Duluth on May 14, reached Bismarck on a Northern Pacific train, and were aboard the Missouri River steamers *Dugan* and *Florence Meyer* en route to the Yellowstone by May 16. Already aboard were Lieutenant Colonel George Buell, Major Charles G. Bartlett, and four companies of the Eleventh Infantry. Most of these troops had been reassigned from the Standing Rock Agency downriver and constituted the initial garrison of Post Number Two.[13]

Meanwhile, another 198 mechanics and laborers departed Saint Paul on May 28, bound for the Tongue River and the site of Post Number One. This project was superintended by Captain Charles S. Heintzelman of the Quartermaster Department. Aided by matériel and labor shipments delivered by nine steamboats operating on the Yellowstone by two transportation companies and the army itself, the construction of the two posts proceeded speedily. Poor and Heintzelman were intent on quartering awaiting garrisons before the oncoming winter.[14] To assist the civilian workers at the Big Horn Post, Buell pressed his infantrymen to carry out an array of supporting tasks. By July 18, for example, his doughboys had cut some two thousand cottonwood logs from the Little Big Horn Valley and floated them to a site near the river's mouth where sawyers at a new steam-powered sawmill cut dimensional lumber from sunup to sundown. Intent on preserving local wood, Buell forbade cutting trees within eight miles of the fort. Even tipi poles abandoned in the Indian village at the Little Big Horn Battlefield were scrounged as fuel for use at Big Horn Post.[15]

By the end of August the construction of the Tongue River post was nearly half completed. The *Saint Paul and Minneapolis Pioneer Press* reported that all the Minnesotans would be home by October, except for some finishers. The projects slowed as summer waned, however, when the garrisons at both posts were put in readiness to join the looming campaign against Nez Perces who were invading the territory from Idaho. News from far western Montana was dire and caused considerable concern on the Yellowstone. On August 9 Looking Glass, White Bird, Joseph, and their Nez Perce followers had badly thrashed a force of Seventh Infantry and allied civilians commanded by Colonel John Gibbon in the Battle of the Big Hole.

The battle took place on the North Fork of the Big Hole River southwest of Butte, and the tribesmen were reportedly traveling eastward through Yellowstone National Park to the buffalo prairie. Miles's troops eventually engaged in the Nez Perce War, but Buell's did not.[16]

Despite the uncertainties associated with the Nez Perce tumult, the quarters, barracks, and storehouses at both posts were gradually completed and occupied by year's end, much to the relief of Buell's command, which had been tent-bound since early summer. The completion of work at both forts continued into 1878. The matter of names was finally resolved on November 8, 1877. Post Number One was officially christened Fort Keogh, honoring one of Custer's deceased troop captains, Myles W. Keogh, and Post Number Two, closest to the Little Big Horn Battlefield, became Fort Custer. Both names had been used unofficially for months.[17]

Forts Custer and Keogh were superbly built and served the army exceedingly well (Custer until 1898 and Keogh until 1900 and then intermittently thereafter as a remount station and quartermaster depot into the early 1920s). Though it had been founded by Buell and the Eleventh Infantry, by 1879 Fort Custer was headquarters for a succession of cavalry regiments and gained renown throughout the army as one of the finest cavalry stations in the nation. Miles, meanwhile, commanded Fort Keogh until December 1880 and policed the Big Open country and northern border tirelessly, denying Sitting Bull's refugees all opportunities to linger or hunt south of the acknowledged Medicine Line. By their very imposing presence, both Fort Custer and Fort Keogh manifested Sherman's and Sheridan's vision that the "Sioux Indians . . . would never regain this country."[18]

Throughout the nineteenth century the U.S. Army was continually challenged by its responsibility to protect the nation's borders and amorphous frontier and the fiscal realities of disbursing and quartering troops. Invariably the nature of the frontier dictated the existence of broadly scattered, exceedingly small, and hastily constructed interior posts that were notably expensive to maintain. Conditions on the nation's coasts were less severe. There essential locations were dictated by geography and generally fixed by mid-century. Each of the nation's coastal forts typically featured imposing masonry construction at some harbor entrance and adequate and stable regular artillery garrisons. On the ever-shifting frontier, in contrast, local circumstances usually demanded nearly spontaneous establishment and predictable abandonment of an array of forts serving immediate but rarely prolonged needs.

In the 1870s the army's strategic thinkers came to desire a system of consolidated "national" forts, and this zeal eventually played a major role in the garrisoning of Sioux Country. Brigadier General John Pope, commander of the Department of the Missouri at Fort Leavenworth, Kansas, and Terry's and Crook's peer, was a leading proponent of troop and fort consolidation. He addressed its merits as early as 1875 in his annual report to the secretary of war. In 1877 Pope renewed his call for consolidation, observing that the danger of Indian troubles was diminishing from year to year. Maintaining central garrisons would create enormous efficiencies for the army. Railroads now reached virtually every region of the country, he noted, and troops could be transported to points of need with considerable speed. The exercise and instruction of the army would be materially enhanced by troop concentration. Pope saw only one exception to the benefits of centralization. Garrisons were still needed at Indian agencies to safeguard Indians and whites alike.[19]

Centralization became a cause célèbre for Sherman and Sheridan in the late 1870s. But in the wake of the Great Sioux War the implementation of this strategy in Sioux Country was driven as much by day-to-day circumstances as by politics, budgets, and institutional desires. In the proximity of the Great Sioux Reservation, for instance, Terry drew attention to the demands of the Black Hills frontier. He declared that troops were needed there to safeguard the burgeoning mining and ranching settlements, the roads leading to them, and the Indians residing nearby. Terry particularly envisioned a new fort on the plains east of Deadwood in the vicinity of the northern Black Hills.[20]

With the scantiest debate and lobbying, Congress approved a new Black Hills fort in June 1878. Within one month companies of the First and Eleventh Infantry and Seventh Cavalry (all commanded by Colonel Samuel D. Sturgis, Seventh Cavalry) were temporarily encamped in the shadows of Bear Butte, on the Dakota plains eighteen miles east of Deadwood. Sheridan visited the northern Black Hills himself in mid-July and selected the site for the new post from several options, choosing a location about five miles southwest of Bear Butte where the forest and plains met. That fall Sturgis and most of his contingent returned to their permanent stations. Terry selected Major Henry Lazelle, First Infantry, to command the small residual garrison, consisting of two First Infantry and two Seventh Cavalry companies. Under Lazelle's general oversight, the raising of this ten-company post was superintended by First Lieutenant George Ruhlen, Seventeenth Infantry. Ruhlen was experienced in military post layout and construction, having just undertaken similar duties at Fort Custer the preceding year. The new Black Hills post was christened Fort Meade in late December 1878, honoring Major General George G. Meade, victor at Gettysburg, who died in 1872.[21]

Lazelle was reassigned as commandant of cadets at the United States Military Academy in April 1879 and replaced by the Seventh Cavalry's Major Marcus Reno, a stigmatized and continually controversial officer since the Battle of the Little Big Horn. In turn, Sturgis relieved Reno when the headquarters of the Seventh was transferred from Fort Abraham Lincoln to Fort Meade in early summer. Like Lincoln, Meade came to be known as a Seventh Cavalry post, which had particular cachet in the decades following the Battle of the Little Big Horn. Whether they were considered a taint or a charm, Little Big Horn veterans like Reno and First Lieutenant Charles A. Varnum plus scores of enlisted men and the famed battle-scarred horse Comanche, ridden at Little Big Horn by Captain Myles Keogh and now a venerated prancing museum piece, resided there.[22]

More important than the lingering curiosity attached to its residents was the role of the Fort Meade garrison in shielding the northern Black Hills from occasional Indian intransigence during the 1880s and 1890s and the more common thievery and rustling by white outlaws and fugitives. Like Forts Custer and Keogh, Meade safeguarded the settlement of a segment of Sioux Country. But unlike those forts, Fort Meade survived as a national military post until 1944. Thereafter it served as a veterans' hospital, a role it still plays today.

The congressional act of June 1878 that authorized Fort Meade also netted Sherman and Sheridan a new post in northern Montana on the Milk River in the shadows of the Bear's Paw Mountains, where the Nez Perce War was largely concluded in September 1877. In the generals' view, a strong northern Montana post would shield the territory from incursions by American Sioux living in self-imposed exile on the Canadian plains immediately north of the border. An up-to-date post would also allow the immediate abandonment of Fort Benton and eventual closure of Forts Shaw and Logan, in the lee of Montana's mountains.[23]

Construction of the Milk River post, soon to be called Fort Assinniboine, fell to Colonel Thomas H. Ruger and the Eighteenth Infantry, which transferred to Montana en masse in April 1879 from Atlanta and Chattanooga in the army's Department of the South. Ruger, an 1854 West Point graduate and veteran of the Battle of Gettysburg and other notable Civil War campaigns, tackled construction with vigor. The chosen site was northwest of the Bear's Paw Mountains. Because that dramatic mountainscape and surrounding plains were virtually treeless, planners initially considered constructing the post of adobe. But quantities of clay were abundant along Beaver Creek, which flowed along the south and east sides of the site. Despite the promise of spiraling costs the army contracted with Charles A. Broadwater, an enterprising western Montana businessman, to make bricks. Broadwater in turn hired some five hundred Métis (mixed-bloods) from the nearby Lewistown, Montana, area. They were soon producing as many as twenty-five thousand red bricks per day during construction.

The unique, all-brick Fort Assinniboine required second and third appropriations from Congress to complete, but by late 1880 construction of this imposing twelve-company post was substantially finished. In 1887 the Great Northern Railroad, advancing across Montana's Hi-Line Country, was instrumental in the founding of the community of Havre nearby and linked the stately new post to the nation's transportation network. Several regional garrisons were soon consolidated; Fort Benton was closed in 1880 and Fort Shaw in 1891. Fort Logan also closed in 1880, but largely owing to the growth of Fort Missoula, a newer post anchoring the mountain settlements farther west. Fort Assinniboine functioned until 1911. Its garrison fought no Indian wars, and the Canadian border was interminably peaceful.[24]

With Congress now vigorously endorsing Sherman's and Sheridan's vision of national forts and the ongoing transformation of Sioux Country, the generals seized the opportunity to fill other noticeable voids in Montana. They particularly fixated on the 250-mile gap between Fort Buford (at the Yellowstone–Missouri River confluence in northwestern Dakota Territory) and Fort Assinniboine. The generals called for a new post on the lower Milk River, perhaps in the vicinity of the Poplar River Assiniboine Indian agency, to secure that stretch of the national border and, more importantly, seal an important avenue linking the American Indian camps in Canada with their kin scattered across the Great Sioux Reservation.[25]

In the late 1870s this section of northeastern Montana remained vulnerable. Substantial numbers of buffalo still roamed the Big Open country and the land farther south, and the camps of Sitting Bull, Gall, Spotted Eagle, Rain in the Face, and Big Road in Canada numbered upward of three thousand people. So sizable a population intimidated the railroaders and cattlemen eyeing the country. The peaceful Assiniboine Indians, meanwhile, occupied a reservation in northeastern Montana north of the Missouri River. Although their Poplar River Agency was customarily guarded by a small contingent of troops detailed from Fort Keogh or Fort Buford, this was also a quiet point of contact for the Sioux. In October 1880 Congress finally endorsed the generals' desire for a permanent garrison at Poplar River, completing, in Terry's words, "the chain which stretches along the northwestern frontier from the Red River of the North toward the Rocky Mountains." At best, however, Camp Poplar River evolved into an inconsequential, coarsely constructed two-company agency post. Terry had envisioned a twelve-company garrison and sturdy brick construction as at Fort Assinniboine, but Fort Buford was close enough, the Great Northern Railroad was looming, and the matter of the Sioux in Canada was rapidly resolving itself. Camp Poplar River survived until 1893.[26]

Montana's west-central plains presented Sherman and Sheridan with a different protection dilemma. Forts Shaw, Logan, and Ellis were mountain-bound posts shielding the territory's gold country and Forts Assinniboine and Custer anchored the northwestern and southwestern corners of the vast Montana range, but nothing safe-guarded the middle. Accordingly, the generals appealed to Congress for a new post in the Musselshell River country to check sporadic Indian raiding there and protect the advance of the Northern Pacific Railroad in the Yellowstone River valley. In June 1880 Congress authorized the construction of Fort Maginnis, named for Montana's stalwart congressional delegate, Martin Maginnis.[27] Fort Maginnis was eventually located east of the Judith Mountains on Ford's Creek, a tributary of the Musselshell River. Like the modest Poplar River camp, Maginnis was an inauspicious post, conventionally quartering five companies of infantry and cavalry that chased occasional cattle rustlers but few Indians until the fort's abandonment in 1890.[28]

Camp Poplar River and Fort Maginnis belied the premise of strong, central garrisons on the nation's transportation grid. Initial construction of Fort Maginnis, in fact, was hampered by low-water conditions on the Missouri River. But both posts contributed importantly to Sheridan's vision of bottling up segments of Sioux Country, as did Forts Assinniboine, Custer, and Keogh. In reflecting on these gains, Colonel John Gibbon, writing for Terry in the Depart-ment of Dakota's 1878 annual report to the General of the Army, called Custer and Keogh "even more important than anticipated." By means of these large and self-sustaining posts, he concluded, "that whole region of country has been rid of the roving bands which infested it after the campaign of 1876, and the country practically opened to white settlement."[29]

Like Montana's new posts, Fort McKinney in the Powder River country of northern Wyoming effectively constrained the tribes-men's ability to access the northern buffalo range. Its predecessor, Cantonment Reno, was founded on the upper Powder River in October 1876 chiefly as a forward staging area for continuing field operations against the Sioux by Brigadier General Crook. The canton-ment's name was changed to Fort McKinney in August 1877, honor-ing First Lieutenant John A. McKinney, Fourth Cavalry, who was killed in Ranald Mackenzie's fight with Morning Star's Northern Cheyennes on November 25, 1876, in the southern Big Horn

Mountains. The squalid, dirt-roofed outpost served the army until June 1878, when it was abandoned and the name and garrison were relocated to the Clear Fork of the Powder River, some forty miles northwest of this initial plains location.[30]

The new, permanent Fort McKinney evolved rapidly. Situated on a well-watered bench against the backdrop of the Big Horn Mountains, McKinney typically quartered seven companies of infantry or cavalry. Its garrison played no significant role in Indian affairs, aside from its foreboding presence in the Powder River country. But it maintained peace on the Open Range, chasing occasional cattle thieves and intervening in the horrendous range war that bloodied Johnson County in 1892. McKinney also enabled the eventual abandonment of Fort Fetterman in 1882. Having fulfilled its purposes, Fort McKinney in turn was abandoned in 1894. Its worth in the course of settlement was substantial. More than a decade earlier in the 1881 *Report of the Secretary of War* Sheridan had echoed his time-worn epitaph about seeing beautiful farms, fields of wheat, oats, and barley, and hundreds of thousands of cattle in an area that "only two or three years ago was the land of the Indians and the buffalo."[31]

The second dominant motive driving Sherman and Sheridan in their transformation of the northern Great Plains military frontier in the post–Great Sioux War era was the pressing need to exercise firm control over the Sioux at or near assigned agencies on their own reservation. As Forts Assinniboine, Custer, Keogh, and McKinney guaranteed that the unceded hunting country and lands beyond no longer belonged to the Sioux and Fort Meade safeguarded the Black Hills gold country, Forts Robinson, Sully, Yates, and others would soon ensure absolute control of the Sioux agencies. Several of these posts survived well into the twentieth century, which speaks to a tempering hesitancy and doubt shadowing Sioux Country, even as other vestiges of the wild and dangerous frontier faded from existence.

Camp Robinson, Nebraska, was long in the throes of Oglala Sioux agency affairs, originating in 1874 to protect the nearby Red Cloud Agency. The Oglalas were moved closer to the Missouri River during the winter of 1877–78, for a while abandoning the

White River and Pine Ridge country and Camp Robinson altogether. But the government's hope that these Sioux would accept
a permanent agency along the Missouri proved futile. In the fall
of 1878 the Oglalas relocated again, this time to White Clay Creek,
Dakota Territory, where the government conceded a home that would
soon be called Pine Ridge Agency. This site was some seventy miles
northeast of the old Red Cloud Agency.[32]

Meanwhile, the Brulé Sioux were similarly relocated in the fall
of 1877, eastward to the vicinity of the former Ponca Indian agency
on the Niobrara River in northeastern Nebraska. Like the Oglalas,
the Brulés also rejected a permanent Missouri River agency and
returned to the west in the fall of 1878, this time settling on Rosebud
Creek, Dakota. Their agency, soon called Rosebud Agency, was
situated some ninety-five miles northeast of the former Spotted
Tail Agency on Beaver Creek in Nebraska's Pine Ridge. The new
Oglala and Brulé agencies were finally located on the Great Sioux
Reservation. The former Nebraska locations had been only irritating
deviations in the 1870s from intended government control of the
Lakotas on their reservation.[33]

Crook first proposed expanding Camp Sheridan to become the
protectorate garrison for the new Pine Ridge and Rosebud agencies
because it was closer than Camp Robinson. Sheridan spurned the
suggestion, however, doubtless aware of Robinson's continuing strategic value on the southern margins of the Black Hills gold country
and on the useful Sidney–Black Hills stage and freight road. Crook
countered that Camp Robinson needed substantial updating and
its reservation needed to be enlarged. Sheridan concurred. Reflecting
its newfound permanence, Robinson's name was changed from
"Camp" to "Fort" in December 1878. In 1883 it experienced the
first of several dramatic expansions. Fort Robinson's soldiers played
continuing prominent roles in northern plains Indian affairs, participating notably in the wrenching Cheyenne Outbreak of 1878 and
the Ghost Dance–driven Pine Ridge campaign of 1890. Its continued
life doomed Camp Sheridan in 1881 and Fort Laramie, Wyoming,
in 1890. Meanwhile, the Fremont, Elkhorn, and Missouri Valley
Railroad reached the post in 1886, linking it to the nation's transportation network. More than other posts, Fort Robinson fit the

generals' vision of a consolidated and connected national military post, doubling uniquely as a Sioux agency watchdog. Robinson survived the frontier, serving as a quartermaster remount depot after the turn of the century and as a World War II K-9 training center and prisoner-of-war camp. It closed in 1948, ending a colorful chapter in local history and the intriguing saga of the Sioux War posts.[34]

The new Rosebud Agency for the Brulé Sioux lay some 140 miles east-northeast of Fort Robinson and well beyond any reasonable oversight provided by that garrison. The commanding generals accordingly obtained congressional consent in June 1879 to establish a more purposeful Rosebud post to be located in north-central Nebraska on the picturesque Niobrara River. A post in this quarter would also provide security for the settlers and cattlemen invading the lush Sandhills country in the heart of Nebraska. Construction of Fort Niobrara commenced in April 1880 when three companies of the Fifth Cavalry and one company of the Ninth Infantry commanded by Major John J. Upham, Fifth Cavalry, arrived from other assignments in Wyoming and Nebraska. Although pine was readily available in the Niobrara Valley, most of Fort Niobrara was constructed of adobe. Initial work on the envisioned four-company post was completed by the onset of winter.[35]

Fort Niobrara's garrison was seldom needed at Rosebud Agency, twenty miles northwest, but that potential still ruled military thought in the 1880s. Colonel John Gibbon, while temporarily commanding the Department of the Platte in 1884, argued that both Forts Robinson and Niobrara were "well located as picket posts for the close observation of the most powerful and warlike tribe of Indians on the continent, but [those] garrisons are entirely too small for immediate offensive operations in the case of an outbreak."[36]

The Black Hills–bound Fremont, Elkhorn, and Missouri Valley Railroad crossed the Niobrara River five miles southwest of the fort in early 1883, connecting the post to the nation's ever-expanding railroad network. And the army's continuing zeal to close small, obsolete frontier garrisons led to the abandonment of Nebraska's Fort McPherson (1880) and Fort Hartsuff (1881) and South Dakota's Fort Randall (1892). These changing circumstances and perhaps Gibbon's prodding led to the expansion of Niobrara's garrison from four to six companies in 1885 and eight companies in 1891. Niobrara's troops were called to the Rosebud Agency in November 1890 during the Ghost Dance frenzy, but trouble abated there while boiling over at Pine Ridge. A decade later the garrison was skeletonized during the Spanish-American War and Philippine Insurrection and the post was slated for abandonment, only to be fully reoccupied in 1902. By then, however, the adobe structures had seriously deteriorated. The army evinced no desire to upgrade the post and in 1906 dispatched its garrison to Texas. Local ranchers and farmers immediately salvaged most of Fort Niobrara's buildings except for a few retained until 1911 as an army remount depot. In 1912 the site and portions of the military reservation were converted to use as a national wildlife refuge, which still exists.[37]

Two posts emerged on the Missouri River in the post–Great Sioux War era from a much more expansive slate. In 1870 no less than seven individual garrisons dotted the eastern boundary of the Great Sioux Reservation. Some originated as outposts shielding advancing steamboat traffic, while others were founded as agency guardians for various Nakota and Lakota Sioux bands.[38] By war's end, only Forts Sully and Yates continued to play a meaningful role as agency guards and overseers of settlement.

A new or second Fort Sully was established in 1866 on the east bank of the Missouri, some thirty miles south of the mouth of the Cheyenne River, replacing a smaller post bearing the same name established downriver in 1863. By the mid-1870s Sully's garrison chiefly shadowed the Cheyenne River Agency, ten miles upriver, which was the assigned home of Sans Arc, Miniconjou, Two Kettle, and Blackfeet Sioux. Fort Sully's troops did not substantially participate in the various campaigns of the Great Sioux War, because Brigadier General Terry drew his combatants more easily from posts farther north in the territory and Minnesota. But Sully's typical four- or five-company garrison was nevertheless fully occupied on the Missouri, particularly when avenues to the Black Hills goldfields were charted across Sioux Country and segments of the reservation were opened to settlement. Unlike Robinson and Niobrara, Fort Sully was never dramatically expanded or redeveloped in the

1880s; but it proved of continuing utility until 1894, leading to the abandonment of Fort Hale in 1884 and Fort Bennett (the official, one-company Cheyenne River Agency post) in 1891. Sully was South Dakota's last Missouri River fort.[39]

From 1870 to 1875 a small garrison of two or three companies guarded the Grand River Agency, administrative headquarters for Hunkpapa and Blackfeet Sioux located at the mouth of the Grand River in central Dakota Territory. The agency and protectorate post were relocated upriver in June 1875 to the west bank of the Missouri, some thirty-five miles south of Fort Rice and sixty miles below the Northern Pacific Railroad's temporary terminus at Bismarck. Like Camp Robinson, the new Post at Standing Rock and the adjacent Indian agency witnessed tumultuous times in the immediate postwar years, with hundreds of tribesmen surrendering arms and horses after returning from seasons of active resistance. In 1877 and 1878 five or six companies were routinely quartered at the post; nine were in residence in the fall of 1876.[40]

The Post at Standing Rock was renamed Fort Yates on December 30, 1878, honoring Captain George W. Yates, Seventh Cavalry, who was killed in the Battle of the Little Big Horn. The Yates garrison witnessed the poignant arrival of Sitting Bull and his small band of followers on August 1, 1881, soon after surrendering at Fort Buford on July 19. The garrison and adjacent agency also figured prominently in the murderous Ghost Dance unrest enveloping the Standing Rock Reservation in 1890. Among the casualties was Sitting Bull himself, who for a long time was interred in the Fort Yates military cemetery. Like Sully, Fort Yates was never counted among the so-called national posts, but it functioned as a Sioux agency guardian until September 1903. Its continuing life in the midst of the Hunkpapas led to the end of Fort Rice in 1878 and Fort Abraham Lincoln in 1891. Though most traces of the post disappeared decades ago, the community of Fort Yates remains the highly visible headquarters of today's Standing Rock Reservation.[41]

Among the remaining military posts dotting northern Dakota Territory, only Fort Buford endured, surviving until 1895 as one of the last in the chain guarding the northern border and remnants of Sioux Country. The Great Northern Railroad passed Fort Buford in 1886, but no great remodeling or enlargement occurred to draw it into the scheme of national forts. It outlived Camp Poplar River by two years, however, and Fort Stevenson (downriver), which was abandoned in 1883. Fort Pembina, located in the extreme north-eastern corner of North Dakota, was also abandoned in 1895. The northern border was never troubled.[42]

The Great Sioux War and subsequent relations with the Lakotas defined military purpose and order across the northern Great Plains in the final quarter of the nineteenth century. No less than twenty-six posts dotted Sioux Country in the mid-1870s, mostly positioned along its margins. These posts, in turn, were supported by another dozen garrisons in the distant corners of the Platte and Dakota departments. The commanding generals lamented that none of their posts in the mid-1870s were strategically located in the heart of the Sioux hunting country where most of the fighting was antici-pated and in fact occurred. Before the close of 1876, however, the fore-runners of Forts McKinney and Keogh were securely planted where buffalo still roamed, and other developments loomed.

In reordering the northern plains garrisons, Sherman and Sheri-dan were driven by the dual objectives of containing the various Lakota bands at assigned agencies on the Great Sioux Reservation and safeguarding the former hunting lands for white settlement. With additional forts like Assinniboine, Custer, Maginnis, and Niobrara, the tally across Sioux Country actually rose to thirty-one permanent military installations in 1880 before widespread consoli-dation commenced. But with the closing of small, obsolete garrisons like Benton, Logan, Fetterman, Hartsuff, and Stevenson, the number of posts fell to twenty-two in 1885 and to a mere nine in 1895.

Fort Assinniboine, Montana, survived into the early twentieth century as the last of the northern plains border forts. The Sioux had ceased to be an issue for that garrison in the early 1880s, but the fort was well built and strategically located and was not aban-doned until 1911. Forts Custer and Keogh, Montana, at first bottled up Sioux hunting country, but their respective missions soon refo-cused on the policing of the nearby Crow and Northern Cheyenne reservations, respectively. Fort Washakie in central Wyoming (earlier called Camp Brown) contributed modestly to the 1876 campaigns but within a few years chiefly policed the Shoshone-Arapaho reservation. While invariably attendant to the demands of Sioux Country, Fort Meade, South Dakota, paid greater attention in the 1890s and later to affairs in the Black Hills, with the advance of railroads and the maturation of communities and mines. Fort Meade also outlasted the frontier, and its many surviving old buildings and quaint Old Army cemetery proudly reflect its Wild West heritage.

Fort D. A. Russell at Cheyenne owed its origin in 1867 to the advancing Union Pacific Railroad. It marshaled troops and supplies for the 1876 campaigns and survived the frontier era as a model national post in a state capital and on the nation's premier transcontinental railroad. It is the only Sioux War–era fort functioning today, surviving from 1930 until 1947 as the renamed Fort Francis E. Warren and since 1947 as Francis E. Warren Air Force Base. Today the legacy of the frontier weighs heavily at Warren, with hundreds of substantial red brick army buildings from the turn of the twentieth century scattered across its vast developed area. Since its redesignation as an air force base, Warren has consistently quartered a major air force missile command; while the base has no airfield, it still has twenty substantial brick stables, an ultimate tribute to the days of cavalry, field artillery, and the Old West.[43]

Forts Robinson and Niobrara, Nebraska, and Yates, North Dakota, lingered as the last of the Sioux reservation watchdog garrisons, although the Indian intransigence of the 1870s gave way to a marked civility by the 1890s and a growing curiosity by the turn of the twentieth century. The Oglalas, Brulés, and Hunkpapas residing on the respective Pine Ridge, Rosebud, and Standing Rock reservations became frequent guests at local garrison functions. Ironically, in September 1934 a handful of aged veterans of the Great Sioux War, along with several hundred other tribesmen from Pine Ridge, came to Fort Robinson to participate in the dedication of a memorial to the death of Crazy Horse. But the events of 1876 and 1877 were fleeting memories by the 1930s. Robinson and the other Old Army posts were mere relics of a colorful and tumultuous bygone era.[44]

4

THE ARMY AND THE
NORTHERN PACIFIC RAILROAD

General Sheridan departed the Upper Missouri region on July 27, 1877, aboard a Northern Pacific passenger train bound from Bismarck to Saint Paul, after completing his month-long exploration of Sioux Country. He could hardly bridle his enthusiasm for the opportunities awaiting adventuresome easterners and emigrants willing to challenge this new frontier. At every pause on his survey of the Big Horn and Powder River basins, the Yellowstone River country, and the Upper Missouri region, Sheridan saw fertile, well-watered valleys and superb grazing lands. He knew that industrious new garrisons at Forts Custer and Keogh and others to come were perfectly positioned to accommodate the inevitable settlement of this newly wrested Indian land. A transcontinental railroad, though momentarily idled at Bismarck, would soon resume tracklaying through the very heart of the northern plains. And once again Sheridan's Army would work in all ways necessary to ensure the successful completion of this Northern Pacific Railroad, just as the army had supported the Union Pacific and Kansas Pacific railroads nearly a decade earlier when they built across the plains of Nebraska, Kansas, and Wyoming.

Even with the Sioux removed to the Great Sioux Reservation or to Canada, the northern Great Plains remained raw and untamed, if decidedly less dangerous than when railroad surveyors explored the Yellowstone Valley in the early 1870s. Although much had changed in the intervening years, much was also at stake. Sherman, Sheridan, and the army continued to work diligently for the benefit of the nation and the army. Sherman justified their support of railroads in many ways. Certainly military operations throughout the plains were materially enhanced by the much speedier movement of troops and stores by rail, not at the pace of a horse. The army benefited economically too: the transportation of property and troops was free from tolls or other charges on land-grant and bonded railroads, which included all the Pacific lines. The West's expanding railroad grid allowed Sherman to close many scattered and unduly costly outposts, concentrating army garrisons at larger, centrally located forts. They could be advanced anywhere as the need arose. The generals certainly appreciated that the spread of railroads throughout the American West had "a most salutary and positive effect in settling our Indian troubles," as George Crook observed in 1877. Sherman crowed that "these railroads have completely revolutionized our country."[1]

The army, of course, had already abetted the Northern Pacific's advance from Minnesota into Dakota Territory. In 1872 it established Fort Seward where the line crossed the James River and Fort McKeen (renamed Fort Abraham Lincoln in 1873) on the west bank of the Missouri River slightly below Bismarck, where the track ended through most of the 1870s. The settlement of the Red River valley west of Fargo and along the railroad west to Bismarck followed. The line promoted itself heavily and readily sold acreage received in land grants carved out of the public domain. Indian resistance was virtually nonexistent in northeastern Dakota, and Fort Seward was abandoned in 1877.[2]

The army had also diligently supported the Northern Pacific's surveying adventures in the Yellowstone River country of Montana in the early 1870s. The work of field engineers and surveyors there, however, was not nearly as unobstructed as in eastern Dakota. The company was simultaneously building grade and laying rail eastward through the Columbia River valley of Washington and Oregon and westward from Minnesota. But the Yellowstone Valley represented a formidable obstacle in the early 1870s in crossing inhospitable Indian country—and nearly all of it Sioux Country.

In 1871 well-outfitted expeditions were mounted from Fort Rice on the Missouri River and Fort Ellis at Bozeman. Railroad officials blithely hoped that they would map the uncharted Yellowstone River countryside, leaving little if any survey work to be completed in 1872. The surveyors based at Fort Rice were led by Thomas L. Rosser, chief engineer of the railroad's Dakota Division and noted as one of George Custer's West Point classmates and a former Confederate general officer. Rosser was accompanied by seven companies of infantry commanded by Lieutenant Colonel Joseph N. G. Whistler of the Twenty-second Infantry. This expedition traced a line through western Dakota and eastern Montana that generally followed the Heart River to its head, spanned the Little Missouri River about where Andrews Creek joins, and followed Glendive Creek west to the Yellowstone. Rosser and Whistler returned to the Missouri River in mid-October without incident. They did not explore the Yellowstone Valley, however, or encounter the Montana-based surveyors.[3]

The Fort Ellis crew, meanwhile, was first directed by civilian engineer Edward D. Muhlenberg. He led a small corps of unescorted surveyors across Bozeman Pass to the Yellowstone and reached the vicinity of the Crow Agency, near today's Livingston. There they awaited two companies of Second Cavalry from Fort Ellis commanded by Captain Edward Ball. Muhlenberg floundered, intent on skirting Crow Indian land by tediously surveying the river's difficult north bank while ignoring the more agreeable south bank. In early November Muhlenberg was succeeded by W. Milnor Roberts, the Northern Pacific's chief engineer, who was accompanied from Fort Ellis by additional troops commanded by Major Eugene M. Baker of the Second Cavalry. By late November the surveyors had advanced some 170 miles east of Fort Ellis. Roberts concluded that the company would need to bridge the river several times and also cross Crow land.[4]

A considerable expanse of unsurveyed land remained in the Yellowstone Valley, and in 1872 expeditions again advanced into Sioux Country from Forts Rice and Ellis. The railroad determined to locate an acceptable line between the area near Pryor's Creek in the west and Glendive Creek in the east. The Fort Ellis escort was again commanded by Major Baker, who this time led eight companies of Second Cavalry and Seventh Infantry. On August 14 Baker's column was attacked by Sioux and Northern Cheyenne warriors below Pryor's Creek, but the tribesmen were repulsed. One soldier was killed and another soldier and three civilians wounded, while two Indians were killed and ten wounded. The surveyors advanced to the vicinity of Pompey's Pillar, east of today's Billings, and were again attacked by Indians. At this point the railroaders concluded that they were inadequately protected and refused to continue downstream. They rather unceremoniously abandoned the field.[5]

The column from Dakota was led by Colonel David S. Stanley of the Twenty-second Infantry, a veteran officer with considerable experience on the Great Plains. Commanding twelve companies drawn from the Eighth, Seventeenth, and Twenty-second infantry regiments, Stanley's column, numbering some six hundred soldiers and railroaders, advanced westward in mid-July. Rosser again directed the surveyors, who this season explored a route across western Dakota generally south of the 1871 line to the head of O'Fallon Creek in Montana and down the creek to the Yellowstone. Indians repeatedly harassed Stanley, who decided against waiting for Baker, not knowing that the major had withdrawn. Stanley started retracing his outbound trail on August 19, returning to Fort Rice on October 15. Neither Baker's party nor Stanley's party materially advanced the Northern Pacific's alignment in 1872, although Rosser refined the line through a portion of the Little Missouri badlands. The failures of 1872 were directly attributable to increased Indian resistance, necessitating a third year of surveying to determine a line in the Yellowstone Valley between Pompey's Pillar and the mouth of the Powder River.[6]

The Northern Pacific organized a single survey in 1873, headed by Rosser and again with a military escort commanded by Stanley. Stanley's force was substantially enlarged that season, tallying thirty companies of Sixth, Eighth, Ninth, Seventeenth, and Twenty-second Infantry and Seventh Cavalry—in all some nineteen hundred soldiers and civilians. The Seventh Cavalry (again commanded in the field by Custer, as had become the norm in the history of this still relatively new regiment) was transferred from Reconstruction service in the South to Dakota Territory to strengthen the expedition's defense capability. The expedition hastened to the location of Muhlenberg's terminated 1871 venture and commenced a careful survey east along the Yellowstone. The pace was tedious, with almost constant harassment from the Sioux. Elements of Custer's command engaged in three sharp clashes: five soldiers were killed and four wounded, while four Indians were killed and another twelve wounded. Rosser's fieldwork was conclusive, however. The surveyors refined a railroad alignment between the Missouri River and Glendive Creek and determined a route along the Yellowstone. But tracklaying did not resume in 1874. By then the nation was deeply mired in the Panic of 1873, and the Northern Pacific was barely able to pay its surveyors and run an occasional train in the Dakota Division. The intense Indian resistance experienced by the surveying expeditions in 1872 and 1873 was equally significant and demanded resolution. Paradoxically, had the Northern Pacific not collapsed financially in 1873 but instead progressed directly to construction in 1874, an all-out war with the Sioux might have come to the northern plains two years earlier than actually occurred.[7]

Work on the Northern Pacific's Missouri Division, as the line from the Missouri River west to the Yellowstone River was known, resumed modestly under Rosser's direction in early 1878. Locomotives, cars, ties, iron, and other stores were moved to the end of track at the river's edge in Bismarck and then across the river in winter on rails and ties laid directly upon river ice. These unique but precarious and always short-lived ice bridges were the norm for the railroad until a three-span iron bridge set upon piers of solid granite masonry was completed in October 1882. In the intervening summers a large transfer boat outfitted with rails ferried cars from bank to bank.[8]

　　Tracklaying west of the Missouri River was capital intensive and cautious at first, as public confidence returned to the railroad. The line's net earnings had grown at a reasonable pace in the mid-1870s and were not markedly impacted by the great debate over the worth of railroad lands in Dakota that the company needed to sell to underwrite its expansion and early operation. Unlike the Union Pacific and Central Pacific railroad companies that built the nation's first transcontinental line in the 1860s, the Northern Pacific received no government subsidies for construction whatsoever. But it did receive a more generous land grant amounting to twenty square miles of land per running mile, which was sold to capitalize the line.[9]

In 1878 tracklaying advanced only ten miles beyond Mandan, the new railroad community on the west bank of the river opposite Bismarck, and earthwork extended barely eight miles farther. But work proceeded at a greater pace in 1879. The rolling prairie landscape in western Dakota was not particularly formidable until the work reached the point where grassy prairie uplands met the tortured badlands of the Little Missouri River, some 135 miles west of Mandan. Rosser's only initial construction hurdle was bridging the Heart River and its tributaries. With an east-flowing river and the rail alignment following its valley, in one stretch across the prairie the Heart required four bridges in the span of ten miles.[10]

At the peak of this activity, some two thousand men and eight hundred teams worked to build the Northern Pacific in Dakota and Montana. Such skillful orchestration was common to railroad construction on the Great Plains. While Rosser's surveys in the early 1870s had determined the railroad's general alignment west of the Missouri River, locating crews now worked as many as fifty miles ahead of grading crews. They established a specific course that considered the necessary cuts, fills, and crossings and the most favorable and least time consuming and expensive construction effort, linking point to point on Rosser's general survey. Bridge, trestle, and culvert crews simultaneously worked between the locating surveyors and grading crews, constructing water crossings by using local stone and timber where possible and otherwise preparing riverbanks for the fabrication of iron bridges. The bridges were purchased in the East, brought up by railcar, and assembled when the line reached each location.[11]

Grading crews armed with picks, shovels, and horse-drawn slip scrapers and wagons worked well ahead of track layers, throwing up a continuous earthen berm measuring some fourteen feet wide at grade level. They used material drawn or "borrowed" from either side of the center line, excavating to a base some twenty-six feet wide at grade in long cuts and slightly narrower in shorter cuts. The workers threw or carted excavated material out of the cuts to the forward or backward lines of the grade in a monotonous process known as cut and fill, thereby creating a well-drained surface for ties and rails. Often a spirited competition arose between grading and bridging crews on the one hand and track layers on the other. The graders and bridgers strove to stay ahead of the track, and the track crews hustled to keep pace with the graders. The ruling grade never exceeded sixty-five feet of vertical change per mile in this division and only fifty-three feet of change in the Yellowstone Division, which was critical to the efficient operation of locomotives and loaded cars.[12]

The definitive and iconic work in railroad construction was tracklaying. In these long transcontinental lines the methods were systematized and much admired. Supply trains constantly advanced ties, rails, spikes, and links to the end of track from siding caches and dumps that themselves were constantly being replenished from sources farther behind. Ties were manhandled from flatcars to small horse-drawn cars, pulled forward over the last rails laid, and again manhandled from car to grade. When empty, the small cars were tipped off the track so that others could be pulled forward; then they were rerailed and used again as railcars came along. In the appropriate sequence, a small car bearing rails came forward, and the iron was manhandled into place. Designated workers gauged the rails and others joined them end to end, using links and hefty nuts and bolts. Simultaneously, other workers dropped spikes at each tie. Thirty or forty men in relative unison drove those spikes, while others tossed more earth and tamped around and under each tie to lock the new track in place on the grade. Tracklaying was a fluid, seamless motion undertaken with urgency. Each man had only one thing to do, was accustomed to doing it, and did not have to wait on the action of anyone else. At times Northern Pacific track was laid at the rate of two or even two and a quarter miles per day. This was a notable achievement but well shy of a record set by Chinese laborers on April 28, 1869. They laid ten miles of track in a twelve-hour day in their final approach to Promontory Summit, Utah, and the celebratory completion of the nation's first transcontinental line on May 10, 1869.[13]

The labor associated with the Northern Pacific's bridging, grading, and tracklaying compares favorably to work on other contemporary transcontinental railroads—the Union Pacific and its Kansas Pacific subsidiary constructing in the 1860s and the Southern Pacific, now laying rail across the American Southwest and vying with the Northern Pacific for the distinction of being the nation's second transcontinental line. But the manner in which the United States Army labored to ensure the Northern Pacific's security and success was almost without parallel. As had been the case with the support rendered to the alignment surveys in the early 1870s, military operations within the Division of the Missouri and Department of Dakota in 1879 again revolved around the needs of the Northern Pacific Railroad. The last shots of the Great Sioux War had been fired in July 1877 in the valley of the Little Missouri River, nearly on Rosser's railroad alignment. The wildness of the landscape ahead as well as the uncertainties posed by the Lakotas and other tribes still migrating in the region dictated the continuous deployment of troops to construction camps, end of track, and points in between. The army rallied to this call with alacrity.

The army's protection efforts began slowly in 1878, but little was required. The Northern Pacific mustered resources and labor in and around Mandan and began inching westward, no more than a day's ride by troops at Fort Abraham Lincoln, four miles south of Mandan. In August Rosser did explore the line westward to the divide between Beaver and Glendive creeks in Montana, accompanied by a Seventeenth Infantry company from Lincoln.[14] But when construction in Dakota gained stride in 1879 General Terry deployed troops accordingly. He dispatched one Sixth Infantry company from Lincoln in April, another from the Sixth in June, and one from the Seventeenth Infantry in July (replaced by yet another from the Sixth Infantry in August), plus a surgeon from Fort Bennett, the small post at the Cheyenne River Sioux agency below Fort Yates. In addition, in June a Seventh Cavalry company from Lincoln escorted

the railroad's vice president, John Stark, engineer Rosser, and others
to the end of track and on to the Little Missouri badlands. The
executives were intent on confirming the alignment through that
rugged landscape. With bridging, grading, and tracklaying scattered
over more than a hundred miles in 1879 from west of Mandan to
the Little Missouri River, these infantry companies rarely worked
in concert as they went about providing security to the laborers
and camps by their mere presence. Indians posed no particular threat
to the workers in 1879, and construction proceeded apace.[15]

In late October, when railroad work had slackened, two of the
army companies and the surgeon were recalled to Fort Lincoln.
Grade had been advanced to one hundred miles west of Mandan
and track fifty-two miles west, with scheduled trains running that
far. Company B, Sixth Infantry, commanded by Captain Stephen
Baker, was not withdrawn from the field but instead ordered to
establish a cantonment in the badlands where the railroad alignment crossed the Little Missouri River. Baker's company had been
in those breaks most of the summer. He chose a site on the river's
west bank and commenced construction immediately, finishing
quarters for the company and a storehouse for quartermaster and
commissary goods by mid-December and quarters for the officers
by Christmas. A stable, laundress quarters, hospital, guardhouse,
and bakery were completed in January. The post buildings, constructed of logs, formed a small quadrangle. Cottonwoods and
cedars were cut from floodplain groves several miles away, while
finishing materials like sheathing, doors, and windows were delivered
from Fort Abraham Lincoln. Baker dubbed his small post Cantonment Bad Lands. On New Year's Day in 1880 Baker reported that
the weather was stormy, game was plentiful, and "no Indian signs
have been discovered."[16]

Baker's camp was soon augmented with the arrival of Doctor
C. C. Miller, a contract physician dispatched from Fort Snelling in
Minnesota, and Frank Moore, a post trader appointed from Bismarck.
Moore established a store on the perimeter of the cantonment that
quickly became the social center of the post, offering a warm stove
and convivial meeting space plus an array of dry goods, groceries, and

liquors. Son of a Missouri River steamboat captain, the enterprising and affable trader was destined to become a prominent
businessman when trains arrived in October 1880 and frontier
enterprise flourished.[17]

Despite a typically fearsome Dakota winter and the withdrawal
of some workers and troops, several hundred graders continued to
labor in the badlands throughout that season. Contract freighters
also continued to forward carts, tools, and assorted iron from the
end of track. Work almost never ceased. Construction in the badlands
was slow and costly, with two long cuts alone accounting for the
movement of 100,000 yards of earth. Trestle work was common, as
the grade wound up to and over the tortured valley's many gullies
and ravines. By the following June grading contractors had crossed
the Little Missouri and were working on the first five miles west of
the river in the gradual ascent of the valley, bound for Montana.[18]

When construction resumed in earnest in the spring of 1880,
the army again mustered troops for another summer of support.
This deployment was notably larger than that of 1879. Construction not only spanned the Dakota badlands but reached the broad
prairie land between the Little Missouri and Yellowstone rivers
and then the Yellowstone Valley itself. This entire isolated area
was far from Fort Abraham Lincoln in the east and Fort Keogh
in the west.

Major Lewis Merrill of the Seventh Cavalry commanded the
1880 deployment, with three infantry companies drawn from the
Eleventh and Seventeenth regiments at Forts Lincoln and Yates
and three companies of Seventh Cavalry drawn from Forts Lincoln,
Yates, and Totten. Additionally, two Fifth Infantry companies from
Fort Keogh were dispatched to his command, ordered at first to
encamp on the Yellowstone River at the mouth of Cedar Creek. The
Sixth Infantry company at Cantonment Bad Lands was not assigned
to Merrill, although it was certainly acknowledged as one of the
forces working to secure the Northern Pacific's construction effort
that season.[19]

Forty-six-year-old Lewis Merrill was a seasoned officer well suited
to this command. An 1855 West Point graduate and brigadier general

of volunteers during the Civil War, Merrill was already well acquainted with western Dakota and eastern Montana. He had participated in one of the closing deployments of the Great Sioux War in the summer of 1877 and the Nez Perce War later that fall. His duty this season, as explained in orders received from General Terry, was simple enough: deploy his command to appropriate points along the line to provide best cover for the railroad's working parties.[20]

In June Merrill established a headquarters camp on the grade, dubbed Camp Houston, located at the head of the Heart River 130 miles west of Mandan. There he retained three of the companies assigned to him. At the same time, Merrill's two Eleventh Infantry companies established Camp Andenreid east of his Heart River camp where the rail line crossed the Green River 98 miles west of Mandan and closest to the end of track. In early July the two Fifth Infantry companies from Fort Keogh established Camp Thorington on the Yellowstone River at the mouth of Glendive Creek and were soon destined to shield graders approaching the valley from the Dakota badlands. Meanwhile, in mid-August the remaining Seventh Cavalry company established Camp McIntosh where the alignment crossed Beaver Creek in Montana, just west of the territorial line.[21]

From these fixed locations, Merrill's scattered troops diligently tended the Northern Pacific's bridgers, graders, and track layers as the railroad continued across western Dakota and into Montana, proceeding slowly through the badlands but with noticeable speed on the prairie. The occasional loss of horses and mules from the contractor's camps, invariably attributed to Indian raiders, triggered army investigations that often fingered white rustlers and not Indians. But actual instances of Indian raiding did occur. In early August warriors demonstrated against a telegraph construction party near Camp Houston and two days later fired into a contractor's horse herd near Houston, killing two horses and running off eighty. Seventh Cavalry Captain Henry J. Nowlan and twenty-eight men responded, recovering the horses but never closing with the raiders. In another instance, a sergeant and seven Seventh Cavalrymen and four Cheyenne scouts trailed Indian horse thieves in early August and actually closed with that small party, killing one, severely wounding two, and recovering the animals. The sergeant was later acknowledged in a General Order for his distinguished action. General Terry came west in July, carefully inspecting the railroad from Mandan to its end of track, pausing at several of the army camps, and conferring with Merrill on the accomplishments and needs of the summer deployment.[22]

Meanwhile, Company D, Seventh Infantry, commanded by Captain Richard Comba, was dispatched to Cantonment Bad Lands in early June from Fort Snelling to succeed Baker's Sixth Infantry company. Comba's men chased occasional horse raiders and kept an observant eye on graders still engaged throughout the badlands. Mostly, however, they tended what he and almost all post commander's called in their monthly reports the "regular garrison and escort duty" associated with the place. This amounted to a fairly unvarying martial routine common at military posts but in this case located at an isolated river crossing in an especially trying landscape.[23]

The Northern Pacific made good progress in the summer and fall of 1880. By late October construction trains were arriving at the Little Missouri River. On November 5 a temporary bridge spanned the stream and enabled track layers to continue working on the ascending grade. Graders, meanwhile, reached Beaver Creek, Montana, in early November and continued pushing westward. They were protected by one of the Eleventh Infantry companies relocated from Camp Andenreid in mid-November to the newly founded and short-lived Camp Breck, near Sentinel Butte, Dakota. A permanent bridge was completed across the river in late November. Scheduled train service commenced immediately between Mandan and Little Missouri Station, while construction trains continued beyond that point. Certainly the most notable event that year occurred on November 10, when Northern Pacific rails reached the Montana line. The occasion was marked with appropriate festivities, including the driving of a ceremonial silver spike.[24]

In late December tracklaying stopped for the winter about thirty miles short of the Yellowstone River. Grading had reached the Yellowstone Valley and progressed up the south side toward the Powder River, and locating crews had advanced the line to the Big Horn River under the watchful eye of Fifth Infantry companies from Fort Keogh. Even as most other work stopped, however, a crew of some three hundred men continued rock excavation throughout the winter on three particularly difficult bluff sections west of Glendive. It was especially important to the railroad that regular service on the line triggered almost immediate business, and pioneer ranchers in western Dakota and eastern Montana soon shipped cattle east to market. According to one railroad historian, in the fall of 1880 as many as thirty-seven cars of cattle were shipped in one day. Shipping cattle proved to be significant business for the Northern Pacific in the years to come.[25]

As work on the line largely closed in 1880, portions of Merrill's command were withdrawn. While some companies redeployed, Comba's company at Cantonment Bad Lands was maintained and now guarded the new station at the railroad's temporary terminus. In mid-October two of Merrill's infantry companies learned that they would overwinter on the line. Companies A, Eleventh Infantry, and B, Seventeenth Infantry, were ordered to establish a camp on Glendive Creek to safeguard railroad parties persisting in that locale. Camp Thorington at the mouth of Glendive Creek was abandoned, and its two Fifth Infantry companies returned to Fort Keogh. The new camp, christened Camp Porter, was established on the line four miles above the mouth of Glendive Creek. And in late November a lieutenant and twelve men from Company F, Seventh Infantry, from Fort Snelling were sent to occupy the railroad's Sentinel Butte Station and guard government and railroad property stockpiled there. Sentinel Butte Station lay at the westernmost crest of the Little Missouri River valley. The railroad provided quarters for these soldiers. The small detachment was attached to Comba's command and rotated periodically with men from Bad Lands cantonment. Duty at Sentinel Butte was short-lived, however, and the guard was withdrawn by the end of March 1881.[26]

When construction resumed in earnest in 1881, the army's related deployment was noticeably judicious, despite the isolated landscape through which the railroad labored. This was a candid reflection of other responsibilities weighing heavily on Terry and the Department of Dakota, including the return from Canada and subsequent stateside movement of Lakota Indians in the wake of their nearly four-year exile north of the border. As many as three thousand American Sioux lived north of the border following the Great Sioux War until neglect and starvation there compelled their return, band by band, beginning in the winter of 1880–81 (see chapter 7). Surrenders were occurring at Camp Poplar River and Fort Buford on the Missouri River and Fort Keogh on the Yellowstone. Monitoring this traffic from Canada across eastern Montana and northwestern Dakota to points of surrender, and then downriver on boats chiefly to Fort Yates, substantially engaged the troops readily available to Terry and limited security efforts for the Northern Pacific to meet essential needs but little more. At that time, Terry simply had no troops to spare and was offered none from beyond the Department of Dakota.[27]

Major Lewis Merrill again commanded the army's 1881 railroad escort. As in 1880, this amounted to scattering troops to a handful of small tent camps along the rail line to guard excavators, bridge builders, graders, and iron handlers. The two infantry companies at Camp Porter focused their support on graders and track layers approaching the budding hamlet of Glendive on the Yellowstone. Upriver, two companies from Fort Keogh again were detailed to Merrill's command. This time Company E, Second Cavalry, and Company I, Fifth Infantry, established Camp Garfield on the south bank of the Yellowstone at the mouth of O'Fallon Creek. Company F, Seventh Cavalry, from Fort Buford again also joined Merrill, establishing Camp Biddle on the north bank of the Yellowstone opposite the mouth of Glendive Creek at the site of the old Glendive Cantonment, which dated to Great Sioux War days. Merrill exercised administrative oversight over Comba's company at Cantonment Bad Lands and the soldier camp established in the Short Pine Hills some 110 miles south of the cantonment, where railroad tie cutters were engaged. That camp, called "Camp Cook [*sic:* Cooke]" and commanded by Captain Charles S. Ilsley, Seventh Cavalry, consisted of two Seventh Cavalry companies and one from the Twenty-Fifth Infantry, all drawn from Fort Meade near the Black Hills. Seventh Cavalry companies from Meade had similarly guarded tie cutters in 1880, but that deployment had not been linked to Merrill's effort on the line. In all, nine companies were deployed to railroad service in 1881. They were overseen by Merrill directly or through reports to his headquarters, established at Camp Porter but separately called Camp Terry.[28]

Track advanced into Glendive on July 4. The town was already booming, its population having exploded from 150 the previous winter to 1,200 or 1,500 in 1881. Glendive marked the terminus of the Northern Pacific's Missouri Division and commencement of its Yellowstone Division, and construction of a roundhouse, water tower, machine and blacksmith shops, and station was well underway. The route west in the Yellowstone Valley posed new challenges. The valley was narrow and hemmed in by massive bluffs on one side or the other. The railroad could either bridge the river at every sharp bend in its course or follow one bank and cut a roadway through rocky precipices whenever they hugged the river's bank. The Northern Pacific adopted the latter course, following the Yellowstone's south bank west 225 miles almost to Billings, repeatedly cutting through bluffs, and even tunneling where necessary.[29]

Construction initially advanced slowly along the Yellowstone. Problematic bluffs were encountered within nine miles of Glendive, and track had advanced a mere thirty miles by mid-September. Significant bridging was also required, including structures over the Powder and Tongue rivers. As in Dakota, bridges in the Yellowstone Valley were first constructed with timber trusses set on piles and cribbing filled with rock but were replaced in time with Howe iron trusses set on stone piers. For all the valley's difficulties with hardrock bluffs, however, difficult construction was offset by long grade tangents across nearly always level bottomlands that required little more labor to build than throwing up enough earth for a roadbed. One of these level sections was sixteen miles long, another thirteen miles, and several five to eight miles. On November 28 track finally reached Miles City, which, like Glendive, boomed. A mere hamlet of several hundred citizens in October, chiefly serving the needs of nearby Fort Keogh and pioneer cattlemen, the town now sported a "floating population" of nearly three thousand.[30]

By late fall Merrill's command had mostly returned from the field. The battalion with the tie cutters in the Short Pine Hills went back to Fort Meade in mid-October, Captain James Bell's Seventh Cavalry company returned to Fort Buford about the same time, and the Second Cavalry and Fifth Infantry companies from Fort Keogh left at the end of October. Camp Porter was ordered abandoned on

November 19, with its infantry companies from the Eleventh and Seventeenth regiments returning to Forts Sully and Abraham Lincoln, respectively. Merrill's service this season was uneventful, despite the constant movement of Indians throughout the area. General Terry gave a fitting epitaph for the 1880 season (fitting as well for 1881 service) in his annual report to General Sheridan:

> Five companies of mounted troops and four companies of infantry, the whole under the command of Maj. Lewis Merrill, Seventh Cavalry, have been employed, during the summer and thus far during the autumn, in protecting the road, its workmen, and contractors. This duty has been well performed. The men engaged in the work of construction have not only been protected from actual injury but preserved from the causeless panics which almost always occur when men, who have no experience on the frontier, are sent into the Indian country.[31]

The winter of 1881–82 allowed more work to be done than in the previous year, and construction parties of all types continued pushing westward. Rail was advanced to the Rosebud Creek crossing by February 16, 1882, and reached the budding hamlet of Forsyth in March, with grading crews working fifty miles beyond. Like many towns along the line, Forsyth was laid out by the railroad, partly to serve its operational needs and partly for financial gain through the sale of town lots after scheduled service began. Ahead lay the Big Horn tunnel, the first of many to come. Located several miles west of the Big Horn River bridge, that 1,150-foot-long tunnel was holed through on March 27 and was ready for track in June. By then, grading crews were 130 miles ahead, near Benson's Landing, which came to be known as Livingston.[32]

The Northern Pacific needed the army for one final season, and once again Major Merrill orchestrated deployments from garrisons near and far. As early as March 1882 an infantry company from Fort Meade was detailed to the headwaters of the Little Missouri River to protect railroad tie cutters again working in that locale. As in years past, ties cut in the Short Pine Hills were floated downriver to a site near the railroad crossing at Little Missouri Station.

This venture uniquely relied on spring runoff for success on what otherwise was an exceedingly shallow plains watercourse. As in 1881, a company from the Twenty-fifth Infantry (Company H this season) was detailed to this duty, assisted in June by Company H, Seventh Cavalry, also from Fort Meade. Their work, in turn, was supported by Company L, Seventh Cavalry, from Fort Abraham Lincoln, directed to the field in late June.[33]

Railroad work in Montana in 1882 largely pushed beyond the margins of Sioux Country, crossing the Crow Reservation and at last reaching the Rocky Mountains, with the prospect of soon meeting construction crews working from the west. Merrill dispersed troops from Terry's Landing near the mouth of the Big Horn River westward to the mouth of the Boulder River, near present-day Big Timber. Company D, Second Cavalry, encamped there, and Company C, Second Cavalry, took station on the north side of the Yellowstone opposite the mouth of the Stillwater River, near present-day Columbus. Meanwhile, Company F, Seventh Cavalry, encamped near the mouth of Pryor's Creek, east of present-day Billings; and Company I, Fifth Infantry, and Company E, Second Cavalry, took station at Terry's Landing, the steamboat freight and passenger transfer station serving Fort Custer, thirty miles south. Merrill established his own headquarters south of the Yellowstone at the west end of Huntley Bluff, near Coulson. As in previous years, these tent camps were given the names of prominent army and railroad personalities: Camp Perin in the Short Pine Hills; Camp Morgan at the Little Missouri crossing; Camp Hughes at Pryor's Creek; Camp Hatch at Stillwater; and Camp Breck at Boulder Creek. Merrill's headquarters was designated Camp Villard, honoring Henry Villard, president of the Northern Pacific Railroad.[34]

After surmounting obstacles like the Big Horn tunnel and bridges over the Big Horn and Yellowstone rivers (the first crossing of the Yellowstone since entering the valley), Northern Pacific track layers approached the vast Clark's Fork Bottom north of the Yellowstone in mid-August. To the chagrin of local promoters, the railroad deliberately bypassed the existing village of Coulson. Speculators there, including a number of influential Montanans, had imagined a great boom from the sale of lands they controlled, only to suffer bust when the railroad instead surveyed the town site of Billings farther west. It established machine shops, a headquarters hotel, and a depot and generally spurred growth there on land it controlled in what one partisan ballyhooed as the "Second Denver." The first train arrived in Billings on August 22. Within four weeks the line was fully operational from there to Saint Paul, and business almost immediately flourished. By early October 354 cars of cattle had loaded out, and by the end of November 566 carloads had been sent east. Meanwhile, track layers continued their push west. On September 1 the gap between the two sections of the main line in Montana had closed to 500 miles.[35]

The line from Billings west to Helena, a distance of 239 miles, was designated the Montana Division. Construction as far as Livingston had the same general physical characteristics as in the Yellowstone Division, although with fewer instances of bluff cutting. Scheduled train service to Livingston began on January 15, 1883. But west of Livingston the railroad departed the Yellowstone Valley and encountered the Belt Mountains, requiring steep grades reaching 116 feet to the mile and construction of a 3,610-foot tunnel at Bozeman Pass. Work on the Bozeman Tunnel began in February 1882, and it opened to traffic on January 16, 1884. To allow tracklaying to proceed in the interim, a switchback line exceeding the allowable grade was laid over the pass into the town of Bozeman, where tracks arrived on March 14 and scheduled service began one week later.[36]

As winter set in, Merrill closed his third and final season of service to the Northern Pacific, dispatching his scattered command back to Forts Ellis, Custer, and Keogh. Merrill had already ordered the return to Fort Meade of the several companies guarding tie cutters in the Little Missouri Valley in September. But he momentarily retained Company L, Seventh Cavalry, at Cantonment Bad Lands because of supposed difficulties with Indians in that area. Except for that momentary and groundless unsettlement, the army's work along the line that year had been stunningly routine.[37]

By now Cantonment Bad Lands had outlived its usefulness too. On November 9, 1882, Captain Richard Comba's Company D, Seventh Infantry, was relieved from duty and entrained for Bismarck and eventual service at Fort Laramie in the Department of the Platte. Comba's annual report completed several months earlier suggests that a conspicuous tranquillity had overtaken the Little Missouri countryside and perhaps had existed much longer than implied in his summary: "Nothing since the date of report for last year September 3d. 1881 has occurred calling for action by the Troops at this Post other than occasional scouting and escort duty." To pack and dispose of the cantonment's public property, Second Lieutenant William H. Sage and a small detachment of Fifth Infantry were transferred from Fort Keogh. When their business was completed, they entrained for Keogh in March 1883. Sage's note in the camp's final monthly Post Return declared: "Post abandoned by withdrawal of troops at 4.30. AM. March 4, 1883."[38]

The railroad's work in 1883 had a renewed vitality, because progress in the east and west suggested the likely completion of the line sometime in late summer or fall. Work that year occurred well beyond the bounds of Sioux Country, and neither Merrill nor any other officer or military command at Forts Ellis, Shaw, Missoula, or elsewhere organized to protect the workmen. The railroad wended its way northwest from Bozeman to Helena and through another massive excavation, the Mullan Tunnel, beneath the Continental Divide west of Helena. Similar crews in Montana pushed from the west, following the valleys of the Clark's Fork, Flathead, and Jocko rivers into Missoula and the Hell Gate River (or Clark's Fork River as it is better known today) east of town to a celebratory meeting of the rails.[39]

The completion of the Northern Pacific Railroad was anticipated by the company president, Henry Villard, who spared neither labor nor expense to host a formal opening that honored the company's triumph. Americans had already taken pleasure in the grand finale of another transcontinental railroad at Promontory Summit in 1869, but that was the accomplishment of two companies. The Northern Pacific was the first single company to span the West. Aiming to draw the nation's attention to this feat, Villard invited financiers, politicians, bankers, journalists, and dignitaries from across America and abroad to join in his celebration. So many individuals accepted his invitation that four excursion trains of ten to twelve cars each were required to carry celebrants to western Montana. A fifth train originated in Portland and carried dignitaries from Washington, Oregon, and California. All were bound for Gold Creek, Montana, and ceremonies scheduled there for September 8.[40]

Villard's excursion began in Saint Paul; dignitaries enjoyed celebrations there and in Minneapolis before traveling west. Smaller festivities occurred at cities along the way, including Fargo, Bismarck, Billings, Livingston, and Bozeman, where music and speeches entertained enthusiastic crowds. Sitting Bull was among those participating in the gathering at Bismarck. The last spike site was located at the mouth of Gold Creek in the Clark's Fork Valley west of Helena. Villard had arranged for the construction of a lavishly decorated wooden pavilion with seating for one thousand. Rails actually had been joined on August 22, so twelve hundred feet of line were removed for a ceremonial relaying by crews from east and west. At 3 P.M. on September 8 Villard signaled the start of the grand celebration, cueing the Fifth Infantry Regimental Band from Fort Keogh to play the "Grand Triumphal March." This score was written expressly for the occasion by the band's chief musician, Kenneth Price. Villard then rose and offered brief remarks, which were followed by speeches from former Northern Pacific president Frederick Billings, secretary of the interior Henry M. Teller, representatives from England and Germany, governors of the states and territories through which the railroad ran, and former president Ulysses Grant, extolling the glory and importance of this new line. At appropriate pauses in the program the infantry band added a martial and celebratory air. During the ceremonial driving of the last spike, telegraph clicks signaling the completion resounded from coast to coast, while fire from two twelve-pounder Napoleon smooth-bore cannon from Fort Keogh reverberated up and down the valley. The Northern Pacific Railroad, stretching from Gold Creek westward 847 miles to the Puget Sound and eastward 1,198 miles to Lake Superior, was finished.[41]

The triumphant completion of the Northern Pacific Railroad also owed a debt to General Sheridan and the United States Army. It was a signal accomplishment in Sheridan's long and highly successful career. For more than a decade troops in his command labored to support this railroad, spending three seasons in the field in the early 1870s. They shielded surveyors exploring western Dakota and the Yellowstone Valley as they struggled to establish an alignment for the railroad. Sheridan's Army waged an all-out successful war with the railroad's principal objectors, but only after horribly bloodying the very land to be crossed by the railroad. Construction resumed after resolution of the so-called Sioux Problem and the financial recovery of the railroad and nation after the Panic of 1873. It continued under the watchful eye of troops for four consecutive years. The army's contribution to the success of the Northern Pacific was tremendous, as acknowledged by the company's earliest historian, Eugene V. Smalley (writing in 1883): "No historical account of the Northern Pacific enterprise would be just or complete without an acknowledgment of the very valuable services rendered by the army of the United States in protecting the surveys and construction of the road, and in reducing to subjection the hostile Indians along its line, and removing them to reservations, so as to open the country to settlement and civilization."[42]

Sheridan's view of this effort was comparably nationalistic. Certainly the Northern Pacific and all railroads allowed for the practical, economical, and rapid movement and supply of troops— a great gain for a small army still serving a frontier constabulary mission. And railroads changed methods of freighting in general. On the northern plains steamboats had ruled the Missouri and Yellowstone rivers for decades, but the advance and completion of the Northern Pacific brought a new economy. Private enterprise and governments, even in Canada, consigned business to the railroad and not the steamboat companies, except for ever-diminishing short hauls. Simple things changed too. Isolated Fort Buford now received mail from both east and west three times per week. And letters from department headquarters in Saint Paul were delivered in five days instead of eight, including a day and a half on a stage from Glendive.[43]

Even as Villard was driving his ceremonial last spike at Gold Creek in 1883, the impact of the Northern Pacific Railroad already had profound consequences throughout Sioux Country. Some had been anticipated, like the ready opening of midwestern and eastern markets for Montana and Dakota beef. Others were serendipitous, such as access to the massive northern plains buffalo herd and to markets eager for hides and then bone. The slaughter of the northern plains buffalo herd simply could not have occurred without the Northern Pacific Railroad, and cattle could never have spilled across the range had the buffalo remained. Sheridan knew this intuitively, having already witnessed the parallel story occurring on the central and southern plains. Sheridan's Army played an undeniable role in the transformation of the northern plains, but in the end it was the glint of Northern Pacific iron rails that brought this ultimate change to Sioux Country.

Interestingly, some contemporaries winced at the transformation unfolding before them. A pioneer in eastern Montana, perhaps in a moment of nostalgia, wrote: "Then came the army of railroad builders. That—the railway—was the fatal coming. One looked about and said, 'This is the last West.' It was not so. There was no more West after that. It was a dream and a forgetting, a chapter forever closed."[44]

5

"THE BUFFALOES ARE GONE"

In the mid-1870s the tribesmen in the Sioux and Northern Cheyenne camps probably never grasped that the buffalo across the northern plains were not nearly as plentiful as in decades gone by.[1] More likely, for these people and other northern plains tribes, the notion of immense, inexhaustible herds remained as vivid as in the past. These extraordinary monarchs of the plains embodied both literal and spiritual essences that sustained daily life, cemented economies, and enriched cultures. Buffalo meat, both fresh and dried, was a healthful and savory Plains Indian staple, augmented by the animal's tallow and marrow. Hides and fur provided robes, shirts, leggings, mittens, belts, lodge covers, bedding, utilitarian wares like straps, bags, shields, ropes, bindings, and even boats. The sinew, bone, and horns became bowstrings, thread, tools, and ornaments. The buffalo inspired social, political, and religious beliefs and rituals. Their seasonal migrations governed the movement of the Plains tribes and fixed the cycles of life.[2] John Fire Lame Deer, an early twentieth-century Brulé Lakota spiritualist, remembered buffalo and that unique time in the West: "The buffalo was part of us, his flesh and blood being absorbed by us until it became our own flesh and blood. Our clothing, our tipis, everything we needed for life came from the buffalo's body. It was hard to say where the animal ended and the man began."[3]

Even during the ebb and flow of troubles and treaties with the whites in the third quarter of the nineteenth century, hunting buffalo remained a constant among the northern plains tribes until the very end of the Great Sioux War. For the signers of the 1868 Fort Laramie Treaty, that necessity was guaranteed in article 11, which stipulated hunting rights north of the North Platte River in Wyoming and Montana and on the Republican Fork of the Smoky Hill River in Nebraska and Kansas. But as tensions mounted between the Sioux and those whites who were bound for goldfields or determined to advance another transcontinental railroad, the hunting rights across the northern plains were first constricted and then destroyed. The ability of the Oglalas and Brulés to hunt buffalo in the Republican River countryside disappeared upon the completion of the first transcontinental railroad linking Omaha, Cheyenne, and Ogden and the Union Pacific's subsidiary line, the Kansas Pacific, crossing Kansas to Denver. These two lines and others prompted the sequential slaughter of the entire southern plains herd. The entitlement of all the Sioux to hunt in the unceded country of Wyoming and Montana was revoked in the first article of the controversial Agreement of August 15, 1876, which also dramatically reshaped the Great Sioux Reservation by excluding the Black Hills. Yet despite these paper prohibitions and the relentless wintertime campaigning waged by Crook and Miles, Sioux and Cheyenne families successfully trailed buffalo in the remote haunts of Wyoming and Montana until the very brink of capitulation.[4]

Repeatedly during the war-torn winter of 1876–77 troops struck secluded Indian camps. While human casualties were generally limited, tipis, personal possessions, and freshly replenished buffalo food stocks were consistently destroyed. When Indian bands surrendered at the agencies in 1877, they all arrived in forlorn and starving condition. The sweet morsels of buffalo meat that the families had consumed in the days and weeks before were becoming memories that many would never again renew. The agencies instead gave the people cattle, sometimes on the hoof and sometimes in "block" (meaning butchered meat), and both elicited disgust.[5]

There was a time in the American West when buffalo were so numerous that they seemed to "blacken" the landscape for as far as the eye could see. Awestruck travelers crossing the Great Plains in the early nineteenth century described viewing buffalo in the most sensational terms: "innumerable" and "immense" herds were so vast as to fill the "view of the country for two weeks."[6] In 1839 Santa Fe–bound traveler Thomas Farnham reported seeing buffalo covering the entire country for three days. On the Arkansas River in 1871, Major Richard Irving Dodge, then of the Third Infantry, wrote that "the whole country appeared one mass of buffalo."[7] Sightings on the northern plains were equally dramatic and inspiring. In the 1860s buffalo were so commonplace throughout Dakota and Montana that they were almost always visible from passing Missouri River steamboats, whether grazing open prairie hillsides or wallowing in water. In 1867 veteran boat pilot Grant Marsh recalled the day near Elk Horn Prairie on the Missouri, 125 miles above the mouth of the Yellowstone River, when the sternwheeler *Ida Stockdale* was stopped for hours by a migrating herd. "In front the channel was blocked by their huge, shaggy bodies, and in their struggles they beat against the sides and stern, blowing and pawing. Many became entangled with the wheel, which for a time could not be revolved without breaking the buckets." No one aboard cared to shoot at the animals, "for the sight was too awe-inspiring a demonstration of the physical might of untamed creation."[8]

Even in 1876 the campaigners encountered buffalo with astounding frequency. Second Lieutenant John Bourke, an aide-de-camp to General Crook, recalled that the men of the Big Horn Expedition marching north in March saw buffalo nearly every day and that buffalo meat appeared at many a meal. Bourke added with a disarming candor that it was stringy and tough because the soldiers could only hit old bulls. Writing for the *Chicago Times,* reporter John Finerty mentioned the frequency with which the men of the Big Horn and Yellowstone Expedition, Crook's summer movement, encountered buffalo. In mid-June on the very eve of the Battle of the Rosebud the soldiers of the column crested a ridge and saw before them a sight "calculated to thrill the coldest heart in the command. Far as the eye could reach on both sides of our route . . . somber, superb buffaloes were grazing in thousands! The earth was brown with them." As Crook's Indian scouts gave chase with a cacophony of rifle fire and whoops and yells, "buffalo after buffalo went down," much to Crook's horror: he was sure that his presence in Sioux Country had been thoroughly betrayed. The men of Nelson Miles's Yellowstone Command had similar encounters. Second Lieutenant William H. C. Bowen, Fifth Infantry, recalled that the march from Tongue River Cantonment to Fort Peck in the fall of 1876 "took the better part of seven days and during that whole time the buffalo in sight were as thick all over the plains as the largest cattle herd in eastern Oregon today [1927], and these herds in sight were but a small part of the whole. They were moving in millions, mile after mile and mile after mile, too many even to estimate."[9]

Invariably characterized as a single mass of animals, as if in one gargantuan western herd, the 24 to 27 million buffalo that roamed the plains in prehistoric times were actually innumerable large and small herds dotting a myriad of micro-ranges throughout the Great Plains. *Bison bison* had indeed evolved an elaborate accommodation with its environment. As the dominant species of the Great Plains ecosystem, buffalo thrived on the nutritious blue grama and buffalo grasses of the plains landscape along with subordinate species as diverse as prairie dogs, pronghorns, and wolves. Certainly the great buffalo herds migrated, though not in vast sweeping movements but in random wanderings that spanned hundreds of miles to take advantage of local terrain, water, and forage. Generally the tribesmen knew where to find herds, which were predictably valley-bound in winter and spring, whether dodging fierce winter snows or grazing on succulent spring grasses, and on the uplands in summer, feasting on nutritious warm-season forage. Hunters knew too that fall's chill signaled change and the renewal of the annual cycle.[10]

Buffalo had a different worth in white society. Bartered robes from Indian country funneled through scattered trading houses furnished easterners with luxuriant sleigh and carriage blankets, bed and sofa covers, overshoes, and prized buffalo overcoats. Ironically, the decline of the robe trade by the early 1870s coincided with significant advances in the domestic tanning industry that allowed for the economical and efficient processing of dry, raw hides.[11] In eastern tanneries, thickly furred winter skins were tanned with the fur on to make covers and clothing, but summer hides also had value, producing fine leather. For a while, one broker's entire supply was consumed by the British army, which valued American buffalo leather for its elasticity and durability. America's expanding industrial complex demanded buffalo leather too, for use as belting on factory machinery.[12]

The northern Indians learned of the progressive destruction of the vast southern plains buffalo herd by word of mouth, especially from Cheyenne kin in the south. The notion of northern and southern ranges and herds had evolved from the days when the great east-west emigrant migrations sliced the range in half. Overlanders bound for Oregon, Utah, and California posed no particular threat to the buffalo. But as the Union Pacific Railroad, its Kansas Pacific branch, and its Santa Fe competitor tracked westward in the late 1860s and early 1870s the southern herd was doomed. The railroads not only penetrated the diverse ranges of the southern herd but provided reliable freighting to vast urban markets clamoring foremost for leather and sometimes for meat. In an opportunistic slaughter between 1872 and 1874, nearly 4 million buffalo were eliminated from the southern plains. By the mid-1870s it was easy to deny the Oglalas and Brulés treaty rights to hunt in the Republican River basin because precious few buffalo survived there anyway.[13]

The northern buffalo herd was always somewhat smaller. At the onset of the Great Sioux War, some 2 million buffalo dotted the Powder River country, the Little Missouri badlands, the Big Open between the Yellowstone and Missouri rivers, and a bevy of smaller scattered ranges across Sioux Country. Greater and lesser fur trading outfits including the powerful American Fur Company had preyed on the northern herd for decades. The tribes functioned as willing purveyors of well-tanned buffalo robes, delivering tens of thousands annually to Missouri River outposts like Forts Benton, Union, and Pierre. The demands of trade and tribal subsistence had a noticeable impact on the herd. Recognizing this, farsighted traders called for the government to ban the robe trade outright as early as 1858. Such pleas went unheeded.[14]

With eastern markets established for buffalo robes and hides, meat, and even bone, the southern herd was methodically slaughtered in a few years. It was inevitable that the northern herd also become fixed in the sights of Sharps and Springfield buffalo-hunting rifles. The convergence of forces was slightly different than on the southern plains, but the outcome was no less uncertain. The deadly forces were fully concentrated by 1880. By then Sioux Country had been cleared of its Indian residents and General Sheridan's array of purposefully scattered new military posts assured the permanence of that outcome. Meanwhile, cattlemen were slowly but deliberately inching longhorns and shorthorns onto the new open range. Buffalo, which offered a mere one-time profit, were in the way. Most important of all, the Northern Pacific Railroad resumed tracklaying west of the Missouri River in 1878 on a straight line from Bismarck to the Yellowstone River. By December 1880 the track had reached Montana and was a mere thirty miles short of the Yellowstone and the budding hamlet of Glendive. A year later the railroad reached Miles City, the dusty Yellowstone River village adjacent to Fort Keogh, already ordained as the principal headquarters of Montana's buffalo hunting fraternity.[15]

The final slaughter was largely the occupation of professional hunters, a distinctive class of generally unsavory characters remembered as dirty, greasy, unshaven, and frequently lousy and yet habitually hospitable and glad to help anyone in time of need.[16] Many had taken part in the systematic destruction of the southern herd. From Fort Benton on the Missouri and Miles City, Terry, Glendive, Sully Springs, and Dickinson on the Northern Pacific, well-equipped hunters ranged into the vast hinterland that harbored the northern herd. The arrangements were simple. Across the range, small, self-reliant hunting teams made forays from permanent camps tucked away in creek bottoms near reliable water and wood. One member typically did the cooking and camp chores while others hunted afoot and usually alone for beasts grazing on nearby uplands.[17]

Buffalo hunting was most common in fall and winter, when the animals' shaggy coats were most luxuriant, but summer hides were taken as well. Well-armed hunters, who preferred to be called "buffalo runners," typically sought small bunches of buffalo grazing or at rest, but most marksmen were also fully adept at killing animals on the run. The stalkers approached their quarry from downwind until they reached an advantageous rise as close to the herd as possible while still maintaining a semblance of brush or rock cover. The oldest cow was usually identified as the leader of the bunch and targeted first. While a thundering rifle clap invariably startled the group, the animals were typically inclined to follow their leader. If the lead cow was successfully killed, the survivors sniffed warm blood, pawed, bawled in wonderment, and did everything but run away. Another wary cow might start to move and would be targeted next. The danger was invisible, with the shots and blood bewildering the cows and calves until all were killed.[18]

Dropping animals one after another was called getting a "stand," and many veteran hunters were skilled at repeating such successes day after day. William Temple Hornaday was a renowned chronicler of this destructive time and also something of a celebrated buffalo hunter. He documented the tallies of men like Harry Andrews, a Montanan who once fired 115 shots from one set in a single hour and killed 63 buffalo. Other Montanans like Frederick R. "Doc" Zahl killed 83 in one stand, and John Edwards killed 75. According to Hornaday, the record on the northern plains belonged to Vic Smith, perhaps Montana's most famous hunter, who in the winter of 1881 killed 107 buffalo in one stand of about an hour's time, without shifting his point of attack. On the southern plains the record was purportedly 112 buffalo.[19]

The number of animals shot during a day was usually governed by the number that could be skinned. Animals shot in winter would freeze solid overnight and those shot during warmer weather would bloat, stretching the hide and making skinning difficult.[20] The pliant hides were stretched on the ground, hair side down, until they either dried or froze. Each grown animal's skin netted hunters from $2.50 to $4, depending on age and sex, so considerable care was taken during skinning to minimize any damaging knife cuts. Pegging the skins to the ground was rarely necessary, but the skinners usually cut their outfit's initials into the thin muscle adhering to the fleshy side. The carcasses, meanwhile, simply littered the prairie. Some hunters retrieved and marketed the hump roast and tongues, but little else was immediately salvaged. Montana pioneer Granville Stuart lamented the pathetic view in April 1880: "The bottoms are liberally sprinkled with the carcasses of dead buffalo. In many places they lie thick on the ground, fat and the meat not yet spoiled, all murdered for their hides which are piled up like cord wood all along the way."[21]

In due course the accumulated hides were transported to the river and rail outlets encircling the range. In the camps the skins were not folded but merely piled atop one another, hair side down. In getting the skins to market, however, the hunters usually folded them once lengthwise down the middle, with the hair side in, and piled them into high-sided wagons. Sometimes as many as a hundred skins could be hauled in a single load pulled by four horses.[22]

Fort Benton's buffalo shipping heyday occurred in 1876 in the prelude to the slaughter when the I. G. Baker and Company steamboating firm transported 75,000 hides to market. Fort Benton shipped twenty thousand hides in 1880, five thousand in 1883, and none at all in 1884. The town's hunters destroyed the scattered herds of north-central Montana, but much larger herds still grazed the Yellowstone River country in the eastern half of the territory. One Minneapolis fur buyer, J. N. Davis, opined that half a million buffalo were to be found within a 100-mile radius of Miles City.[23]

Even as the slaughter ensued, the presence and immensity of the northern buffalo herd made lasting impressions on those not caught up in the killing frenzy. Oliver P. Hanna, a roustabout and hunter in the Fort McKinney area in Wyoming, held an army contract to furnish the fort with five thousand pounds of wild meat weekly; his only lament was securing enough wagons to cart the flesh to the post. As late as 1881 buffalo remained so plentiful between Forts Fetterman and McKinney and north through the Little Big Horn and Little Powder River valleys of Montana that they caused cattlemen great anxiety. "They scared the range horses and stampeded them to the foothills," groused one woeful cowman.[24]

Perhaps those same animals very nearly overran Fort Custer in 1881 before a detachment from the garrison was ordered to the plain south of the post to skirmish them away figuratively if not literally. When an immense buffalo herd descended from the northern Yellowstone River bluffs overlooking Miles City and Fort Keogh in 1882, a squad of Fifth Infantrymen killed enough to fill six army wagons with fresh buffalo meat destined straight for the fort's kitchens.[25] Lieutenant William H. C. Bowen of Miles's Fifth Infantry provided a cogent view of the slaughter and its consequences in a reminiscence published in 1927. Buffalo meat, generally a by-product of the destruction, had selective value. "Thousands of buffalo were killed for their tongues alone," Bowen asserted, and thousands more for the strips of tenderloin along the backbone. "Tongues were retailed at Miles City and at Fort Keogh at the rate of 25¢ each or $3.00 per dozen. The tenderloin was retailed at 10¢ per pound." Bowen noted that the contract price for fresh beef by the quarter to the troops was 3¢ per pound at that time and officers were allowed to purchase choice cuts at the same price. He remembered an instance in the summer of 1881 when duties called him from Fort Keogh to the Poplar River Assiniboine Agency on the Missouri River, 125 miles away. "The carcasses of dead buffalo dotted the plains for the entire distance and the air fairly reeked with the odor of rotten flesh. A good athlete could easily have jumped the whole distance from carcass to carcass without touching foot to ground except at the river and ravine crossings."[26]

Second Lieutenant Joseph M. T. Partello, Fifth Infantry, recalled seeing a herd of some 75,000 buffalo crossing the Yellowstone in the vicinity of Fort Keogh in 1883, presumably bound north for Canada and hounded all the while by "Indians, pot-hunters, and white butchers." Less than 5,000 of that mighty mass, he claimed, ever lived to reach the Medicine Line.[27] Hunter-naturalist Hornaday was less illusionary. In fact, barely 275 survived the migration, he asserted, by taking refuge in the labyrinth of ravines and creek bottoms west of the Musselshell River and in the badlands at the head of Big Dry and Big Porcupine creeks. Hornaday extolled the extreme efficiency of the hunters, calling their labors a "life and work . . . at its best." "The only thing against it," he lamented, "was the extermination of the buffalo."[28]

During the peak of the slaughter, barroom and boarding-house banter in the gateway towns focused on favorite and prosperous killing grounds. Easily the most popular prospect was the vast Big Open, the triangle of land north of Miles City bordered by the Yellowstone on the south, the Musselshell to the west, and the Missouri River to the north. Lieutenant Partello figured that as many as 250,000 buffalo still inhabited this countryside in 1882. Dozens of other outfits preferred roaming south of Miles City and Glendive, particularly in the breaks and prairie between the Powder and Little Missouri rivers. Meanwhile, hunters from Medora, at the Northern Pacific's crossing of the Little Missouri, to Bismarck ranged south and east of the Little Missouri onto the headwaters of the Grand and Moreau rivers. Buffalo were hunted to extinction in every square inch of Sioux Country, from the obvious large ranges astride the Yellowstone River to the farthest reaches of the Milk and Marias rivers north of the Missouri, the Judith Basin, the Big Horn Basin, and all of western Dakota.[29]

The slaughter of the northern buffalo herd peaked and essentially ended as the winter of 1882–83 passed. Not even the buffalo hunters themselves were aware that the end of the great hunt had arrived so abruptly. Most outfitted again in the fall of 1883, sought out their favorite ranges that until then had been so profitable, but invariably ended the season in near or total failure and bankruptcy. Not only the millions but the thousands were gone forever.[30] A rancher traveling across the northern plains as the slaughter came to an end noted that he was "never out of sight of a dead buffalo and never in sight of a live one."[31] First Lieutenant Hugh L. Scott of the Seventh Cavalry, then stationed at Fort Meade, Dakota, also recorded this abrupt disappearance. "I traveled with [First Lieutenant Luther R.] Hare five hundred miles in search of buffalo in September, 1883. They had been plentiful the year before but now we did not even see a recent track. We met an old Sioux Indian who had been searching all summer and had killed one old scabby bull. Many thought they had gone north into Canada. The Indians thought they had gone underground to rest and would come again, as they were told in their ancient legends had happened before. But the buffalo never returned."[32]

Hornaday attempted to quantify the slaughter. A principal informant was J. N. Davis, the Minneapolis fur buyer. In Davis's accounting, the first shipments of buffalo skins from Northern Pacific Railroad stations in Montana and Dakota occurred in 1881 as the line was still advancing westward. He received some fifty thousand hides that year. The number of hides consigned to Davis totaled about 200,000 in 1882 and 40,000 in 1883. Davis reported that in 1884 he "shipped from Dickinson, Dakota Territory, the only car load of robes that went East that year, and it was the last shipment ever made."[33] Other buyers reported similar peaks in 1882 and the virtual bottoming of the market by 1884. Joseph Ullman, a fur importer-exporter with offices in New York and Saint Paul, reported to Hornaday that "[i]n 1884 we purchased less than 2,500 hides, and in my opinion these were such as were carried over from the previous season in the Northwest, and were not fresh-slaughtered skins." He added that "[i]n 1885 the collection of hides amounted to little or nothing."[34]

The notion promoted by Lieutenants Partello and Scott that some buffalo escaped the American slaughter by passing to a Canadian sanctuary was sometimes embraced in the hunting camps but amounted to nothing more than a delusion. Those buffalo that somehow crossed the Missouri and neared Canada were killed by white hunters working the river and by the Blackfeet, Assiniboines, Crees, and Métis residing along the border. Canada was only an illusionary sanctuary. Its original plains buffalo population had been hunted to extinction even before the American slaughter began. When Sitting Bull's followers took tormented refuge in Canada in the late 1870s, they frequently tested fate by hunting buffalo on American soil, because none existed in Canada. They also competed with native Canadians for the limited wild game that somehow survived on the distant prairie. Canada proved no haven for the American Sioux or the buffalo.[35]

Of course, it is inaccurate to say that every buffalo bull, cow, and calf had been annihilated when the great slaughter ended. At the start of the 1883 hunting season, an alleged ten thousand buffalo still ranged in western Dakota, particularly along the headwaters of the Moreau and Grand rivers more or less midway between the Black Hills and Bismarck. This herd was speedily reduced to about eleven hundred animals early that fall before Sitting Bull, Running Antelope, and perhaps a thousand of their followers arrived on the scene in October and promptly killed the rest. These Hunkpapas had been released by their agent expressly to partake in this unique opportunity, and the hunt became a great if momentary celebration in Indian country. White hunters had killed the rest. Vic Smith recalled that "when we got through the hunt there was not a hoof left."[36]

The naturalist and budding conservationist William Hornaday himself contributed notably to the final extermination of the buffalo. Driven perhaps by simple curiosity and perhaps by the sensational news of the slaughter, the Smithsonian's chief taxidermist (then thirty-two years old) took occasion in early 1886 to inventory the buffalo skins and skeletons in the collections and found them wanting in specimens suitable for public display. Hornaday relayed word of this deficiency to his superiors, who promptly arranged his trip to Montana to collect buffalo before the species was extinct altogether. Hornaday imagined the need for eighty to a hundred animals; twenty to thirty of these would provide skins and complete skeletons, and another fifty or more would yield skulls. Informants in Montana had located a small herd of buffalo on Big Dry Creek north of Miles City, half the distance to the Missouri River. As for the morality of killing perhaps the last of the wild buffalo, Hornaday and his Smithsonian superiors rationalized that in this way the American public could at least see what their most famed mammal looked like; otherwise cowboys would kill them all and leave the carcasses to decay. "There really was no choice," Hornaday lamented.[37]

When Hornaday reached Miles City on May 9, reports on the whereabouts of surviving buffalo were less than encouraging. Fort Keogh's commanding officer, Colonel John D. Wilkins, Fifth Infantry, knew of none in the locales traveled by his troops. By telegraph Hornaday learned from an officer at Fort Maginnis that no buffalo were known to survive in the Judith Basin, and a rancher from Wyoming reported that none remained in the Powder River country to the south. On the brink of failure even before leaving Miles City, Hornaday fortuitously heard again from Henry R. Phillips, the rancher on Little Dry Creek who had previously reported that a few buffalo might still be found in the vicinity of the Big Dry.[38]

Hornaday outfitted at Fort Keogh, obtaining camp equipment, a wagon, and a five-man Fifth Infantry escort, and on May 13 crossed the Yellowstone River, angling north toward the valley of the Big Dry. Aside from killing two young pronghorns on the third day, the opening of Hornaday's hunt was both uneventful and frustrating.

The hunters established a permanent camp eight miles west of Phillips's ranch on the Little Dry, some ninety miles northwest of Miles City, and learned from Phillips and some of his cowboys that thirty-five head of buffalo had recently been seen in the breaks between Phillips Creek and the Musselshell River, south of the Big Dry.[39]

The targeted country (some forty miles east to west by twenty-five miles north to south) was entirely uninhabited, Hornaday complained. It was treeless, without running water, and extremely hilly and broken. This tract of buffalo country was impassable for wagons, so Hornaday released the government carriage and its soldier escort. He and three companions (Andrew H. Forney of the National Museum, George H. Hedley of Medina, New York, and a Cheyenne Indian guide named Dog) began circuit riding the tortured countryside. Aside from capturing a buffalo calf whose mother eluded pursuit, killing one buffalo bull, and collecting some of the bleached skeletons and skulls that generally littered the prairie, Hornaday's initial month-long hunt was a decided failure. He determined to return in the fall, however, when the hairy coats of these survivors would be in their wintertime prime.[40]

Hornaday returned to Miles City on September 24, 1886, this time accompanied only by W. Harvey Brown, a twenty-four-year-old student at the University of Kansas and a summer volunteer at the National Museum. Hornaday engaged the services of three cowboy guides and hunters in Miles City and again was furnished with transportation, supplies, and a small infantry escort at Fort Keogh. The outfit crossed the Yellowstone on the twenty-fifth and within several days drew into camp on the Big Dry, some ninety miles north of Miles City. As in May, the wagons and escort promptly returned to Fort Keogh, though one of its members elected to remain with the outfit until the close of the hunt. The search for buffalo commenced immediately, but animals were not spotted until October 13. One of the cowboy hunters fired on this small bunch but killed none; they eluded him as he gave chase.[41]

On October 14 Hornaday joined the cowboys and the others and trailed seven buffalo for more than twenty miles through rugged terrain and wet gumbo. The sticky, clay soil made for easy tracking.

At the head of Taylor Creek Hornaday finally spotted the pursued group plus seven more. The hunters crept to within several hundred yards of the bunch and fired a volley at the resting animals but missed entirely. They were more successful, however, when the animals rose and ran. Four of fourteen were killed that day and four more two days later. Among the second four was a large old bull that was dropped late one afternoon a considerable distance from the camp. When the crew returned the next morning to skin and skeletonize this particular carcass, they discovered to their considerable surprise that Indians had already thoroughly cleaned the animal, taking the tongue, meat, and hide and cracking the leg bones for the marrow but leaving behind the unskinned head. They had painted one side red and the other yellow. Only later did Hornaday learn that this was the handiwork of eleven Assiniboine men from the Fort Peck Agency on the Missouri, who were also in the area hunting buffalo.[42]

Over the next several days Hornaday's circuitous travels through the rugged Little Dry and Taylor Creek countryside netted six more animals, bringing the total killed to fourteen. They had vigorously stirred up the survivors, whose fresh hoof prints betrayed their presence. Feeling the need to allow them to quiet down, Hornaday moved his camp to the Musselshell River, thirty miles west, where he hunted deer and upland birds but found no signs of buffalo except for bones. On November 17, the hunters returned to their permanent camp and resumed the quest. Four old buffalo cows were discovered and killed almost immediately, bringing the harvest to eighteen. Hornaday figured that he could kill thirty and pressed his hunters, even though the crew's horses were exhausted from daily chases after nearly a month of hunting.[43]

Hornaday's outfit killed its twentieth buffalo on November 20. After his frustrating springtime hunt, Hornaday had now narrowed his threshold requirement to twenty animals, though the prospect of killing thirty still tantalized him. With the weather turning against him, however, he sent his Fifth Infantry hunting companion to Fort Keogh on November 23 to retrieve the army wagons. Despite frigid temperatures and frequent snows, Hornaday's hunters continued the chase. On December 6 he and one of the cowboys chanced upon three buffalo, including an enormous old bull that was easily the largest yet seen. Hornaday spurred his horse and with a hurried shot shattered the bull's foreleg and brought him down. He quickly turned his attention to the fleeing cows and pursued one. But it had already crossed a deep, snow-filled gully and escaped before Hornaday could cross the same chasm. He returned to the downed bull, which rose and attempted to flee as he approached. Before killing the beast, Hornaday reveled in "the rare opportunity of studying a live bull buffalo of the largest size on foot on his native heath." He even paused to sketch the scene in his notebook and then fired a final killing shot through the lungs, "which soon ended his career." Nearly all the adult bulls taken by Hornaday's party carried old bullets in their bodies. The trophy bull bore four bullets of varying sizes, including one sticking fast in one of its lumbar vertebrae.[44]

Having taken twenty-three animals, on December 14 Hornaday and his party headed for Miles City, where they spent a week returning equipment and boxing specimens for shipment to Washington. Their take was modest, almost humble, compared with the daily slaughter occurring during the heyday of buffalo hunting and was clear evidence that the great northern herd was all but eliminated from Sioux Country. It was a bitter testimonial to the day in American history when the few wild survivors of the 2 million buffalo that once roamed the Montana, Wyoming, and Dakota prairies were destroyed for skins and skulls rather than being corralled and bred for the edification of succeeding generations—a notion that was unfathomable, of course, at the time.[45]

Hornaday was not the only institution-bound scientist worrying about the imminent destruction of the remaining buffalo and its implications within the museum world. Officials at the American Museum of Natural History in New York City realized that their collections also lacked a sufficient number of buffalo skull and skin specimens. In 1887 the museum dispatched one of its founders, the eminent American naturalist Daniel Giraud Elliot, to Montana to comb the same landscape between the Yellowstone and Missouri rivers where Hornaday had collected his specimens; but the countryside was entirely barren. For three months Elliot searched the region in vain, not finding even one living buffalo.[46]

Hunters encountered and killed a few other well-scattered loners for several more years. Hornaday wrote that his expedition had left perhaps fifteen animals alive in the divide between the Yellowstone and Missouri rivers, but those were mostly killed by cowboys in 1887. An old bull was killed near Billings in 1888, reportedly the last wild buffalo seen in Montana. In 1886 seven buffalo were discovered east of the Missouri River in the Prairie Coteau country near Grand Rapids, Dakota, southeast of Bismarck. A bull was killed and a calf captured. Another of that group was killed in 1888, and the fate of the others went unreported. In 1884 a solitary buffalo was killed in Pleasant Valley in the southwestern Black Hills, acknowledged as the last seen in that corner of the Dakota Territory. In 1889 some twenty-six buffalo were observed grazing in southern Wyoming's Red Desert, and their fate, too, was unreported but predictable. The infrequent sighting and killing of solitary survivors created sensational national news for a very short while longer.[47]

In January 1889 Hornaday attempted to tally the free-roaming buffalo surviving in the United States and counted only 85, including the shadowy, doomed small groups southeast of Bismarck and in Wyoming's Red Desert. Elsewhere in North America, some 200 buffalo supposedly survived in Yellowstone National Park, where they lived under a precarious mantle of federal protection in an era well before the birth of the National Park Service and a firm, enforceable preservation ethic. According to Hornaday, 550 survived in the vicinity of Great Slave Lake in far northwestern Canada, perhaps because of the extreme seclusion afforded by that habitat. Another 250 buffalo were scattered in zoos and private herds, including 18 in the show stock of William F. "Buffalo Bill" Cody's internationally celebrated Wild West exhibition.[48]

For the remaining free buffalo, predation remained a persistent threat. The Yellowstone National Park herd was in constant jeopardy throughout the 1890s, even though federal regulations in the national park outlawed killing them. In the years before the creation of the National Park Service in 1916, the U.S. Army policed the park.

Soldiers patrolled the vast 2-million-acre preserve and commonly encountered evidence of poaching, including market hunters serving hotels inside the park. In nearby gateway communities like Cooke City and Gardner buffalo hides and heads openly fetched from one hundred to four hundred dollars. Even live calves were sought. Catching illegal hunting *inside* the park proved a vexing problem for the wardens. When poachers were caught, their punishment typically amounted to little more than the confiscation of their hunting outfits and banishment from the park. Rarely were poachers punished by confinement in the Fort Yellowstone guardhouse on the park's northern border or in any other jail, and in due course most returned to their old haunts with new gear. The winter of 1893–94 was a particularly profitable season for Yellowstone's buffalo poachers, who captured a number of calves in the vicinity of Gardner and succeeded in slaying 116 animals that had drifted west and out of the park. When a subsequent count turned up barely 20 survivors, agitation from preservationists across America led Congress to pass federal legislation outlawing the killing of Yellowstone's buffalo under penalty of a thousand-dollar fine or imprisonment. Reduced to a handful, the herd survived into the twentieth century despite noticeable continued annual predation.[49]

The wholesale slaughter of the buffalo left behind a bleached residue of skeletons littering the plains that in turn gave rise to a profitable if brief trade in buffalo bones, available free for the picking. From the early 1870s onward, midwestern plants profitably processed buffalo bones scavenged from the Great Plains into bone charcoal or boneblack, a product then in great demand as a material for filtering and purifying sugar syrup. Other bone products included glue, neatsfoot oil, and fertilizer. When southern plains bone stocks were diminished, attention rapidly turned northward, where Missouri and Yellowstone River steamboat companies and the Northern Pacific Railroad stood ready to haul new bone concentrations to market.[50]

The nation's principal buffalo bone processors included the Michigan Carbon Works of Detroit, the Northwestern Fertilizer Company of Chicago, and the Empire Carbon Works of East Saint Louis, Illinois. Of all the processors, the Michigan Carbon Works most aggressively pursued Sioux Country's buffalo bone debris, dispatching agents to river and railroad towns across Dakota and

Montana to buy pickings and offering from $8 to $12 per ton depending on transportation considerations. Local bone pickers, in turn,
radiated from the region's hamlets, targeting the successive bone
stands dotting the vast outback. When Hornaday hunted north of
Miles City in 1886, he observed that the landscape between the
Yellowstone River and Red Buttes, some thirty miles northwest,
had already been picked clean of buffalo bones; but from that point
onward the wreckage of the vanished herds was plain to see. Itinerant
pickers carted tons of bones to railroad yards and sidings throughout the region, where they were piled into huge ricks before being
shipped east. Even Sioux and Assiniboine Indians from the Fort
Peck Agency in northeastern Montana and Métis from northern
Dakota availed themselves of momentary opportunities to collect
and haul bones to local buyers.[51]

The buffalo bone trade was as short-lived as the herds themselves once the wanton slaughter commenced. By the early 1890s
the bone ricks were largely empty; the easy gleanings from the prairie
had already been harvested and shipped away. When demand out-
stripped the supply of buffalo bones, processors sought alternative
raw materials and developed new technologies. Fertilizer companies
turned to mineral phosphates and sugar refiners to developing an
electrical process that replaced boneblack. During the course of the
trade, some 2 million tons of bones worth a reported $40 million
were collected, adding an ignoble if quietly profitable footnote to
the legacy of the buffalo in Sioux Country.[52]

The extermination of the free-roaming plains buffalo elicited mixed
and often extreme reactions from plainsmen and government agents.
Some observers were simply elated. E. S. Topping doubtless spoke
for an entire generation of contemporary Montanans when he wrote:
"As these animals are driven off the range, the space they occupied
is filled with domestic cattle, and the absence of buffalo insures a
cessation of [the] Indian wars."[53] But General Terry saw it differently.
When he received a disturbing report in September 1881 from an
officer at Fort Keogh on the wanton slaughter of buffalo occurring
north of the Yellowstone, he forwarded it to General Sheridan with
a remarkably intelligent and farsighted endorsement. Although the
killing of the buffalo would "solve the Indian problem," he candidly

observed, "the slaughter of animal life in such a way is abhorrent to me." The ever-strident Sheridan, however, added his own endorsement as the communiqué was forwarded to Sherman: "If I could learn that every buffalo in the Northern herd were killed, I would be glad. The destruction of this herd would do more to keep Indians quiet than anything else that could happen."[54]

Modern-day observers and apologists have asserted that senior army officers like Sheridan and Sherman played a straightforward role in the extermination of the American buffalo, citing the generals' rhetoric as evidence. Others point to a perceived shadowy government conspiracy between the Grant administration and the army to rid the plains of buffalo as some form of wayward Indian policy. But no such policy existed. Rhetoric did not kill buffalo; nor did the army, aside from opportunistic sport and mess-hall hunting. In fact, the army in Montana actually abetted Indian buffalo hunting in the 1860s and 1870s by developing permits and providing escorts that enabled and promoted off-reservation hunting, much to the consternation of territorial newsmen, settlers, and stockmen. Acknowledging the army's protectionist measures, Montana pioneer Duncan McDonald wrote to the Deer Lodge New North-West in 1878, expressing his belief that for nonhostile Indians, "the army is without doubt the Indian's best friend."[55]

In the end, the widespread killing of buffalo in Sioux Country and throughout the Great Plains was caused by access to the range provided by railroads, prosperous new national and international markets for buffalo garments and belting leather, evolved industrial technologies in the East capable of handling the glut of hides, and, perhaps most important of all, an irrepressible clamor for a new economic order across the plains. The ultimate consequences for the buffalo and the Sioux were strikingly similar. The reflection of the Lakota visionary John Fire Lame Deer again seems profound: "There are places set aside for a few surviving buffalo herds in the Dakotas, Wyoming and Montana. There they are watched over by Government rangers and stared at by tourists. If brother buffalo could talk he would say, 'They put me on a reservation like the Indians.' In life and death we and the buffalo have always shared the same fate."[56]

6

THE BEEF BONANZA

The legacy of cattle ranching on the northern plains in the several decades immediately following the Great Sioux War remains a captivating and enduring saga. As the cattlemen themselves expressed it, "grass and water were as free as air."[1] In late nineteenth-century historian Frederick Jackson Turner's vision of the successional transformation of the American frontier, the cattlemen occupied and ultimately tamed the unfenced open range. The era of the so-called Beef Bonanza marked the ultimate use of a vast, semiarid land and brought symbolic closure to a decades-long frontiering process that transformed the West. This story is much more complex and nuanced than Turner's simple thesis suggests, of course, and laced with interesting characters, innovative thinking, and environmental catastrophe atop an inherently rich western landscape indeed remade once both the Sioux and buffalo were no longer present.

Cattle were known in the vicinity of Sioux Country well before the climactic Great Sioux War. They appeared on its margins at places like Forts Union, Pierre, and Laramie during the mid-nineteenth century, when fur traders dominated Euramerican enterprise on the northern plains. Cattle were also driven and led by emigrants traveling the great overland trails to Oregon, Utah, and California at mid-century. They even pushed across a corner of the Sioux homeland when Texas stock was trailed through Wyoming and Montana in the late 1860s to western Montana's burgeoning gold-fields. Inevitably, wherever concentrations of people to be fed existed in the West, whether at mining camps, Indian agencies, or budding communities, cattle were first delivered and in time raised locally to meet an ever-growing demand.

The invasion of Sioux Country by cattle and cattlemen, of course, could only occur in an orderly sequencing of events that first pushed the Sioux, Northern Cheyennes, and other Indians from the land of their forebears into the firm grip of agency control, where agriculture and other civilizing practices were introduced. Then the buffalo had to be eliminated, because many on the plains feared that Indians might revert to their old ways and whites knew that buffalo could never be domesticated. Easy access to significant markets had to be guaranteed as well, but the Union Pacific, Northern Pacific, Great Northern, and Chicago and Northwestern railroads quickly linked the northern Great Plains with dense eastern populations and markets.

The spread of the Beef Bonanza across the northern plains in the post–Sioux War years had a distinct push from the southern margins of Sioux Country. Men like John W. Iliff, Seth E. Ward, Hiram B. Kelly, and Adolph Cuny had been successfully raising cattle on the prairies east of the Rocky Mountains between Denver and Fort Laramie since the late 1850s. Iliff, the first so-called cattle king of the northern range, grazed nearly seven thousand head of cattle in 1870 between Crow Creek in southeastern Wyoming and the South Platte River and as many as twenty-five thousand just seven years later. Most of Iliff's cattle fed the populations of Colorado's mining communities and nearby army camps; but after the coming of the Union Pacific Railroad to Cheyenne in 1867, they were also sent to Chicago markets.[2] Ward, long a Fort Laramie sutler and frontier entrepreneur, ran some two hundred head near that fort, chiefly for sale to the local post commissary. Kelly ran five hundred head on Chugwater Creek midway between Fort Laramie and Cheyenne, and Cuny had one thousand head between Fort Laramie and Fort Fetterman. These were among Wyoming's pioneer cattlemen, but others operated north of Cheyenne, east on the richly grassed plains between Cheyenne and Sidney, Nebraska, and on the Laramie Plains west of the Laramie Mountains in south-central Wyoming.[3]

By the mid-1860s the brood herds sustaining these early entrepreneurs typically came from Texas, where Iberian longhorn cattle (a breed descended from Spanish stock) grazed the diverse ranges. Generally untended during the Civil War, these longhorns multiplied phenomenally. Texas cattlemen who were seeking new opportunities to markct thcir animals after the war learned that they might earn thirty to forty dollars per head if the cattle were delivered to northern mining camps, railroad construction crews, and Indian agencies. The prevailing rate in Texas at the time ranged from three to ten dollars per head. These Texas cattle were rough, lanky, long-horned animals, with thin loins and rumps and coarse, stringy meat. But they reproduced easily and could be managed and might actually shed their unsavoriness if fattened before slaughter. In any case, toughness or tastiness counted little to the Texans, who asserted that their range beef was "good enough for factory workers, reservation Indians, drunken and dissipated soldiers at the army posts, and the 'paddies and chinks' who were the 'gandy dancers' on the railroad construction crews."[4] The northern "stocker" market proved an irrepressible lure. Some 260,000 Texas longhorns were driven north in 1866, with an equal or a greater number following each year well into the 1880s.[5]

The spread of cattle ranching across the eastern half of Wyoming in the late 1870s in the wake of the Great Sioux War was much like a classic military envelopment. First, cattlemen crossed the North Platte River and fanned northward through the Old Woman, Rawhide, Sage, Cheyenne, and Hat valleys, all local landmarks during the protracted course of the Sioux War. Then they spread north and northwest into the vast Powder River Basin lying between the Black Hills and Big Horn Mountains. These ranchers, including Wyoming pioneers like John Hunton, James Hervey Pratt, Nick Janis, and Alexander "Heck" Reel, routinely supplied beef and hay to neighboring forts and Sioux agencies and were as well known to army contractors and Indian agents as Iliff (who died unexpectedly in 1878 at age forty-six), Ward, and Cuny. In the early years of the Beef Bonanza, army and Indian markets remained the principal local outlets for Wyoming cattle.[6]

In the late 1870s the energy pouring into Wyoming's newest enterprise ran unchecked. Cattlemen coveted the fresh landscape "thrown open to settlement," as Wyoming pioneer Oliver P. Hanna remembered it.[7] A newsman described "the boundless, gateless, fenceless pastures" of the public domain, resplendent with nutritious grasses, which required minimal operating expenses aside from a few cowboys, some corrals, and a branding iron.[8] Although some 523,000 cattle were reportedly grazing Wyoming's plains by 1880, up from 218,000 recorded only five years earlier, that was still far short of the number demanded by ranchmen to stock the range fully. So great was the demand for cattle during the boom, in fact, that buyers like brothers Moreton and Richard Frewen, operating on the headwaters of the Powder River in the late 1870s, variously sourced their needs in Colorado *and* Oregon and were still frequently frustrated by an inability to acquire necessary stocker animals. At the end of the 1870s Texas suppliers were equally tempted by prospective sales in Montana and in 1879 alone trailed 100,000 longhorns there as pioneer ranchers inched east from the mountains onto the prairies.[9]

In the late 1870s and early 1880s Wyoming's cattlemen perfected a local adaptation of the so-called Texas System, an operating scheme in which all ranchers had an equal share of the grazing lands and water resources of the open range in their sectors of the territory. A rancher's stock roamed freely with all other cattle and might wander hundreds of miles. The herds received no supplementary feeding or protection and reached market maturity by feeding on grass alone. The cattlemen agreed that no one would gather stock from December until the coming spring roundup without informing neighbors and giving them fair opportunity to examine the animals before driving them away. In 1880 the Wyoming range was divided into six vast roundup districts. The free-ranging stock was gathered, sorted, branded, and culled for market or return to the range, usually in June. Even drives to market became cooperative ventures.[10]

The stock growers' spirit of collaboration, born out of the self-interest of maximized profit generated at minimized expense off a communal range, gave rise to formal associations that established and enforced the rules of the range and policed the violators. Wyoming's association was the first in Sioux Country, founded in November 1873 as the Laramie County Stock Growers' Association. Just to the east, the Stock Association of the Western District of Nebraska incorporated in February 1875. Montana's association followed in February 1879. Numerous other associations existed, including the Black Hills Live Stock Association, organized in 1880; the Eastern Montana Stock Growers' Association, organized in 1883; and the Little Missouri River's Bad Lands Live Stock Association, founded in 1884. All were eventually absorbed by respective larger statewide bodies.[11]

A phenomenon more characteristic of the Wyoming boom than elsewhere on the northern plains was foreign investment in the cattle industry. It included both the underwriting of individual American ranchers and the emergence of British and Scottish companies functioning independently on the range. In the late nineteenth century Great Britain was a prime importer of American beef and was tantalized by reports of lush Texas breeding grounds and cattle driven to Colorado and Wyoming, where the prairies were covered with "self-made hay." The desire to engage and profit from American ranching became an obsession among British and Scottish capitalists. By the early 1880s they were deeply invested in a number of western ventures, including the Swan Land and Cattle Company, north of Cheyenne; the Dakota Stock and Grazing Company, with vast holdings in the Cheyenne River and Hat Creek valleys in Wyoming, Dakota, and Nebraska; and the Powder River Cattle Company, a joint venture involving the Frewen brothers. This colorful if fitful sidelight to cattle raising added a cosmopolitan twist to the northern ranges and its social clubs. But these opportunists suffered equally from the market and natural vagaries that soon overtook the industry's pell-mell expansion across Sioux Country.[12]

In the late 1870s and early 1880s the demand for stocker cattle in Wyoming and across the northern plains reached the extreme limits of supply. The call for Texas longhorns increased from year to year, as Texas herders continually struggled to meet the demand. All along, the Texans had three outlets for their cattle: the northern plains, which was especially well suited for yearling and two-year-old cattle; eastern markets, which particularly sought young steers for sale to local farms and ranches; and midwestern feeders seeking grown steers for fattening before slaughter. When Wyoming cattlemen could not obtain all the longhorns they wanted to fill home ranges, they turned to Colorado, the Midwest, and Oregon and Washington. Although Durham cattle from the Northwest and Angus and Hereford cattle from the Midwest were not considered as hearty as Texas longhorns, Sioux Country ranchers were eager to have them. They paid attractive prices that more than compensated for the costs of trailing animals across the Rocky Mountains from Oregon or transporting them by rail from Iowa or elsewhere in the Midwest.[13]

During the early boom years, Wyoming cattle that were not marketed locally typically found their way to packinghouses in Chicago, Omaha, and Kansas City (Chicago was the distinct preference). In 1882 top grade packers weighing from 1,100 to 1,350 pounds yielded $9.35 per hundredweight in Chicago, having perhaps initially cost a western rancher $14 for a two-year-old heifer, $15 for a two-year-old steer, and $8 for a yearling. Against this gain came the expenses of managing the stock on the open range, trailing it to outlets like Cheyenne or Sidney, and rail transportation to destination stockyards. The cattlemen's associations wrangled continuously with the railroads over shipping costs, which added from $6.90 to $12.50 per head, along with the weight losses incurred from Wyoming to market. To reduce those losses, some cattlemen drove their stock farther east to places like Ogallala, which for a while was Nebraska's leading cow town. Without local packing houses and improved refrigerator cars, however, the western ranchers were continually vulnerable to the vagaries associated with distant markets. Despite these problems, enthusiasm for the industry ran unchecked, and Wyoming cattlemen proudly made an annual trip to Chicago to market their stock.[14]

Montana's cattle story parallels Wyoming's to a degree, though the envelopment of Sioux Country (consisting of Montana Territory's vast eastern half) originated in the mountain West. Since the early

1860s the gold camps and scattered military garrisons had stimulated the self-sufficiency in cattle production that was necessary to sustain a thriving population. Pioneer Montanans like Nelson Story, Johnny Grant, Conrad Kohrs, Philip Poindexter, and William Orr, who nearly all had entered the territory as prospectors, soon turned their energies to ranching in the luxuriant Bitterroot, Beaverhead, Deer Lodge, and Gallatin valleys that dotted the western mountains. The notion of an open range also existed in 1860s Montana, but it had different connotations there. The mountain West was unfenced and thus "open," but Montana's western valleys were typically grazed only seasonally. In summer cattle were driven to the timbered highlands, and the lower valleys were reserved for winter pasturage. Moreover, those well-watered fertile lowlands were coveted by others, especially when sheepmen, dairy herders, and farmers competed for the same natural advantages.[15]

In the long run Montana's valley-bound cattlemen were constrained both by competing demands for the land and by the lack of new markets outside of the gold camps. Montana cattle were occasionally driven to the Mormon settlements and Union Pacific and Central Pacific railheads in Utah and southwestern Wyoming, but these long drives across high passes were especially hard on range stock. The ranchers' quest for new ranges in the mid-1870s took them cautiously northward and eastward into the Sun and Smith River valleys and Judith Basin. These new grazing lands bordered on untamed Indian country, but the small army garrisons at Camp Baker and Fort Benton offered protection, as did Fort Ellis at Bozeman.

Throughout the 1870s the prospect of reliable connections to eastern markets beckoned, as surveyors for the Northern Pacific Railroad explored the Yellowstone Valley. When the railroad resumed construction westward from Bismarck in 1878, its marked progress provided a powerful incentive for western ranchers to seize Montana's eastern ranges. Meanwhile, new army garrisons at Forts Custer and Keogh (founded in 1877 and 1876), Fort Assinniboine (established in 1879), and Fort Maginnis (authorized in 1880), all purposefully situated throughout the territory to safeguard the opening of this sector of Sioux Country, provided immediate new markets for

Montana beef and necessary protection as cattlemen fixed their attention on the evolving buffalo country. An additional notable market for Montana beef also loomed in Canada: at its North-West Mounted Police posts situated along the American border, on its own Indian reserves, and for its own railroaders advancing the Canadian Pacific transcontinental line.[16]

In the Judith Basin in central Montana the Judith Cattle Company, owned by Thomas and John Power and Joseph H. McKnight, pioneered the spread of cattle onto that new range and represented the first substantial leap into Montana's Sioux Country. The Power brothers were business giants in Montana, operating steamboats and other ventures from Fort Benton, while McKnight was long the post trader and a regional entrepreneur operating at Fort Shaw in the Sun River valley. Other outfits like the Montana Cattle Company and Pioneer Cattle Company followed the Judith Company into that prosperous but rugged outback watered by the Judith and Musselshell rivers. William Hornaday chased and killed some of the last of the free roaming northern plains buffalo in this same locale in 1886.[17]

Ultimately the arrival of the Northern Pacific Railroad abetted Montana's cattlemen more than any other single force, opening immediate outlets in Saint Paul and Chicago and accessing a section of Sioux Country far larger than the Wyoming range. The same market hamlets that served as collection centers for the hide hunters (notably Miles City, Terry, and Glendive) also became cattle towns. They facilitated the initial distribution of stocker cattle to the new range and the subsequent seasonal concentration of market-ready animals for shipment to eastern packers. Miles City emerged as eastern Montana's premier cattle town, another Ogallala or Abilene.[18]

Ironically, some of the ballyhoo in the booming cattle business came from an unlikely source: a Second Cavalry veteran of the Great Sioux War. Major James Sanks Brisbin, who led the relief of Fort Pease in February and March 1876 to open military action in the prolonged conflict and later witnessed the burial of Custer at the Little Big Horn, published a book in 1881 titled *The Beef Bonanza; or, How to Get Rich on the Plains.* Although Brisbin surveyed the prospects of the entire western range, he particularly espoused the worth of the northern plains and especially Montana, his home throughout the 1870s and early 1880s. Brisbin called the Montana range the finest grazing ground in America. "Its grasses cure naturally on the ground," he wrote, "and even in winter, cattle and sheep, which run out all the year round, are found fat and fit for the butcher's block." Brisbin proclaimed that the cattle business could not be overdone: there was always a market for meat. Dismissed by many contemporary reviewers as unduly optimistic, Brisbin's polemic captured the fervor of cheap land, fabulous profits, and the idealism and enthusiasm pervading the cattle empire during the boom years of the late 1870s and early 1880s.[19]

The flood of cattle invading eastern Montana in the 1880s came from every quarter, and for a while the area appeared to offer ample room for all comers. Foundation stock was trailed from Oregon and Washington, usually via Idaho and the Monida Pass west of Yellowstone National Park. The Northwest provided desirable short-horns and other polled breeds like Durham and Hereford cattle long favored by mountain ranchers and already common in the herds spreading east from the Sun River and Judith Basin country. Easterners delivered cattle too, although one derisive observer considered them "pampered barnyard stock . . . used to being fed by hand."[20] The commonest stock remained Texas longhorns, driven overland on the now famous Texas Trail that skirted the Kansas-Colorado border, crossed the Nebraska Panhandle, passed west of the Black Hills, and typically ended somewhere on the Powder or Little Powder rivers in southeastern Montana. From there Texas stock was sold and disseminated to ranches throughout the territory south of the Yellowstone River and was sometimes pushed onward toward Miles City and a river ford west of Fort Keogh, where the herds fanned onto the ranges of the "North Side."[21]

Like other northern plains cattlemen, the Montanans were not especially enamored with longhorns, which had poor lines and too many off colors and resulted in inferior-looking herds. Even more aggravating were their quarrelsome disposition and the long horns themselves, which interfered with shipping. But the animals could be obtained in quantity and were easily finished on the northern ranges. A longhorn turned onto Montana's luxuriant grasses could

weigh three hundred to four hundred pounds more than a counterpart grown to maturity in Texas. Two-year-old trailed cattle were
typically double-wintered on the Montana range before being shipped
to slaughter.[22]

The spread of cattle throughout eastern Montana began as a
trickle in 1879 and swelled to vast proportions in 1881 and 1882.
Scores of trail herds numbering two thousand to three thousand
head each were turned loose on Montana's open range. In 1881 the
Scott and Hanks Cattle Company drove twenty thousand head from
Nevada to its ranch on the Powder River, one of the largest drives
ever recorded in Montana. In 1882 the Niobrara Cattle Company,
operating in Nebraska and Montana, trailed some ten thousand
cattle from Oregon to ranges on the Powder River and Mizpah
Creek. The Northern Pacific Railroad reported shipping 41,700
cattle into Montana from the East in 1883, with 13,000 unloaded at
Miles City alone and 12,000 at Billings. Montana pioneer Granville
Stuart offered a startling report of the surge: in 1880 some 250,000
head, including dairy cattle and work oxen, were tallied in the whole
of Montana Territory, but by the fall of 1883 more than 600,000
head were on the range. And still the numbers grew. In 1884 the
Northern Pacific reported the delivery of nearly 100,000 head; as
many as 12,800 were unloaded at Glendive in a single day. In 1885
a Texas livestock journal reported that the drive out of Texas that
year numbered 385,000 head, with perhaps 100,000 reaching Montana. Inside the territory, the movement of new stocker animals
in the mid-1880s spanned the Yellowstone and sprawled across all
sections of the Big Open. No one reported whether the Montana
range was fully stocked or noted that competition from sheepmen
was proving vigorous. The saturation of the range, though not yet
seen, loomed near at hand. With it came a travesty unique to the
story of the Beef Bonanza.[23]

In large measure the spread of cattle across the western half of
Dakota Territory at the close of the Great Sioux War is a story very
much like Montana's in its parallel link with the arrival of the
Northern Pacific Railroad in the region in 1879 and 1880. The enterprise spanned the Little Missouri's vast east and west margins and

ultimately all of the neighboring Upper Missouri country. But Dakota's story distinctly focuses on the Little Missouri River country in the northwestern quarter of the territory.

The Little Missouri River, a unique Great Plains stream with resources and topography distinct from others, originates in Wyoming in the shadows of the northern Black Hills. It courses north, first as a shallow rivulet barely a few yards wide and eventually as an unhurried, always muddy, but reasonably reliable river angling north and then east toward the Missouri in today's North Dakota. By the time its turgid waters reach the Dakota Territory, about where the corners of present-day North Dakota and South Dakota meet Montana, its shallow, unassuming character is modified by the distinctive nature of the highly eroded landscape through which it flows and which, of course, it continually helps shape. This dramatic, tortured-looking badland has deceptive qualities. It is seemingly uninviting because of its ruggedness, stressed by blistering summer heat and frigid winters, yet its grazing qualities immediately caught the attention of early plainsmen. A Northern Pacific Railroad contractor was startled to see men cutting good-quality hay in the Little Missouri badlands in January 1880. The badlands, he declared, "are destined to become of much note. Cattle behind the bluffs . . . are thoroughly protected from wind and snow, and they can find good grazing the winter through."[24] This dichotomy pitting impression versus reality was already intuitively understood by the region's Indians, who recognized the Little Missouri's inherently sheltering nature and knew that large native ungulates like buffalo and elk prospered there.

The Little Missouri watershed lay partly outside the Great Sioux Reservation. Its Dakota and reservation portion was ceded by the Sioux in the so-called Agreement of August 15, 1876. According to article 1, the Belle Fourche River and 103rd meridian came to define the reservation's western boundary north of the Black Hills.[25] When ratified by Congress in February 1877, the agreement threw open the entire drainage area. The cattle invasion of the Little Missouri and its margins in Montana and Dakota had two general points of entry. From the south ranchers like Erasmus and John Deffenbach, William Dickey, and Henry Weare had operated on the northern periphery of the Black Hills during the peak years of the gold rush. They chiefly marketed their beeves to the mining camps and, after 1878, the new army garrison at Fort Meade. By mid-1877 the landscape north of the Black Hills was steadily claimed, as established herders and newcomers alike fanned from the Belle Fourche, Redwater, and Little Missouri headwaters.[26]

This infiltration was cautious at first, particularly on the eastern and northeastern margins of the Black Hills, where ranches butted against the Sioux reservation. Yet the richness of this vast new range beckoned. Pioneer badlands rancher Howard Eaton's Custer Trail Ranch was located some five miles south of the Northern Pacific Railroad's crossing of the Little Missouri, the northern point of entry. He reported in a bemused way how cattlemen cautiously inched their way into the Little Missouri country, proclaiming as they reached every subsection of the new range: "This is good enough for me." "But," Eaton countered as he peered off in the direction of the Black Hills, "it is even better for 120 miles south of us, than where the large herds are now."[27]

After first coming to the badlands to hunt in 1880, Eaton and a partner, Eldridge G. Paddock, developed the Custer Trail Ranch with six hundred cattle imported from central Minnesota. The operation expanded in 1882 when Eaton and Arthur C. Huidekoper, a fellow Pennsylvanian who had also come to hunt the badlands, formed the Custer Trail Cattle Company, with Huidekoper funding the purchase of additional cattle and also horses and sheep. In the next several years Eaton and his brothers (Charles and F. Alden Eaton), often with Huidekoper's underwriting, operated the Custer Trail Ranch, the Little Missouri Horse Company south of the railroad at the Logging Camp Ranch, and the Badger Cattle Company, located at the SOHO Ranch some forty miles north of the Northern Pacific's tracks.[28]

During the early 1880s the Little Missouri country north and south of the railroad boomed, with dozens of large and small cattle companies sprawling across the ranges throughout the long and picturesque badlands valley. The Berry, Boice Cattle Company, owned by D. B. Berry and Henry C. Boice, was located some thirty-five miles southwest of the railroad's Little Missouri crossing. The Bad Lands Cattle Company was owned by Hiram B. Wadsworth and W. L. Hawley, who established themselves on the river fifteen miles north of the railroad; and Pierre Wibaux, a wealthy twenty-five-year-old Frenchman who had come to America lured by opportunities in the cattle trade and established a prominent ranch on Beaver Creek (a Little Missouri tributary on its west side near the Montana line) in 1883. Another Frenchman of even greater prominence was the Marquis de Morès (born Antoine-Amédée-Marie-Vincent Manca de Vallombrosa), who appeared in Dakota in 1883. Like Wibaux, twenty-four-year-old de Morès fancied the opportunity to capitalize on the booming western cattle bonanza, but his angle was different. De Morès imagined a meat-packing enterprise on the Dakota range itself, on the Little Missouri River.[29]

Dickinson and Little Missouri were the commercial centers supporting this explosion of cattle across western Dakota. Dickinson was a previously unheralded Northern Pacific siding located on the plains about midway between Bismarck and the Little Missouri River. The unpretentious hamlet of Little Missouri was platted in 1883 at the railroad's river crossing. Of the two, Dickinson, founded in 1882, quickly developed into the Dakota Territory's preeminent northern cow town. It rivaled Miles City to the west and places such as Ogallala, Nebraska, and Dodge City, Kansas, in the number of cattle received and shipped during the heyday of the bonanza. First noteworthy as a loading yard for buffalo hides during the close of the great hunt, Dickinson's stock pens witnessed the offloading of thousands of eastern stocker cattle bound for the Killdeer Mountains and Knife River country north of the railroad and the lush ranges of the Heart and Cannonball River headwaters south of the tracks as well as thousands more annually inbound from the range and destined for eastern slaughterhouses.[30]

The settlement that became Medora, meanwhile, was born on the west side of the railroad's Little Missouri River crossing when the army established the small Bad Lands cantonment in November 1879 to safeguard construction of the Northern Pacific in that locale. The railroad siding near the cantonment sported a section house known as Pyramid Park. The company preferred that name instead of "Badlands" or any other less inviting name that might scare prospective land buyers and settlers. The Pyramid Park Hotel, operating chiefly as an outfitting lodge for hunting and tourist parties, was established adjacent to the railroad's section house in October 1880. A month later a post office opened at the cantonment, named "Comba" after Captain Richard Comba of the Seventh Infantry, who then commanded the army camp. Observers were led to wonder what name would ultimately stick.[31]

The arrival of de Morès on the Little Missouri in April 1883 settled the naming matter almost instantly. Rejecting "Pyramid Park" and "Comba," de Morès bestowed the name "Medora" on the community that he envisioned developing on the east side of the river, in honor of his American-born wife, Medora von Hoffman. At the heart of his new community was a proposed packing plant. Medora blossomed almost overnight. Expansive development by de Morès complemented the customary Wild West attributes of other cow towns. The town eventually featured two hostelries, the Pyramid Park Hotel located west of the river and the new de Morès Hotel east of the river, plus seven saloons, the *Bad Lands Cow Boy* newspaper, a handful of other businesses, and a scattering of rough shacks. The picturesquely situated hamlet flourished, and its residents took particular pleasure in the presence of the Frenchman and other luminaries who detrained regularly at the station.[32]

The meat-packing adventure of the Marquis de Morès in Medora is unique in Sioux Country. Born out of high-minded intention, extraordinary capital investment, and a vigorous assault on the complexities of marketing beef and mutton, it led to regrettable failure and financial losses, though mostly draining the assets of his wealthy father-in-law and not himself. Cattlemen on the Great Plains had long wished for packing plants in their midst as a way of freeing themselves from the burdensome costs of transportation, commissions, and distant packers. A successful French securities investor, de Morès had met and wed the daughter of an American Wall Street banker and in 1882 gained employment in his father-in-law's New York City bank. Like many investors worldwide, de Morès was soon caught up in the American cattle craze. He particularly saw an opportunity to engage in a recent innovation in the meat-packing industry, the shipment of dressed beef in refrigerated railroad cars from places like Chicago to the cities of the East. De Morès carried the thought one step farther. If dressed beef could be shipped in refrigerated cars from Chicago, why not slaughter, dress, and ship directly from the western range itself?[33]

The advance of the Northern Pacific Railroad across Sioux Country and the cattle boom in Dakota and Montana were prominent news in America at the time. Lured by his friend Pierre Wibaux, and with financial backing assured from his father-in-law, de Morès set out for Dakota to explore prospects for himself. His arrival at the Little Missouri railroad station on April 1, 1883, is well recorded, along with his christening of the new hamlet of Medora on the river's east bank with a bottle of fine French wine and his explorations of the countryside and meetings with area cattlemen. De Morès arranged to purchase land belonging to the railroad to provide close-in pasturage necessary to maintain a steady supply of slaughter cows and a site to develop his abattoir and community. Some residents called de Morès the "crazy Frenchman," but others realized that his scheme had possibilities.[34]

De Morès called his enterprise the Northern Pacific Refrigerator Car Company, indicative of the need to process *and* ship dressed beef. The construction boom engulfing Medora in 1883 was highly newsworthy across the entire northern plains and Upper Midwest. A slaughterhouse with cooling and cold-storage rooms, a new hotel, a clubhouse for workmen, the palatial de Morès residence on a hilltop overlooking the town, and workmen's residences emerged throughout the summer. The slaughterhouse was finished by the end of September and operations began in October, employing butchers lured west from Chicago. The plant had a capacity of 150 beeves per day.[35]

The keys to success lay in gaining a reliable supply of range cattle, maintaining steady daily kills at the slaughterhouse, securing dependable sources of refrigeration ice across the rail network, and gaining acceptance of dressed Dakota and Montana range beef in eastern markets. Each of these proved problematic to de Morès, and none was more vexing than the matter of securing reliable access to eastern markets. Large established packing houses owned by

Swift and Armour proved to be ruthless, entrenched competitors. They already had access to nearly every meat market in the East and boasted of marketing grain-finished beef, not tougher grass-fed beef straight off the western range. Undaunted, in 1884 de Morès made measurable sales in Saint Paul and Chicago and developed a string of cold storage facilities spanning from Helena and Billings in the west to Duluth, Saint Paul, and Chicago in the east. Ever the salesman, de Morès even imagined transporting dressed Dakota beef to Buffalo, New York, on refrigerated Great Lakes steamers and the development of allied industries in Medora, such as tanneries and soap, shoe, and glue factories.[36]

In the end, the de Morès enterprise collapsed. Despite the expansion of his slaughterhouse capacity to three hundred head per day, in 1885 his butchers rarely processed even eighty head per day. De Morès lacked sufficient close-in feeding facilities and usually operated only five or six months per year instead of year-round. And the quality of cattle varied from season to season. Sometimes consigned beeves were simply "too poor to kill," according to the *Bad Lands Cow Boy* in 1885, and had to be grazed "until fit for slaughter." De Morès shipped six carloads of dressed Montana cattle to New York City in August 1885 amid great fanfare, thereby finally if momentarily penetrating the elusive New York marketplace. But his butchers rarely processed fifty head per day during the summer of 1886. With losses continually mounting, his father-in-law came to Medora in the autumn of 1886 and closed the plant.[37]

De Morès himself abandoned Medora in the spring of 1887 and never returned to Dakota. His packing plant was sealed up as if being saved for a day when the economics of the industry would change. In 1908 the plant, still filled with machinery, burned to the ground. An iron boiler and a towering brick chimney are all that remain today. The palatial de Morès home in Medora was abandoned intact, as if he was anticipating a grand return someday. But even in his absence, memories of de Morès's vision and audaciousness have never diminished. The town honors his name in statuary and the preserved site of his abattoir. And the graceful de Morès residence, virtually unchanged from the day of his departure, retains its splendor as a lavishly tended North Dakota historic site.[38]

The Marquis de Morès notwithstanding, easily the most note-worthy individual to engage in the cattle business in the Dakota Territory and perhaps all of Sioux Country was Theodore Roosevelt, who arrived in Medora on September 7, 1883 (about the time the de Morès slaughterhouse was finished). This twenty-four-year-old budding New York politician and ardent sportsman had come to the Dakota Territory to hunt buffalo. Joseph A. Ferris, a Medora shop and stable keeper, guided Roosevelt about the badlands for two weeks on a vigorous hunt that wore Ferris thin while invigorating his asthmatic client. The hyperactive New Yorker developed a wild enthusiasm for investing in Dakota land and cattle. The two men often discussed ranching in the badlands. At one evening camp-fire late in Roosevelt's hunt, he cross-examined Ferris, his brother Sylvane Ferris, and Bill Merrifield, their friend and business partner, about the costs of stocking a cattle ranch adequately and properly managing that stock. Before the evening was out Sylvane Ferris and Merrifield found themselves agreeing to run cattle for Roosevelt. They knew of an available herd, so Roosevelt wrote a check on the spot for one-third down ($14,000), becoming an instant cattleman and timeless Dakota legend.[39]

The cattle herd that Ferris and Merrifield knew to be available belonged in part to Hiram B. Wadsworth and W. L. Hawley of the Bad Lands Cattle Company, with Roosevelt's new partners holding shares. Roosevelt acquired that herd and its Maltese Cross brand and established a ranch bearing the same name on the Little Missouri some eight miles south of Medora. In 1884 he bought another several hundred head and established Elkhorn Ranch, twenty-five miles north of town. At his peak as a rancher, Roosevelt ran some three to five thousand head on both ranches, a small number when compared to other operators yet colossal when twinned with the already heralded Roosevelt name.[40]

Roosevelt regularly returned to Medora. He reveled in western cowboying and ranching and took an active role in annual roundups. In turn, the West is known to have shaped Roosevelt. He wrote eloquently and often of his ranching and western hunting experiences. Roosevelt found solace at his Elkhorn Ranch in February 1884 following the deaths on the very same day of his mother, Martha (known to the family as "Mittie"), and his beloved twenty-two-year-old wife, Alice, who died from complications during childbirth. Roosevelt embraced the ruggedness, individualism, and self-determination that characterized northern plains cowboys and life on the Dakota range. Although he had disposed of his ranch properties by the early 1890s, he continued to visit the Little Missouri country whenever possible. When he was running for vice president in September 1900, his campaign train stopped in Dickinson and Medora. His old friend Joe Ferris came aboard to greet him. The two reminisced about their meeting nearly seventeen years earlier and their physically exhausting buffalo hunt. As the train coursed through the badlands, every crag and butte reminded Roosevelt and Ferris of the days when they rode that wild country together. Roosevelt was palpably moved. "The romance of my life began here," he said. William McKinley and Roosevelt won their election that fall; after McKinley's tragic assassination just one year later, Roosevelt became president.[41]

Cattle found their way to other niches across the former Sioux Country during the great boom. For example, they spread north of the Missouri River on either side of the Montana-Dakota line under the mantle of protection provided by the garrison at Fort Buford. There men like Alvin Leighton, Walter Jordan, and the Hedderich brothers (George, Clint, and Gus), among others, prospered in business and ranching endeavors on Missouri tributaries like the Big Muddy and Little Muddy rivers.[42] Cattle also spread throughout the Sandhills and Niobrara River countryside of central and north-central Nebraska in the late 1870s and early 1880s, facilitated by protections afforded by army garrisons at Forts Hartsuff and Niobrara.[43] The Big Horn Basin of west-central Wyoming had been buffalo country when Sheridan and Crook explored it in the summer of 1877 and was only peripherally connected to Sioux Country in its farthest southwestern extreme. The area filled with ranchers and cattle in the late 1870s during the general boom engulfing Wyoming and then southeastern Montana in the early 1880s.[44] Yet another prospective cattle boom awaited. This one occurred in the West River country between the Missouri River and Black Hills in the southwestern quarter of the Dakota Territory, which remained Sioux reservation land until the late 1880s. The outcome was the same.

During the phenomenal northern plains cattle boom in the wake of the Great Sioux War, stockmen were abetted by the removal of the Indian barrier, the slaughter of the northern buffalo herd, and the steady advances of railroads in filling Wyoming, Montana, and Dakota with cattle. Conditions in the early 1880s were ideal. The financial depression of the early and mid-1870s was over, and abundant domestic and foreign capital was again freely available. Western steers brought a good return in the Chicago marketplace. Reporters lauded the opportunities for the poor to grow rich in cattle and the rich to double or treble their worth. And the land was free. In 1875 Wyoming recorded 218,000 cattle on the range, then generally limited to the distinct southeastern quarter of the territory. In 1885 the number was 779,000. In 1875 Montana tallied 309,000 cattle on its ranges, which were distinctly mountain centered. In 1885 it reported 975,000 head scattered throughout its expansive mountain valleys and eastern prairie. Dakota's numbers are not so readily available, but the total for the Black Hills district alone in 1884 is put at 700,000 to 800,000 head. Scholars agree that by the mid-1880s the Sioux Country was about topped-out with cattle. The heralded Beef Bonanza had been an unqualified success. The open range system worked. A land that had been overgrassed and undergrazed had been put to a higher use. What could possibly dampen the nation's exuberance or the generals' smug self-satisfaction over having civilized Sioux Country?[45]

In hindsight, the open range system that characterized the era of the Beef Bonanza across the northern plains and elsewhere in the West was fraught with many vulnerabilities. Some stock brought to the northern plains wintered reasonably well, but animals from the East fared poorly, tending to stand still in winter as if waiting to be fed. A succession of easy winters across Sioux Country in the early 1880s belied the ordinary fearsomeness of that season and the northern countryside, where winters were more typically characterized by subzero temperatures lasting for weeks or more, coupled with killing winds and snows. The winter of 1885–86 was especially warm with little snow, and the following summer was uncharacteristically dry and warm. The normally luxuriant grasses of the northern ranges barely grew that season and were greatly overgrazed by the overstocked herds. Long past were the days when beavers dammed rivulets and creeks at regular intervals along their normally winding courses and thereby contributed to the general watering of the plains. In the period of the cattle boom and before it most of the beavers had been trapped out; their dams were now deteriorating, causing creeks to dry even more quickly and compounding the extreme aridity of 1886.[46]

As the summer of 1886 waned, some wary stockmen read natural signs like earlier migrations of waterfowl and wild animals growing unusually heavy coats of fur and pointed to the surety of a hard winter ahead. But with the ranges full and cattle prices depressed, few stockmen heeded the ominous signals. The calamitous winter of 1886–87 is still lamented on the northern plains. The first storm hit the Dakota ranges on November 4 and rapidly swept all of Sioux Country, lasting for many days and filling coulees, depressions, and river bottoms with finely packed snow. Extremely cold temperatures followed the blizzard, reaching forty degrees below zero. Then came blizzard upon blizzard throughout the months of November, December, and January, with snow piling four and five feet deep on the level and drifts touching rooftops. The little grass that existed was buried under layers of snow. Stage roads closed. Trains ran only intermittently. Schools closed for the entire season. Newspapers across Wyoming, Montana, and Dakota began reporting horrendous stock losses varying from eight to twenty percent at midwinter and predicted losses from fifty to seventy-five percent by the season's end.[47]

Newly arrived stock from the East and footsore and weakened trail stock from Texas were immediately vulnerable to the brutal crush of winter. Less hearty animals crowded into coulees and creek bottoms and froze to death or were smothered by blowing and drifting snow. Native stock that had been on the range one or two years fared only slightly better. Without any feed more substantial than sagebrush and cottonwood boughs, they succumbed too.

Ice crusts formed on top of the snow that lacerated the animals' noses and cut their legs. Even the heartiest cattle died singly and in huddled masses.

Finally, in early March 1887 a "Chinook" blew across the plains. This unique warm wind universally welcomed east of the Rockies loosened winter's grip and melted the snow at an unduly rapid pace. Within days creeks and rivers flowed again and carried the carcasses of countless dead cattle downstream amid cakes of ice and debris. According to a writer watching the Little Missouri River: "Onc had only to stand by the river bank for a few minutes and watch the grim procession ceaselessly going downstream to realize the full depth of the tragedy that had been enacted within the past few months."[48] Montanan Granville Stuart echoed a sentiment that others soon voiced across the plains: "A business that had been fascinating to me before, suddenly became distasteful. I wanted no more of it. I never wanted to own again an animal that I could not feed and shelter."[49]

The losses across Sioux Country varied from range to range and region to region. Roosevelt's friend Gregor Lang of the Neimmela Ranch on the Little Missouri lost eighty percent of his stock. Roosevelt's Elkhorn and Maltese Cross ranches lost some ninety percent of their animals. The Continental Land and Cattle Company, one of the largest outfits operating north of the Black Hills, reportedly entered the winter of 1886–87 with 65,000 head on the Little Missouri and Box Elder and Little Beaver creeks in Montana and Dakota but counted only 16,000 head the following spring. Alexander Swan, one of Wyoming's venerable "cattle kings," owned 29,000 fat cattle in the spring of 1886 but rounded up only 9,000 the following June. Conrad Kohrs of western Montana claimed losses of fifty percent. Granville Stuart could not believe that the loss was so great until his spring roundup recorded only 900 calves branded as compared with 8,000 the year before. Horrendous stories of this sort were repeated throughout the northern plains. Western Montana fared somewhat better than elsewhere, with losses varying from forty to fifty percent in the Musselshell and Judith Basin regions and less in the Sun River country. In the heart of Sioux Country, however, reported losses ran as high as ninety to ninety-five percent and averaged seventy-five to eighty percent in the estimation of the *Mandan Daily Pioneer*.[50]

The heavy runoff in the spring of 1887 created a good crop of grass. Some ranchers recovered, but many more went into receivership that summer as creditors demanded payment. Those most responsible for the boom lost the most. Large companies that had imported huge herds purchased at high prices on borrowed money at high interest rates disappeared almost overnight. Despite continually languishing cattle prices in 1887, market-ready animals were shipped to slaughter. The range was practically cleared of stock. The halcyon days of the open range, marked by the pell-mell surge of cattle coupled with the unquestioned belief that they could care for themselves and only needed rounding up, culling, and shipment to market to net unspeakable profits, were over.

What evolved instead was a fenced range, as small ranchers, sheepmen, and farmers also demanded access to this rich country. Herds were smaller and managed with deliberate care: ranchers provided shelter for weaker animals and cut hay for emergency feeding. Surviving cattlemen tempered their financial expectations too. With so many bankrupt cattle barons and the vast open range increasingly segmented, the hope for enormous profits at minimum expenses gave way to pragmatic satisfaction derived from reasonable returns on a scale compatible with the new conditions. Depressed cattle prices continued to plague the industry throughout the 1890s and seriously handicapped recovery in Sioux Country.[51] Grass was still king, but only memories of the open range remained. Ironically, history was repeating itself. Now the "civilizers" themselves had reason to remember a unique but fleeting time in Sioux Country.

7

Cycles of
Despair and Death

There was no joy in the massive Sioux and Northern Cheyenne village at Little Big Horn as the sun set on June 25, 1876. It had been a day of utter chaos and terror for the villagers. They had first been surprised in the mid-afternoon by soldiers attacking at the southern margins of their sprawling camp. After repulsing those aggressors, they engaged other bluecoats in a spirited and glorious fight on the high banks east of the river. The tribesmen killed them all, including their leader, George Armstrong Custer. The warriors then returned to the first attackers, who had now burrowed themselves into the bluff tops upstream of the village. Before the sun disappeared entirely on that hot Sunday, the villagers reconfigured themselves into a much tighter circle at the northernmost end of the camp and commenced drumming and wailing. A cacophony of peculiar sounds floated across the valley that some of the survivors of Reno's and Benteen's troops interpreted as evidence of a great celebration. In reality they were collective cries of mourning for deceased fathers, uncles, brothers, and sons.

The fighting with the entrenched soldiers resumed at dawn on June 26, despite admonitions from some that they should abandon the camp. Reports of other soldiers advancing on the village, this time from downriver, ultimately triggered the Indians' flight. The skirmishing on the bluffs ended abruptly, and the Little Big Horn battle was over. Weary, parched soldiers soon stood and watched an incredible procession as thousands of Indians trailed south through the afternoon. Women carried young children. The villagers rode ponies and drove others, tugging travois heavily laden with camp provisions and wherewithal. Officers in the entrenchments declared that this was the largest body of Indians they had ever seen: one dark mass two or three miles long and half a mile wide, plus twenty thousand or maybe twenty-five thousand horses. As the parade of Lakotas and Cheyennes moved up the Little Big Horn Valley, Captain Thomas McDougall of Company B, Seventh Cavalry, recalled that he and some of his comrades gave the tribesmen three cheers. It may have been a gesture of smug good riddance or perhaps a sign of humble respect for a valorous foe.[1]

The great Indian assembly, numbering more than seven thousand at its peak, began disintegrating even as it progressed up the Little Big Horn Valley. Some bands were searching for easier hunting and pasturage, and others simply wished to distance themselves from that horrific scene and the dangers posed by a prolonged association with the massed body. By the fourth night the survivors reached the foot of the Big Horn Mountains. Comforted that soldiers were not on their trail, the people celebrated their great victory over Custer and his cavalry. For a short while an ease enveloped the Northern Nation, as these disparate bands of largely nonagency people called themselves. Scouts informed Sitting Bull, Crazy Horse, Crow King, Gall, Little Wolf, and other headmen that Terry's and Gibbon's soldiers had withdrawn north to the Yellowstone and that Crook's bluecoats remained on Goose Creek, a good distance to the east and south. The peaceful interlude allowed time for the men to hunt buffalo on the plains and deer and elk in the mountains, for women to cut new lodgepoles and pick summer berries, and for all to continue the victory dancing.[2]

But the Big Horn Mountain respite was short-lived. The sizable encampment required vast pasturage, which soon became a pressing issue. A surprise encounter south in the mountains on July 7 between warrior-hunters from the village and soldier scouts from Crook's camp triggered yet another flight. This time the villagers moved slowly north and east, first down the Little Big Horn, then across the Wolf Mountains to the headwaters of Rosebud Creek, then down the Rosebud for several days. By July 14 they had turned east into the Tongue River valley. Game was scarce throughout the journey. Much of the Rosebud Valley had been grazed short and burned when they had occupied it just weeks earlier. As the Northern Nation reached the Tongue, it was increasingly evident to all that the substantial needs for grass, fresh water, wood, and game dictated the complete dispersal of the surviving coalition.[3]

In early August the great Indian alliance that had achieved its signal victory over Custer splintered completely. Some bands, mostly the summer roamers, returned directly to the agencies on the Missouri River or in the Pine Ridge country. Others scattered south, east, and north in pursuit of buffalo. While the Northern Nation was united, it had proved itself invincible. Although no one at the time knew or even imagined it, the indomitable allies at Little Big Horn would quickly become the hunted and trapped. During the winter of 1876–77, Sheridan's Army reinforced itself and began an aggressive, relentless pursuit of increasingly vulnerable and weakened Sioux and Cheyennes that finally ended the active phases of the Great Sioux War.

At stake in the Northern Nation's decision-making in late 1876 and early 1877 were issues such as the freedom of movement in the vast Sioux Country of old, the ability to hunt buffalo freely on the northern range, access to the varied pleasurable and sacred haunts scattered throughout the northern plains, and, above all, the perpetuation of the lifeway that they had cultivated over many generations. The alternative to these freedoms—the constrained life at the agencies—was a shadowy prospect at best and an abhorrent one for some. No individual or band resolved this dilemma of choice and its consequences easily or quickly. Some Lakotas were reasonably familiar with the trappings of agency life, having lived in the proximity of trading houses and military posts for years, especially along the Overland Trail in Nebraska and Wyoming. Many of those people, who were mostly Oglalas, Brulés, and Sans Arcs, easily absented themselves in summer to hunt buffalo and rendezvous with kin and as easily returned, often with little or no notice. Among the more visible returns to the agencies now were Little Wolf's Northern

Cheyennes, who appeared at Red Cloud Agency in February 1877, and the more than 500 followers of Morning Star and Standing Elk, who arrived on April 21. At the Spotted Tail Agency, 917 Miniconjou and Sans Arc Lakotas under Touch the Clouds, Roman Nose, and Red Bear arrived on April 14. Other notable appearances and surrenders occurred at Tongue River Cantonment on the Yellowstone River and at the Standing Rock and Cheyenne River agencies on the Missouri River.[4]

Easily the most prominent surrender in 1877 occurred on May 6, when Crazy Horse led 889 followers into the Red Cloud Agency, the proximate home of most Oglalas, though never of Crazy Horse himself. The influential warrior-leader was otherwise almost never seen at such centers of white enterprise, having last been observed at Fort Laramie in 1865 and identified there again in 1870, when he was spotted among raiders who were firing upon soldiers out hunting ducks near the North Platte River. Sitting Bull, Crazy Horse's wartime counterpart, crossed the Medicine Line into Canada in the same week that Crazy Horse surrendered in Nebraska, joining hundreds of Lakotas already there.[5]

The reconciled people enjoyed certain comforts at the agencies, including regularly issued foodstuffs and staples and the pleasures of unrestrained kin relations. But the people were carefully monitored, and travel was severely restricted. They also soon faced a succession of misfortunes, including sometimes successful government attempts to relocate some of them to distant places, the deaths of prominent leaders, an abortive peace mission to Canada aimed at achieving the return of the American Indians there from a land not so very welcoming after all, and sequences of land cessions that continually diminished the Great Sioux Reservation originally defined by the 1868 Fort Laramie Treaty. While victory at Little Big Horn may have been the Northern Nation's wartime zenith, impositions and strife in the ensuing years caused an unfathomable social and cultural divide and took some into the abyss.

Serious trouble first befell the Northern Cheyennes. The Northern Cheyennes allied with the Lakotas during the course of the Great Sioux War were much like their Lakota friends. Contemporary observers noted that they plainly resembled the Sioux in habits and appearance and even that their language incorporated a great many Lakota words. The Cheyennes, who migrated to the Great Plains in the mid-eighteenth century from the Upper Midwest, quickly adopted the buffalo hunting and nomadic culture shared by the Lakotas and other tribes who came before them. In the early nineteenth century the Cheyennes roughly divided into northern and southern groups. The southern body was drawn to amenities and traders on the central plains, while the northerners developed a comparable affinity for similar entities on the northern plains and a growing affection for the Sioux. The northerners and southerners maintained kin relationships and religious traditions through time. But episodes like the Sand Creek Massacre in 1864 and subsequent warfare between the Southern Cheyennes and the army made the tribal division increasingly visible, as did their respective treaties. Among other terms, the 1867 Medicine Lodge Treaty obliged the southern people to adopt a reservation in the Indian Territory. Medicine Lodge quietly distanced the Northern Cheyenne people even more.[6]

Meanwhile, the northerners joined the Sioux in the dramatic and successful Bozeman Trail War in the mid-1860s. The treaty made at Fort Laramie in 1868 resolved that conflict and established a new political order on the northern plains. The particular agreement with the Northern Cheyennes and Northern Arapahos stipulated that they would accept permanent homes in the Indian Territory with the southern portions of their tribes, or in some section of the country set aside for the Sioux in accordance with their new treaty, or on lands set aside for the Crow Indians in accordance with their treaty. The Fort Laramie Treaty further decreed that decisions about permanent residence would be made within one year. In due course the Northern Cheyennes declared their attachment to the Red Cloud Agency and the Sioux. Fearing that the Lakotas would poison Cheyenne relations with whites, the government reneged on the residency provision in September 1874, bluntly asserting that the northerners would have to relocate to the southern reservation whenever so directed by the president but could remain at Red Cloud until then. This was bitterly opposed by the northerners, who viewed it as a direct threat to their geographic and political unity and a disruption of cultural traditions developed and strengthened over time. E. A. Hayt, the commissioner of Indian affairs, assessed the situation correctly in 1877, noting that the relocation of the northerners was an option that "could not be induced . . . by any persuasion or command unsupported by force."[7]

Despite Hayt's observation, the return of the war-weary Northern Cheyennes to the Red Cloud Agency in February and April 1877 sealed their fate. In a conference at Red Cloud in May, George Crook and Ranald Mackenzie met with Morning Star, Little Wolf, Standing Elk, Wild Hog, and other headmen and began aggressively pushing for a move to Indian Territory. Morning Star and Little Wolf stridently reminded the officers that they had received rations with the Sioux since 1868 in conformance with their treaty. Mackenzie countered by declaring that the will of the government dictated their move to the south. Of the headmen, only Standing Elk favored relocating to the Indian Territory, because he had relatives there. His dissent unduly colored the discussion and helped sway it in the government's favor. Mackenzie hurriedly informed General Sheridan in Chicago that the Cheyennes had assented to move after all, and within days it was so ordered.[8]

Confused, astonished, half forced and half persuaded, 937 Northern Cheyennes commenced a seventy-day trek to the Darlington Agency adjacent to Fort Reno in west-central Indian Territory on May 28, 1877. The trip was uneventful, but almost immediately upon arriving the northerners expressed dissatisfaction with their new agency. They were unacclimated to the lower elevation and humid climate of Oklahoma, and many were homesick for friends and conditions in the north. Their reception by southern kin was also perplexing. Northerners who favored the relocation were openly welcomed, but others were greeted with palpable hostility. Sickness quickly overcame the northerners: nearly sixty people died in the first year at Darlington. Conditions for the disaffected did not improve in 1878. Morning Star, Little Wolf, and Wild Hog saw nothing ahead but continued shortages of food, sickness, and inhospitable treatment. They increasingly favored returning to the north, despite the certain risks and difficulties associated with such a flight.[9]

Observers were wary of the northerners' increasingly evident intent to break from Darlington. In early September of 1878 companies of Fourth Cavalry were dispatched from Fort Reno to encamp near the Cheyennes and watch for suspicious movement, and other troops were deployed northward from Fort Sill. Contact between the northerners and agent John D. Miles was frequent during this period of heightened tension. When the Cheyenne leaders openly sought permission to return to the mountains and plains of the north, the agent consistently demurred, warning that if they departed soldiers would come after them. At the brink, Little Wolf boldly declared his intent to go north to his own country. If soldiers followed, he begged that they would allow him and his followers to get a distance from the agency. Then they would fight: "we can make the ground bloody at that place."[10]

At center stage in the mounting crisis were Morning Star (called Dull Knife by the Sioux) and Little Wolf, two steadfast defenders of the traditional Cheyenne lifeway whose names have become synonymous with the Cheyenne legacy in the Great Sioux War and this heroic escape to home country on the northern plains. At seventy years of age, Morning Star was an Old Man Chief with a long history of resisting the whites. He had been a Dog Soldier in his youth, a reflection of his extreme prowess as a warrior, and had fought prominently in Red Cloud's War, including the infamous Fetterman massacre in December 1866. In July 1876 Morning Star's band was surprised by Wesley Merritt at Warbonnet Creek and turned back to the Red Cloud Agency, albeit briefly, in that highly visible and symbolic encounter. In November Morning Star was among those trapped with virtually every other Northern Cheyenne in the devastating fight with Mackenzie's troops in the Big Horn Mountains.[11]

Now aged forty-eight, Little Wolf also had long been a prominent warrior leader. A headman in the Elk Horn Scraper military society since young adulthood, Little Wolf had drawn the attention of army officials at Fort Laramie in the 1850s in skirmishes along the Overland Trail. He figured prominently with other Northern Cheyennes in the Bozeman Trail War in the mid-1860s. In 1876 Little Wolf and his band were counted in the Little Big Horn village, although they arrived after Custer's annihilation. Several of Little Wolf's people, in fact, had discovered crates of hard-bread abandoned on Custer's back trail; when this was reported to Custer, he hastened his pace to the Little Big Horn and the precipitation of that battle. Little Wolf and his people were present en masse in the Big Horn Mountain battle on November 25.[12]

Under cover of darkness on the evening of September 9, 1878, some three hundred Northern Cheyennes led by Morning Star and Little Wolf fled Darlington. Their absence was noted at dawn. Troops on the scene commenced pursuit immediately, while others in Kansas and Nebraska were alerted and dispatched to points of probable convergence, particularly along the Kansas Pacific and Union Pacific railroads. Three days later near Turkey Springs, Indian Territory, the Cheyennes clashed with trailing Fourth Cavalrymen from Fort Reno commanded by Captain Joseph Rendlebrock. Three soldiers were killed and three wounded before both sides disengaged. On three other occasions on subsequent days the tribesmen clashed with pursuing troops as they wended their way north in western Kansas. Lieutenant Colonel William H. Lewis, Nineteenth Infantry, succeeded Rendlebrock on September 23. In an engagement on Punished Woman's Fork of the Smoky Hill River four days later, Lewis was mortally wounded. Again the Cheyennes successfully eluded the soldiers. Frightened Kansans, meanwhile, mobilized for self-defense and ultimately bore the brunt of the Cheyenne flight as the tribesmen raided for fresh horses and cattle and killed settlers on their way north. Notwithstanding prohibitions laid down by the chiefs, forty Kansans were killed by Cheyenne warriors.[13]

Despite troop deployments along the Union Pacific Railroad in the Department of the Platte, the Cheyennes successfully advanced northward in Nebraska, crossing the railroad east of Ogallala on October 4 and entering the Sandhills. There Morning Star and Little Wolf fatefully separated. Morning Star held firm to the belief that the northerners were now safe because they had reached home territory. He preferred to head straight to White River and the Red Cloud Agency (not knowing that the agency had been relocated to the Dakota Territory since his own departure). Little Wolf stridently opposed dividing the bands, arguing that they should continue together to the Powder River country. Once separated, Little Wolf and his followers, numbering about half of the refugees, did not continue north but instead turned deeper into the Sandhills, that vast, grass-stabilized dune field covering all of central Nebraska. Interspersed with inviting rivers and wetlands, the remote Sandhills provided easy avoidance of pursuers and abundant game.[14]

While Morning Star and his followers pressed onward, troops from Fort Robinson advanced east and south. On October 23 two companies of Third Cavalry commanded by Captain John B. Johnson chanced upon them on the Niobrara River and captured them. Johnson observed that the Indians did not wish to fight but were weary and hungry. Despite the apprehensiveness of some warriors, the band surrendered weapons and ponies and was taken to Fort Robinson and domiciled in an unoccupied barrack. For the next several weeks the Cheyennes' stay at Robinson was reasonably convivial. The Indians were seemingly oblivious to the political maelstrom trailing them. Sheridan wanted them returned to Indian Territory immediately and the outbreak ringleaders exiled to Florida. Kansans, meanwhile, pressed for the transfer of the fugitives to civilian authorities and to trial for murder, theft, and the destruction of property.[15]

The Indians were initially ordered to return to Kansas. But when winter set in, Crook recognized that the Indians could not be moved without winter clothing. The Indians were fearful of being in Kansas, and the rhetoric in talks involving Morning Star, Wild Hog, and Captain Henry W. Wessells, Jr., Third Cavalry, who commanded Fort Robinson, turned increasingly antagonistic. Morning Star reminded Wessells that the Cheyennes were on their own ground. "I will never go back. You may kill me here; but you cannot make be go back," he asserted. With the refusals becoming ever more strident, on January 4, 1878, Wessells sealed the barrack and restricted food, water, and fuel. This unconscionable checkmate persisted for five days until the imprisoned Cheyennes broke free en masse after dark on January 9 and fled west up White River.[16]

With troops immediately on their heels, freedom was improbable. On several occasions soldiers closed with the fleeing Indians, who scattered into the breaks of the Pine Ridge west of the post and fought with weapons secreted upon their arrival at the fort and a few others captured during the outbreak. By the end of the next day thirty-five Cheyennes had been recaptured and twenty-seven lay dead, including an infant. Over the next twelve days troops from Forts Robinson and Laramie pursued some fifty Cheyenne holdouts, chasing them across the Pine Ridge and Warbonnet Creek and into the Hat Creek Breaks thirty miles northwest of Fort Robinson. On January 22 the survivors encircled there "fought with extraordinary courage and fierceness, and refused all terms but death." Of thirty-two Cheyennes who resisted to the last, seventeen men, four women, and two children lay dead. Nine persons survived, six with serious wounds.[17]

The carnage at Fort Robinson outraged the nation and worked to counter the enmity in Kansas, where Wild Hog and six other men were taken to stand trial for the killings there. The Kansas indictments were ultimately dismissed, and the defendants were returned to Indian Territory. Meanwhile, fifty-five Cheyenne women and children were moved from Fort Robinson to the Pine Ridge Agency on January 31. Morning Star, along with several family members and warriors, appeared at Pine Ridge three weeks later, having eluded the soldiers and survived the bitter winter.[18]

Little Wolf and his followers also successfully evaded the soldiers, finding haven for three months in the Sandhills on a timbered fork of the Niobrara River and occasionally raiding in the North Platte Valley. In February they resumed their trek to Montana, determined to join Two Moon and other Northern Cheyenne kin at Tongue River Cantonment, now Fort Keogh. Skirting the eastern margins of the Black Hills and Bear Butte while making their way north and west to the Yellowstone River, on March 25 Little Wolf and his followers surrendered to First Lieutenant William Philo Clark, Second Cavalry. Clark, an acquaintance from Camp Robinson and Red Cloud Agency in the time before the removal and already prominent in the surrender and death of Crazy Horse, conceded a provisional asylum at Fort Keogh while Northern Cheyenne affairs were resolved by the government.[19]

For nearly four more years the Northern Cheyennes lived without a permanent home. Little Wolf and his followers remained in Montana with Two Moon's people while Morning Star, his followers, and others initially remained at Pine Ridge Agency in Dakota Territory. Little Chief and his followers also relocated to Pine Ridge Agency in October 1881 after first having been moved from Montana to the Darlington Agency in October 1878, even as Morning Star's and Little Wolf's people were fleeing northward. Nearly seven hundred other northerners remained in Indian Territory. About half of them eventually chose to stay with the Southern Cheyennes because of family ties. In 1879 the United States Senate investigated the circumstances of the Northern Cheyennes' transfer to the south. The investigation exposed the deceit surrounding the removal and uncovered conditions of starvation, sickness, and maladjustment in Indian Territory. The Senate committee concurred with movements afoot to allow the Northern Cheyennes to remain in the north and others to return from the south. In November 1884 President Chester A. Arthur ordered the establishment of the Tongue River Reservation as a permanent home for the tribe. Many people had already been living informally on a small reserve spanning portions of Rosebud Creek and Tongue River since May 1882.[20]

Morning Star joined Little Wolf and others on the Tongue River in November 1879. The aged chief understood the movement to establish a permanent home in Montana; but he died, embittered according to some, in 1883 before the matter was fully resolved. He was seventy-five years old.[21] Little Wolf's final years were deeply conflicted. In December 1880, while intoxicated, he murdered a man named Starving Elk after finding his daughter, Pretty Walker, consorting with him. A possessor of chief's medicine, Little Wolf forfeited his tribal status, imposed on himself a sentence of banishment, and gave away his property, including his horses, as an act of contrition. Little Wolf lived until 1904, walking wherever he went. White settlers on Rosebud Creek remembered him as a gentle, dignified old man who loved children. At the time of his death, he was seventy-four years old. In 1917 ethnohistorian George Bird Grinnell brought the remains of Morning Star and Dull Knife from distant burials to side-by-side graves in the Lame Deer, Montana, cemetery, where they continue to inspire the fierce self-determination of the Northern Cheyenne people to this day.[22]

In the months following Crazy Horse's surrender at Red Cloud
Agency in early May 1877, the enigmatic chief remained the center
of attention. Government agents sought to direct his influence to
the cause of acculturating the Northern Nation. But his disenchant-
ment at Red Cloud was evident almost from the start. With great
concern and pessimism, he watched the removal of the Northern
Cheyennes to Indian Territory at the end of May and recoiled at
persistently repeated rumors that the White River agencies were
also to be moved, east to the Missouri River and far beyond the
traditional homeland of the Oglalas and Brulés. Crook had promised
Crazy Horse that he and his followers would be released from Red
Cloud Agency later in the summer to hunt buffalo in the Powder
River Country, but as summer waned that opportunity was denied.
Crazy Horse had signed on as a scout for the army. Crook wanted
Sioux warriors to assist in any prospective fighting with the Nez
Perce Indians as that turmoil invaded Montana from the west. But
the notion of having surrendered the ways of the warrior in May
only to be reengaged in a war against another tribe sat poorly with
the vaunted chief, as did the withdrawn permission to hunt buffalo.
In the matter of scouting, however, Crazy Horse relented. He informed
Lieutenant Clark that he would join the fight against the Nez Perce.
Agency interpreter Frank Grouard garbled that translation, perhaps
deliberately, telling Clark that Crazy Horse meant to go north
and resume fighting whites. Another interpreter, Louis Bordeaux,
corrected the slip; but Clark thought that Crazy Horse was threatening war.[23]

Whether it was due to the garbled translation or not, Clark,
Crook's agency watchdog, never shook the notion of Crazy Horse
bolting from Red Cloud Agency. The matter was exacerbated by the
chief's continued insistence that he be allowed to go north to hunt.
Crazy Horse's vacillation on the matter of scouting against the Nez
Perce compounded the mistrust. Clark relayed these mounting
concerns to the commander of Camp Robinson, Lieutenant Colonel
Luther P. Bradley, Ninth Infantry. Bradley, in turn, passed them to
Sheridan in Chicago, who directed Crook to investigate the matter
personally. Crook visited Camp Robinson on September 2. He was
briefed on the Crazy Horse travails, including Grouard's mistranslation,

and instructed Clark to arrange a council with the chief and other Red Cloud Agency headmen. Upon learning of the summons, Crazy Horse quickly announced that he would not attend and that he did not want to talk anymore because "no good would come of it."[24]

As Crook and others prepared for the meeting on September 3, a warrior named Woman Dress warned interpreters William Garnett and Baptiste "Bat" Pourier that Crazy Horse in fact intended to appear, leading sixty men. He would shake Crook's hand but hold it firm while those sixty Indians killed the general and everyone with him. Garnett and Pourier brought Woman Dress to Crook, and the warning was repeated. Shaken and counseled by Clark to forego the meeting, Crook ordered the arrest of Crazy Horse and then departed for Cheyenne.[25]

Crazy Horse's apprehension was planned for the morning of September 4, 1877. Eight companies of cavalry commanded by Major Julius W. Mason, Third Cavalry, led the sortie. Clark accompanied them, supported by Indian scouts and warriors from camps nearby. Any surprise was lost well before the column neared Crazy Horse's village, located some six miles northeast of the agency. As the troops approached, Crazy Horse fled undetected to Spotted Tail Agency, twenty-five miles east, seeking the camp of Touch the Clouds. Meanwhile, Mason's party returned to Robinson and passed word to Camp Sheridan that Crazy Horse was somewhere nearby. Crazy Horse and Touch the Clouds were old friends and discussed the inescapable tension at Red Cloud. Both chiefs then rode to Camp Sheridan, seeking to arrange the relocation of Crazy Horse's village to Spotted Tail Agency. Agent Jesse Lee, first lieutenant, Ninth Infantry, pledged to use his influence to arrange the transfer but also made it clear that Crazy Horse would first have to return to Camp Robinson and explain himself in this matter and the welter of other distortions whirling about. Lee offered to accompany Crazy Horse and assured him that he would not be harmed, which seemed to placate the sullen leader.[26]

The ride from Sheridan to Robinson consumed most of September 5. Crazy Horse arrived at 6 P.M. Few comprehended his dire circumstances, though Lee had received a message from Clark en route informing him that Bradley wanted Crazy Horse taken directly to the adjutant's office. Meanwhile, Bradley had received a communiqué from Crook, reaffirming Crazy Horse's arrest and that he was promptly to be taken under strong escort to Fort Laramie and Cheyenne and be entrained there for Omaha. As Crazy Horse rode onto the Camp Robinson parade ground, he easily sensed his precarious situation. Armed warriors from the local camps, mostly unfriendly to the chief, clustered on the south and west perimeters of the quadrangle. A growing throng of supporters positioned themselves behind Crazy Horse's small entourage from Spotted Tail Agency and Camp Sheridan. Bradley could be seen pacing the veranda of his quarters on the northeast side of the grounds. All the officers' quarters were situated on a slight rise overlooking the parade ground. Before him, at the adjutant's office and guardhouse next door, a small knot of soldiers stood attentively. Lee consulted with Second Lieutenant Frederick Calhoun, Fourteenth Infantry, then detailed as post adjutant. He was the brother of Seventh Cavalry officer James Calhoun, killed with Custer at the Little Big Horn. Calhoun confirmed that a meeting with Bradley would not occur and that Crazy Horse was to be surrendered to the officer of the day, Captain James Kennington, Fourteenth Infantry.[27]

Lee pressed the matter with Kennington too and was once more rebuffed. As Crazy Horse dismounted in front of the adjutant's office, Little Big Man, a former friend but now a bitter rival, took hold of him and escorted him into the building. Touch the Clouds and other Spotted Tail Indians followed. Lee crossed the parade ground and confronted Bradley directly. Again the commander refused to hear out the chief. Aiming to mollify Crazy Horse, Lee returned to the adjutant's office and reported that Bradley would see him in the morning but that he would be kept under guard that night. Lee knew better, of course. Sometime after the arrest and deep in the night, Crazy Horse was to be rushed away, bound for Fort Marion at Saint Augustine, Florida, where Indian chiefs from other wars were imprisoned.[28]

Sandwiched between Kennington on his right and Little Big Man on his left, Crazy Horse was ushered from the adjutant's office to the guardhouse, the next building to the north. The throng of observers continued to grow, now numbering several hundred Indians, including the revered Oglala elder Red Cloud. In addition to securing prisoners, the guardhouse was the station for Camp Robinson's daily guard: sixteen men fully armed and equipped who were detailed over a 24-hour period to the internal security of the post and particularly the storehouses, stables, corrals, and guardhouse itself. Working in relief, at any one time one-third of the complement tended walking stations while the remainder relaxed in the guardhouse, under arms still but usually relatively carefree, but not this afternoon. By all accounts, Crazy Horse did not comprehend the full impact of his arrest until he entered the guardhouse and saw the armed relief guards fidgeting on their dais, all with eyes riveted directly on him. He was viewed as the Indian responsible for Custer's death, and these men were veterans of that war. To the right Crazy Horse saw the barred confinement cell, now occupied by seven other prisoners, with iron shackles on the floor.[29]

Finally grasping the gravity of his circumstances and still in the clutch of Kennington and Little Big Man, Crazy Horse recoiled violently, thrashing free from his escort's grip. He drew a trader's knife concealed in his belt and swung it wildly at Little Big Man and others who dared to grapple with him. In a feverish rush, Crazy Horse exploded through the guardhouse doorway. The assembled throng outside pressed close, some northerners advancing to Crazy Horse's defense and others seemingly bent on his destruction. Steadfast at the guardhouse doorway at Guard Post Number One, bayonet fixed to his Springfield rifle, was Private William Gentles of Company F, Fourteenth Infantry. In the melee Kennington screamed out, "Stab the son of a bitch! Stab the son of a bitch!" As Crazy Horse emerged, Gentles, a no-nonsense twenty-year veteran soldier, instinctively assumed the "guard" stance, thrusting his rifle forward so that its butt was tight at his waist and the foot-long triangular bayonet extended forward at eye level. With Crazy Horse's slightly arched back slamming toward him, Gentles lunged, stabbing the warrior-chief in the small of his back, piercing a kidney and lung. As Gentles withdrew the bayonet, Crazy Horse slumped to the ground instantly, mortally wounded.[30]

The crowd was momentarily hushed in shock. Touch the Clouds, close at hand, knelt and comforted his friend while He Dog, another old friend, warned others to back off. Doctor Valentine T. McGillycuddy, one of the garrison surgeons, pushed his way through the throng and examined the prostrate warrior's wound. Blood dripped from the penetration in the back and from Crazy Horse's nose and mouth, confirming that a lung had been pierced. Over the din, Kennington ordered guards to carry Crazy Horse into the guardhouse; but when McGillycuddy protested the captain pointed to the adjutant's office instead. There Crazy Horse was laid upon blankets on the floor as the doctor administered morphine to ease the intense pain. Crazy Horse soon fell unconscious and remained in that state most of the evening. A small throng hovered at his side, including McGillycuddy, Touch the Clouds, Bat Pourier, and Crazy Horse's father, Worm. Though he rallied briefly at 10 P.M. and conversed with his father and Lieutenant Lee, Crazy Horse again lapsed into a coma and died at 11:40 P.M. Touch the Clouds drew a blanket over Crazy Horse's face, laid a hand upon his breast, and quietly proclaimed: "It is good; he has looked for death, and it has come."[31]

At dawn Worm and Crazy Horse's stepmother transported their son's body to Beaver Creek, south of Camp Sheridan, where it was anointed with vermillion, dressed in new buckskins, wrapped in a buffalo robe, and honored in a series of Lakota mourning rites. Camp Robinson and Red Cloud Agency remained in a tense state for several days. While the tone was bitter, no retaliations or defections occurred. Within a week the excitement had eased measurably.[32]

Local reactions to the news of Crazy Horse's death were mixed. Crook's agent, Lieutenant Clark, boldly asserted that "Crazy Horse's death is considered by most of the Indians as a right good thing for all concerned." He did not and perhaps could not account for the hardened ill-will of the northerners, for whom Crazy Horse's killing was an unexplained and inexcusable betrayal, which would evoke a response shortly. Jesse Lee, culpable in the arrest plot, mourned his involvement for the remainder of his life and also consistently blamed others for what he saw in his mind and heart as a "pathetic and tragic end." Newspaper reports were strikingly neutral in judgment, most depicting Crazy Horse's death in sensitive or tragic terms.[33]

The reverberations of Crazy Horse's killing had barely subsided in the White River camps when a delegation of headmen from the Red Cloud and Spotted Tail agencies returned from Washington with other disquieting news. They had learned that the government fully intended to relocate the White River agencies to the Missouri River. In great measure, this was unfinished business from the time of the Fort Laramie Treaty of 1868, which among many articles had stipulated a single agency for the Sioux "near the center of said reservation, where timber and water may be convenient," in Dakota, not Nebraska. But multiple agencies for the various Lakota bands had evolved subsequent to the treaty. Several were located on the Missouri, where the river and its steamboats had efficiently served Upper Missouri commerce and Indian affairs since the 1830s. The river, moreover, defined the eastern margin of the Great Sioux Reservation prescribed by the treaty. From the start, however, the Oglalas and Brulés had steadfastly rejected agencies beyond their traditional homelands in western Nebraska and eastern Wyoming and had gained repeated concessions from the Indian Bureau that allowed agency sites along the North Platte River east of Fort Laramie and then on the White River. Nebraskans fumed all the while, since these agencies were in their state and not in Dakota, and the government ceaselessly bemoaned the added costs incurred in delivering Indian goods by rail and wagon to western Nebraska.[34]

As had occurred with the Northern Cheyennes five months earlier, the relocations were orchestrated swiftly and under duress. In late October 1877 the scattered villages surrounding both agencies were uprooted. Some eight thousand people, including nearly two thousand northern Indians, began long overland treks to the hated Missouri River. The Oglalas traveled northeast along the valley of the White River, destined for the mouth of Yellow Medicine Creek some fifty miles south of Pierre. The Brulés generally followed the divide between the White and Niobrara rivers east, bound for the former Ponca Indian agency on the Niobrara, fifteen miles above its confluence with the Missouri. Companies of Third Cavalry from

Camp Robinson accompanied both movements, as did local cowboys driving cattle to provide food for the relocations.[35]

Weather slowed the movements but failed to obscure the repeated shifting of northern Indians, mostly Miniconjous and Sans Arcs, from Spotted Tail's caravan to Red Cloud's. Many of the northerners had taken refuge at the Spotted Tail Agency after Crazy Horse's killing. Their increasing discontent was palpable, with many of the tribesmen openly threatening to break for the north. Despite Clark's attempts to return the northerners to their assigned caravan, spokesmen among them adamantly asserted that "they belong to the North and not to either Spotted Tail or Red Cloud Agency, that their agency is at present on the Cheyenne River."[36] That assertion was partly based in fact, since Miniconjous and Sans Arcs rightly belonged to the Cheyenne River Agency north of Pierre, despite having aligned more recently with the White River bands. Clark relented but harbored increasing concerns over such movements, fearing that they foreshadowed an outright bolt from the caravans. Clark already recalled the disappearances of small bands of Miniconjous from the White River agencies in the days immediately following Crazy Horse's death, including the followers of Fast Bull and Crazy Horse's relatives.[37]

By early November as many as 250 lodges of Northern Indians were tallied in the Red Cloud column. Among the northerners, leaders like Red Bear, Low Dog, and Black Fox did indeed countenance flight to Canada. Red Bear's closest friend, Spotted Eagle, already resided in Sitting Bull's camp north of the Medicine Line. The feared breakaway occurred in the dim wintry daylight of November 17. Red Bear's followers simply abandoned camp that morning and struck north across the White River badlands. Clark and agent James Irwin, both traveling at the head of the strung-out Red Cloud caravan, were promptly notified. The lieutenant dispatched Touch the Clouds, Crazy Horse's old friend and a moderate since returning from active participation in the Great Sioux War, to overtake the northerners and persuade them to return. Touch the Clouds reached the northerners, but his attempts at persuasion were rebuffed. In all, some six hundred people joined the flight north.[38]

The breakaways successfully fled to the northwest. They crossed the Cheyenne River near the fork of the South Cheyenne and Belle Fourche rivers, skirting Slim Buttes, scene of the great battle with General Crook's troops in September 1876, and reached the Yellowstone River in the vicinity of the O'Fallon Creek confluence. As they continued north, the northerners evaded patrols dispatched by Colonel Miles from Fort Keogh and reached the Missouri River in early January 1878. They crossed below the mouth of Milk River and soon thereafter joined Sitting Bull's coalition of American Indians in Canada.[39]

The departure of most but not all of the northerners from the Red Cloud caravan heightened the dissension among those who remained. These Indians were already reluctant transferees, and many chafed at the aggressive assimilation efforts being pressed upon them. Moreover, the onset of winter had slowed travel to a virtual crawl. Chief Red Cloud counseled among his headmen and concluded that they would travel east no farther but would stay on the White River for the winter, some eighty miles short of the Missouri. Upon hearing reports of the defections and Red Cloud's intransigence, Sherman and Sheridan were furious and ordered that foodstuffs be withheld from the camps and that the Indians only be rationed at the Yellow Medicine Creek site. But Irwin and Crook sided with Red Cloud's people, countering that this was consistent with promises made by the president that these Indians could select locations for their new agencies. Crook knew, moreover, that local commands were ill prepared for further unrest. Both he and General Terry already had substantially deployed available troops from the Platte and Dakota departments in response to the Nez Perce conflict. The initial orders were revoked, and Red Cloud's followers were allowed to remain on the White River through the winter. Spotted Tail's people, meanwhile, encamped on the lower Niobrara River as prearranged, while the debate raged anew on the matter of homes for the Oglalas and Brulés.[40]

Continued efforts to persuade Red Cloud and his followers to accept a Missouri River agency brought nothing but rhetorical hostility. The Oglalas preferred an agency on White Earth Creek in the lee of the revered Pine Ridge and about as far west of the Missouri River as possible without crossing into Nebraska. Spotted Tail's Brulés favored an agency near the junction of Dakota's Rosebud Creek and the Little White River, on the southern periphery of the reservation about midway between their former agency home on Beaver Creek in Nebraska and the Missouri River. A government commission examined both sites in July 1878 and reported that the Indians had selected two of the best locations in the region. With permission to depart westward, the Brulés commenced their relocation from the Ponca Agency almost immediately, using wagons and harness provided by the Indian Bureau and with Indians as drivers. By September 1 the new Rosebud Agency was reasonably functional. Meanwhile, the relocation of the Oglalas tarried into mid-November. Their new agency soon assumed the name "Pine Ridge." As at Rosebud, the adoption of new geographically based names lessened the identifications with chiefs Spotted Tail and Red Cloud, as desired by the Indian Bureau. Coincidentally, in their flight north from Indian Territory, Morning Star's and Little Wolf's Northern Cheyennes reached Nebraska as these Brulé and Oglala relocations were occurring.[41]

Doctor Valentine McGillycuddy, the surgeon who tended the dying Crazy Horse and succeeded James Irwin as Pine Ridge agent on March 10, 1879, aptly and rather sensitively summarized the plight of the Oglalas, and most relocated tribes, in his 1879 report to the commissioner of Indian affairs:

> Since 1863, when Fort Laramie, Wyoming, was the abiding place of these people, they have up to the present moved eight or ten times, sometimes a distance of three or four hundred miles. The responsibility for these repeated removals cannot be charged to the Indians. Locality and love of home is as strongly marked, if not more so, in the American savage as in the white man. The return of the Cheyennes and Poncas during the past year, from a forced transfer to a southern home in the Indian Territory, back to their northern hunting grounds, across a broad stretch of partly settled country, and in spite of military and civil authority, is but a reminder of this.[42]

The turmoil and chaos that characterized Indian affairs in the southern half of Sioux Country in the years following the cessation of open hostilities associated with the Great Sioux War had its parallel in Montana and Canada. The postwar asylum of Sitting Bull and thousands of American Sioux on British soil constituted a border entanglement that vexed both governments for nearly five years. The war's first Lakota refugees crossed the border in October 1876, and Sitting Bull crossed in early May 1877. A year later he welcomed the arrival of Crazy Horse's relatives and other disaffected northerners from the White River camps. Their story of an imagined sanctuary, swelling numbers, overtures from the American government for their return to the United States coupled with subtle and then overt encouragement from the Canadian government to depart, and eventual capitulations distinctly prolonged the legacy of the Great Sioux War. It also necessitated concurrent military maneuvering throughout the far northern plains to ensure the transformations then fully underway.

Notions of a so-called Medicine Line (a discernible demarcation separating north from south, with different political systems, traders, and friends and enemies) dated to well before the onset of hostilities in Sioux Country in the 1870s. The Forty-ninth Parallel dividing the western prairie politically largely originated at the time of the Louisiana Purchase and was ratified in the Treaty of 1818 that clarified certain midcontinental international boundary matters after the War of 1812. That agreement defined this central portion of the border as running from a corner of Lake of the Woods in northern Minnesota westward to the Rocky Mountains. Although the line was unmarked for decades thereafter, border residents, mostly Indians and mixed-bloods, comprehended its existence and consequences. North of the line, Hudson's Bay Company traders ruled the landscape well into the nineteenth century, engaging in a highly competitive and lucrative trade in furs. The company's influence reached beyond the border too until the early 1830s, when John Jacob Astor's American Fur Company established itself on the Upper Missouri at bastions like Forts Union and McKenzie. The border's residents traveled freely between north and south, hunting widely and seizing the advantages of the sharp competition between the companies, trading

furs for firearms, blankets, hardware, and liquor. The Hunkpapa
Sioux were among those whose lifeways were heavily influenced
by this freedom of transborder movement. Hence it was easy for
Sitting Bull and his followers to seek haven in Canada in 1876 and
1877 among a people in a land they had known for generations.[43]

The Medicine Line gained a certain notoriety in the early 1870s
when American and Canadian surveyors plotted the border, erecting
eight-foot-tall iron pylons on the Minnesota-Manitoba line and
five- to eight-foot-tall stone cairns or earthen mounds on the line
separating the Dakota and Montana prairie from the North-West
Territories. The monuments were spaced at three-mile intervals,
but this pencil-thin edge was no barrier at all. Yet despite the lack
of fences or checkpoints, the border was certainly known and was
said by some to have "strong medicine," because it had the power to
stop the U.S. Army in its tracks. It offered the beckoning realities
of relief, hope, and sanctuary to the Lakotas at the close of their war
and earlier to the Santee Sioux in the wake of their 1860s Minnesota
War. The Medicine Line was also a beacon for the Nez Perce Indians
on their own northbound flight through Montana in 1877.[44]

In addition to offering political haven in Canada, the borderlands
of the Medicine Line themselves were an inviting and long-appre-
ciated prairie region, interspersed with unique highlands (particularly in Canada) that provided good hunting. Although striking
features like the Sweet Grass Hills and Bear's Paw Mountains dotted
the American side, the region's dominant physical attributes lay
north of the border. Most notable was the Cypress Hills, a broad
upland on the western margins of today's Saskatchewan. Rising
more than nineteen hundred feet above the surrounding prairie
and well watered and timbered, the Cypress Hills resembled the
Black Hills of Dakota, though on a smaller scale. The Cypress
Hills also featured Fort Walsh, a palisaded North-West Mounted
Police post founded in 1875 to extend Canadian law into a region
overrun with American whiskey traders from Fort Benton, who
were the source of considerable trouble, particularly among local
Indians. Wood Mountain Post, a smaller police station nestled in
another wooded upland or escarpment distinctive from the encompassing prairie, was 160 miles east of Fort Walsh across a vast

short-grass prairie. For the American Sioux, this Canadian refuge (Cypress Hills in the west, Wood Mountain in the east, and the prairie in between) offered good hunting, especially for buffalo, and opportunities for regular trade for food, weapons, and, most importantly now, ammunition.[45]

Major James M. Walsh commanded the North-West Mountain Police force in this district. A courageous and flamboyant inspector who was almost Custer-like in appearance and dress, Walsh met often with Sitting Bull and other Sioux leaders. He developed a commendable rapport with them, while of course exhorting them to obey the laws of the queen's country and warning them that they would not be allowed to continue their war against the Americans from the Canadian side of the border. The Lakotas assented; Sitting Bull assured Walsh that "he had buried his arms on the American side of the line before crossing to the country of the White Mother." But the Lakotas repeatedly sought permission to purchase ammunition for hunting, whether from their Métis friends or from Jean Louis Légaré, a French-Canadian trader operating near Wood Mountain Post. Walsh acquiesced but monitored ball, powder, and cartridge purchases closely.[46]

As the numbers of American Sioux in Canada continued to swell, relations between the two governments became strained. Washington and its agents had made clear the terms to be levied on these tribesmen: unconditional surrender of weapons and horses in accordance with the Rule of 1876, just as was already occurring at agencies throughout Sioux Country. Canada faced the increasing displeasure of its own native Indians, who saw ravenous Sioux intruding on the hunting grounds, and the prospective burden on the government's budget if the American Indians were tended in any way. The Canadian government urged Washington to drop its demand for unconditional surrender, in the hope that this appeasement might lure the American Indians home. The United States, meanwhile, quietly wanted Canada to intern the Sioux north of the border and treat them as Canadian Indians. But Washington also agreed that it was necessary to demonstrate that an effort was being made to persuade the Sioux to return to American soil. After a considerable debate the secretaries of war and the interior were instructed in August 1877 to dispatch a commission to meet with Sitting Bull.[47]

Brigadier General Alfred Terry, commander of the Department of Dakota (the military jurisdiction immediately south of the Medicine Line), headed the so-called Sitting Bull Indian Commission, which was soon also known simply as the Terry Commission. After briefly organizing in Saint Paul, Terry departed Minnesota on September 14, bound for Fort Benton, Montana. Fellow commission members accompanying him included diplomat Albert G. Lawrence of Rhode Island, representing the Department of the Interior and a veteran, along with Terry, of the Black Hills Commission of 1875; Captain Henry C. Corbin, Twenty-fourth Infantry, serving as secretary and otherwise assigned to duty in the Executive Mansion in Washington; and Jay Stone, a stenographer hired in Saint Paul. Also traveling with Terry was his aide, Captain Edward W. Smith, Eighteenth Infantry. Because it was already late in the Missouri River boating season, the party traveled by rail via Omaha to Corinne, Utah, and by stage to Helena and Fort Shaw. Joining the commission in Omaha were Jerome B. Stillson of the *New York Herald* and Charles S. Diehl of the *Chicago Times.* Terry was joined in Helena by Company E, Seventh Cavalry, commanded by First Lieutenant Charles C. DeRudio, and at Fort Shaw by Company H, Seventh Infantry, commanded by Captain Henry B. Freeman. These units escorted the commission as it continued north toward Canada.[48]

Terry reached Fort Benton on October 6 and that evening learned of the engagement between troops led by Colonel Nelson Miles and the Nez Perces at Bear's Paw Mountain, some seventy-five miles northeast of the fort. Miles received the surrender of most but not all of the Nez Perces. Some Nez Perces escaped that entanglement and reached Canada, and their sorry plight would color events in the days ahead. The commission continued north on October 10 and was joined on the twelfth by Companies F, G, and H, Second Cavalry, which replaced DeRudio's company, now relieved from escort duty. The Second Cavalry companies had just participated in the Bear's Paw engagement. The commission reached the Medicine Line, which reporter Diehl referred to as the "stone heaps," on October 15. They were cordially greeted by Lieutenant Colonel

James F. Macleod, commissioner of the North-West Mounted Police from Fort Macleod (west of the Cypress Hills), along with Major Walsh and a complement of red-coated mounted policemen, all smartly wielding pennon-fluttering lances. Macleod, Walsh, and their police contingent escorted the party from the border north to Fort Walsh. Terry's cavalry escort, by international courtesy, could not pass the border and encamped on the shores of Wild Horse Lake. Captain Freeman and the infantry company continued north with Terry, however, detailed as wagon drivers and camp attendants but disarmed before crossing to British soil.[49]

Terry's mission was much anticipated north of the Medicine Line. For nearly two weeks Major Walsh had made every effort to persuade Sitting Bull and fellow chiefs, then mostly encamped near Pinto Horse Butte forty miles west of Wood Mountain Post, to cross the open prairie to Fort Walsh so that the commission would not have to seek out the Sioux camp. At first Sitting Bull was reluctant to meet with Terry, telling Walsh that the Americans always lied and would tell the Sioux nothing that they could believe. The arrival of battered Nez Perce refugees from the Bear's Paw engagement further hardened this view.[50] Already more than a hundred Nez Perce Indians, all bedraggled and many seriously wounded, had found their way across the Medicine Line and into the Lakota camp. The Sioux sharply berated Walsh. "Why do you come and seek us to go and talk with men who are killing our own race? You see these men, women, and children, wounded and bleeding? We cannot talk with men who have blood on their hands. They have stained the grass of the White Mother with it."[51] But Walsh's calm and persistence paid off. Eventually Sitting Bull and twenty other headmen agreed to accompany him to Fort Walsh to council with the Americans.

On the morning of October 17 the commission convened in Walsh's quarters to study the message from the president to be presented by Terry that afternoon. Three interpreters were on hand: Baptiste Shane, official interpreter for the commission; Constant Provost, interpreter at Fort Walsh; and André Larivée, a Métis interpreter friendly to Sitting Bull and designated to represent his interests. Terry painstakingly read the document aloud, pausing and explaining as he went, intent on ensuring that its meaning was fully understood. Misinterpretation could not be a cause of failure.[52]

At 3 P.M. on October 17 Sitting Bull and the other chiefs were led into the largest room in the Fort Walsh headquarters. He and Macleod shook hands vigorously, but he passed the Americans by without shaking their hands and joined followers who were seating themselves on buffalo robes at the center of the room. The meeting space had been arranged simply, with only several tables and chairs. But it was rearranged when Sitting Bull complained that he could not see the American commissioners. They moved their chairs to the front of their table, directly before the chiefs. Observers crowded along the walls: reporters Stillson, Diehl, and John J. Healy (representing the *Benton Record*); American and Canadian officers, including Captains Smith and Freeman and Major Walsh; and another half-dozen red-coated mounted policemen. Among Lakota headmen present in addition to Sitting Bull were Bear's Cap (Bear's Head), Spotted Eagle, Flying Bird, Whirlwind Bear, Medicine Turns Around, Iron Dog, Man That Scatters the Bear, Little Knife, The Crow, Yellow Dog, and probably also Rain in the Face. The Indians were informed that Baptiste Shane would interpret and that Provost and Larivée would listen and ensure that the words and intent were accurately conveyed. For reasons never explained, the council did not open with a time-honored pipe ceremony.[53]

When all were settled, and with no fanfare whatsoever, Terry rose and launched into his prepared address. As always, such messages opened with a call for peace. The president wanted lasting peace, Terry said, regardless of acts of hostility committed in the past: he would offer a full pardon and make no attempt to punish anyone. Terry reminded the chiefs that they were the last to surrender and that all the other bands had come to the agencies, where they were received as friends and given food and clothing. Terry acknowledged that the others had been required to give up their horses and arms, which were sold to purchase cattle for the Indians to enable them to become cattle breeders. Such terms would also be expected of those now in Canada. "The President cannot and will not consent that you should return to your country armed, mounted, and prepared for war." Too much white and Indian blood had already been shed, Terry admonished. "It is time for that bloodshed to cease." In his tersest tone, Terry offered one final reproach: "It is our duty to assure you, you cannot return to your country and your friends unless you accept these propositions. Should you attempt to return with arms in your hands, you must be treated as enemies of the United States." He then asked Sitting Bull and the others to weigh these terms carefully and give an answer.[54]

Throughout Terry's speech the Indians sat quietly, puffing on their pipes. Reporter Jerome Stillson noted that they "continued to smoke, smoke, smoke . . . , until the room reeked." Then Sitting Bull rose and through the interpreter talked of the long history of bad treatment suffered at the hands of the Americans. "You come here and tell us lies, but we don't want to hear them. Don't you say two more words. Go back home where you came from." Several other Indians also offered remarks, echoing the same tone set by Sitting Bull. Terry asked Sitting Bull whether he should report to the president that his offers had been refused. Sitting Bull replied: "If we told you more, you would not pay any attention to it. That is all I have to say. This part of the country does not belong to your people. You belong on the other side; this side belongs to us."[55]

On that note the council unceremoniously ended. As the Indians departed, Sitting Bull and the chiefs again showed effusive respect for Macleod and the policemen present but coldly ignored the Americans. Almost from the start, the Sitting Bull Commission was viewed as a failure, but Terry had conscientiously discharged his duty. And Terry and the commissioners saw deeper realities. No longer did they perceive Sitting Bull as a threat to the American frontier. Sitting Bull feared Miles's troops, and reopening hostilities from the Canadian sanctuary would make him "an enemy of both governments." Terry also believed that in time Sitting Bull and his followers would become so accustomed to their new surroundings that they would come to regard the area as their permanent home, just as had happened with so many Santee Sioux after the Minnesota War in 1862. The commissioners also believed, however, that limited acts of hostility seemed probable as long as Sitting Bull freely roamed the border. Stillson's *New York Herald* perhaps best summed the attitude of the commission and American government: "We wish the Great Mother the joy of her new subjects."[56]

As months and then years passed in Canada, the fragile realities of the Canadian exile became ever more apparent to Sitting Bull and the Lakotas. For a while after the commission departed the Indian numbers continued to swell, including the arrival of some 205 lodges belonging to the Crazy Horse band in the spring of 1878. At its peak at about that time, the group of exiled bands numbered slightly more than 500 lodges, plus perhaps 45 belonging to the Nez Perces, and tallied upward of 3,000 people, including some 270 Nez Perces.[57] Throughout this period the Lakotas faced increasing day-to-day difficulties, including the open resentment of Canadian Indians and diminishing hunting successes on the Canadian prairie, especially for buffalo. This hunting pressure in fact led to the virtual extinction of the Canadian plains buffalo well ahead of the general slaughter occurring on the American northern plains in the early 1880s and necessitated cross-border forays, however dangerous. Such hunts were carefully planned. When they occurred, Indian camps were usually pitched on the Canadian side to protect women and children. But these incursions were easily detected by the Americans and brought quick retaliatory responses from troops at Fort Benton, the new Fort Assinniboine (established on the Milk River in the summer of 1879), and the Poplar River Agency and other areas along the Missouri River.[58]

One hunting foray south of the Medicine Line in July 1879 demonstrated the zeal with which Colonel Miles's troops from Fort Keogh steadfastly guarded the border when reports of incursions occurred. Lured by substantial numbers of buffalo south of the Big Bend of the Milk River, Sitting Bull and six hundred of his followers made a big kill. But before all the butchering was finished, two companies of cavalry accompanied by Crow and Cheyenne scouts struck remnants of the band and began a fight consisting initially of scattered, long-range shooting. Miles soon came on with infantry and howitzers and drove off the Sioux with exploding spherical-case cannon rounds. Five Lakotas were killed, and many others wounded. Miles chased the Sioux to the border but did not cross, and the crisis passed. Major Walsh was also patrolling the border.

He came upon the Sioux as they were settling north of the line, saw the havoc inflicted by the Americans, and went to the border to confer with Miles. Walsh brought several Lakotas with him, including Long Dog, an accomplished Hunkpapa war chief. Walsh and the Sioux again offered assurances that they intended to stay north of the line, but such crossings continued.[59]

Despite Walsh's personal calming influence and continued intercession, the Canadians' unwillingness to tolerate the American Sioux was hardening. The Canadian government was already grappling with the difficulties of caring for its own Indians, especially with the disappearance of the Canadian buffalo. It steadfastly refused to feed and shelter the American Indians or to offer formal sanctuary, coldly asserting that these were American and not Canadian Indians. Most importantly, the government feared increasing diplomatic tension with the United States as more and more Sioux crossed south of the Medicine Line searching for food and in doing so threatened border security. Canadian relations with the American Sioux took a drastic turn in July 1880 when Major Walsh was reassigned to Fort Qu'Appelle, 140 miles northeast of Wood Mountain. Walsh's government had grown disenchanted with his persistent outspoken support of the Lakotas and grew to believe that letting starvation take its course would soon drive the Sioux back to American soil. His successor, Superintendent Lief N. F. Crozier, refused to court Sitting Bull as Walsh had done and traveled among the camps tersely counseling surrender.[60]

In the end, hunger trumped everything. In a disintegration of the unique assembly of bands in Canada not unlike the one that occurred in the wake of the Little Big Horn Battle four and a half years earlier, pragmatic leaders led followers, band by band, across the Medicine Line to their homeland. Individuals and small groups, particularly southerners like Oglalas and Brulés from the Red Cloud and Spotted Tail agencies, were among the first to return in the summer of 1879, barely one year after arriving in Canada. Then Sitting Bull's people began appearing. Hunkpapa chief White Gut led forty families to the Fort Peck Agency on January 28, 1880, and complied with plainly understood surrender conditions. A trickle soon became a tide: by the end of April, more than eleven hundred nonagency Sioux had come to Fort Peck, surrendering their horses and weapons. Spotted Eagle, Rain in the Face, and Charge the Eagle led their followers to Fort Keogh on October 31, 1880, surrendering arms and ponies and welcoming the foodstuffs distributed from the army's commissary storehouses. Perhaps the greatest blow to Sitting Bull's hegemony occurred in January 1881 when Gall departed Canada, leading his followers first toward the Poplar River Agency and then to Fort Buford, at the confluence of the Yellowstone and Missouri rivers. By May 1,125 Sioux were encamped at the fort, under the close guard of troops commanded by Major David H. Brotherton, Seventh Infantry. Steamboats transported them to Fort Yates at the end of that month. On June 13 steamers carried another 1,641 Sioux downriver from Fort Keogh.[61]

In the end, only Sitting Bull and a few others held out. Conflicted, starving, and unable to counsel with his foremost friend in Canada, Major Walsh, Sitting Bull finally accepted the inevitable. Assisted by another friend of Sitting Bull, trader Jean Louis Légaré, 188 people rode or were carried in carts and wagons from Wood Mountain to Fort Buford, somberly entering the post on July 19. The importance of this occasion was not lost on Brotherton, who put off surrender formalities until the next day while immediately tending to the welfare of the forlorn and hungry arrivals. Sitting Bull's formal surrender on July 20 in Brotherton's quarters reflected the poignancy of a leader who had held steadfast for so long to tribal independence and a lifeway that had now all but vanished. Proud still, even at this emotional surrender, Sitting Bull faced a crowd in Brotherton's quarters that including a newsman, an array of American officers, a North-West Mounted Police officer, and fellow surrendering chiefs and headmen. Sitting Bull gestured to his son to give Brotherton his Winchester carbine and then uttered these words: "I surrender this rifle to you through my young son, whom I now desire to teach in this manner that he has become a friend of the Americans. I wish him to learn the habits of the whites and to be educated as their sons are educated. I wish it to be remembered that I was the last man of my tribe to surrender my rifle."[62]

Sitting Bull's band remained at Fort Buford for ten days and then boarded a steamboat bound for Fort Yates. As that boat nosed into the Fort Yates landing on August 1, a great melancholy overtook Sitting Bull, who wept uncontrollably. He lamented to his friend Running Antelope: "This is the first time I have had to surrender and give up." Running Antelope put an arm around his friend and said: "Brother don't weep, everything will come out all right."[63] But Sitting Bull's unshakable despondency unsettled agents at Fort Yates and Standing Rock Agency. Three weeks later he and 171 others, almost exclusively Indians who had surrendered with him at Fort Buford, were forcibly relocated downriver to Fort Randall, on the Missouri near the Dakota-Nebraska border. They were held as virtual prisoners of war there for nearly two years.[64] By all accounts these months were the unhappiest and most uneventful period of Sitting Bull's life. But the forced exile brought about an abrupt change in his demeanor. As one of his biographers noted, "He seemed to understand the magnitude of his fall. No longer did he talk of a reservation on the Little Missouri, or the old life of the hunt free from a white man over him. He was now at peace with the world and intended to remain so."[65]

A few American Sioux representing the tribe's seven bands remained in Canada and never did come home. Some 250 kept their guns and horses. Many resided at Willow Bunch, a small Métis community near the Wood Mountain police post, and some at Moose Jaw, a bustling railroad town eighty-five miles north. For decades these people suffered extreme poverty and the indifference of the Canadian government. In 1910 they were finally granted a small reserve west of the Wood Mountain post. Few lived on the land. By then most of the Canadian Lakotas were city dwellers.[66]

Sitting Bull's return from Canada marked the last of the unfinished business directly related to the Great Sioux War, which ended one way of life for the Lakotas and set the course for another. But the legacy of that war would trail through the decades to come. The transition to reservation life was more hurried and perhaps slightly less stressful for some but drawn out and extremely painful for others. No longer did the Lakotas enjoy a hunting life, especially chasing buffalo across the vastness of the Sioux Country of old. In fact, when surrenders occurred and extant food stocks were exhausted, many would never again be nourished by buffalo. The taste of that meat would become a memory, and buffalo by-products would be the objects of a rarified cultural patrimony. Life at the agencies and reservation meant ration days, beef, and trumped-up hunts of cattle on the hoof occurring within the confines of corrals. Without buffalo and the freedom of the hunt, the elaborate organization of tribal circles and societies held diminishing meaning. The tasks of preparing meat, robes, and skin tipis and clothing no longer had the same validity. Woven cloth replaced skins. Cabins replaced tipis. And the elaborate organization for war, intrinsically connected to buffalo, became almost irrelevant too. Gone were the honors associated with contesting the buffalo prairie, facing an enemy, taking horses, and counting coup and the courage demanded by war.[67]

Instead came government programs that "relentlessly chewed up the old ways." Agents stressed the promise of a new self-sufficiency through agriculture, whether crop farming or stock raising. But scattered attempts at row cropping on the Great Sioux Reservation, never more than a half-hearted experiment anyway, suffered from the same vagaries as elsewhere on the plains—plagues of grasshoppers, drought, and hail—and proved a decided failure. Attempts at stock raising held slightly greater promise. The Indians cared for the cattle provided them by the Indian Bureau; but the same devastation caused by the terrible winter of 1886–87 wiped out Indian cattle too, and the experiment largely ended when breeding stocks were not replaced. Political systems also faced duress. The U.S. government attacked the power of the chiefs, asserting instead that supreme authority rested with the agents. Strong-willed overseers like Valentine McGillycuddy at Pine Ridge and James McLaughlin at Standing Rock asserted extraordinary control over their charges. But weak agents existed too, and agents came and went, resulting in continual political upheaval and unrest.[68]

The spiritual life of the Sioux also came under terrible duress. Medicine men faced civil penalties in Indian courts for providing spiritual counsel or practicing the rituals and incantations of their calling. The Sun Dance was banned. The loss of this centerpiece of the social and religious fabric of Sioux life created an enormous void that was never filled, despite attempts by missionaries to replace it with Christian teachings. Missionaries brought some comfort to the Sioux and gained a certain acceptance, so long as their preaching did not demand too insistently that the old ways be cast aside. Efforts at education met similar mixed reactions and results. Some Indians sensed the importance of education in helping to cope with the white people and the new world, but they feared the erosion of Sioux identity, particularly when young children were carted off to distant boarding schools where hair was cut short, boys were dressed in military uniforms, and they all were assigned the chores of white children. Day schools at the agencies were less repugnant than distant boarding schools but were still only cautiously accepted. Confusion and resentment clouded the 1880s, and adults and children alike were torn by the conflicting values relentlessly thrown at them.[69]

Spotted Tail, prominent patriarch of the Brulé Sioux, was among the first of the great old chiefs to contend with the remorseless press of reservation life and also the first to die. After the dreadful attempt at relocating his people to the Missouri River in the winter of 1877–78, Spotted Tail had taken a new home at Rosebud Agency in south-central Dakota, added another wife to his large family, and sent his own children to the Carlisle Indian School in Pennsylvania. He was widely respected by army officers and their wives at nearby Fort Niobrara, where occasional social contact occurred. But Spotted Tail had also gained the enmity of younger leaders at Rosebud, including Crow Dog, a peacekeeper and chief of a lesser sort, who particularly resented the goodwill that seemingly always trailed the elder leader. Crow Dog resented even more the heavy-handed authority that Spotted Tail exerted among the Brulés and perhaps envisioned his own ascendancy if Spotted Tail was eliminated.

Purportedly to take vengeance against Spotted Tail for having stolen his new wife, Crow Dog shot Spotted Tail dead on August 5, 1881. Tried in federal court in Deadwood in 1882 for the murder, Crow Dog was convicted and sentenced to hang. Upon appeal, however, the United States Supreme Court reversed the local verdict, ruling that the Dakota territorial courts had no jurisdiction over crimes committed by Indians on Indian land and that Crow Dog had settled the murder by tribal custom when he paid blood money to Spotted Tail's family. Crow Dog lived to old age but never succeeded

Spotted Tail as head chief of the Brulé Sioux. With Spotted Tail's tragic death, the Brulés lost a clear-headed pragmatic leader who counseled peace but also tirelessly defended the rights and entitlements of his people. His death was a special blow to the white leaders. As General Crook commented at a critical moment in the Great Sioux War: "Spotted Tail . . . is the only important leader who has had the nerve to be our friend."[70]

The cultural and societal travesties that befell the Lakotas in the wake of the Great Sioux War had yet another overwhelming dimension that compounded the difficulty of issues such as obedience, conformance, religion, and education and included a relentless assault on the land. The Sioux already had been driven from a landscape that once spanned nearly the entire northern plains—the Sioux Country of old—and were now finally confined to a single reservation more or less encompassing the southwestern quarter of the Dakota Territory, minus the Black Hills and adjoining Little Missouri River exclusions. Under dispute were some 9 million of nearly 22 million acres of Sioux land that were deemed by some to be "surplus." Some of this supposed excess was timbered, some arable, and all perfect for grazing. Coveting these acres from the margins were growing numbers of Dakota land boomers who believed that this supposedly surplus land was not needed by individual Indians and was all perfectly suited for general homesteading by whites. The boomers interpreted individual need in terms of the 1862 Homestead Act that prescribed an allotment of 160 acres per adult, virtually free for the taking. Lakota land interests defined in the 1868 Fort Laramie Treaty had set aside the reservation in its entirety for the benefit of all the Lakotas, yet these interests received only a feeble defense from government agents, who were invariably sympathetic to boomers and their political representatives.[71]

Initial attempts in the early 1880s to set aside six smaller reservations carved from within the Great Sioux Reservation, ceding the remaining acreage in exchange for cattle, were marked with fraudulent misrepresentations and blatant pressure exerted on the bands. They stirred up Indian reformers, who reminded the Senate that any such matter required the signatures of three-fourths of all adult males residing on the reservation, as stipulated in the 1868 treaty. The question stalled, but Dakota railroaders, ranchers, farmers, and freighters merely bided their time. The movement did arouse ever-heightening mistrust and resentment at the agencies. Meanwhile, Congress passed the long-debated Dawes Severalty Act of 1887, which provided for individual 160-acre allotments to Indians living on reservations, the surveying of western reservations, and the opening of surplus land for sale to whites. The Dawes Act conceded the existence of a special condition in dealing with the Sioux, requiring conformance with article 12 of the Fort Laramie Treaty, the "three-fourths of all adult males" provision.[72]

Empowered by Dawes, Dakota boomers again moved swiftly to reopen the land question. In 1888 Congress directed the secretary of the interior to appoint a commission to broker the carving up of the Great Sioux Reservation, but the attempt failed once more because of the commission's inability to gain the necessary signatures. Captain Richard H. Pratt, the righteous, dogmatic superintendent of the Carlisle Indian School and head of the commission, suggested that an agreement should be put in place without the required signatures. This stirred even more resentment and mistrust at the agencies, but inroads were being made. The failure in 1888 led to yet another land commission and the passage of the Sioux Act of 1889, which contained more generous concessions than Pratt had offered, including a larger per-acre payment, the extension of educational benefits, and payment of certain administrative expenses associated with surveying and opening the land.[73]

The chairman of the 1889 commission was none other than Major General George Crook, then commander of the Military Division of the Missouri in Chicago (Sheridan's post during the Great Sioux War). An adversary during that war, Crook had become well known among the Sioux, showed a welcome, calming demeanor, and was actually trusted by many. In fact, the taciturn general had emerged in the late 1870s as a respected defender of Indian rights who had come to Red Cloud's aid during the bungled relocation effort in 1877 and advocated for Ponca chief Standing Bear in government proceedings brought against him in 1879. Crook understood Sioux psychology and tribal politics better than others did, but on this mission he also proved to be an able agent for the government.

With infinite patience and, when necessary, a stern paternalism, Crook met with the chiefs and headmen at each of the Sioux agencies in early summer, cajoling those he could and sidestepping others when necessary. His weeks of effort paid off: in the final tally 4,463 of 5,678 eligible males, slightly more than the three-fourths needed, signed the cession agreement. The division of the Great Sioux Reservation and the opening of 9 million acres became a nearly immediate reality. One old Sioux with a long memory put the commission's work aptly: "They made us many promises, more than I can remember, but they never kept but one: they promised to take our land and they took it."[74]

In gaining Sioux approval, Crook offered many assurances on matters related to the land agreement and various earlier treaties. But in the end the president and Congress reneged on most. Crook had not lied when offering guarantees of a sustained ration, a matter of grave concern at the agencies, but it looked as though he had. Congress, in an economizing mood, reduced the Sioux appropriation in 1889 and left the Indian Bureau no alternative but to cut rations. The reduced ration, halved in many instances, was a travesty that led to extreme suffering and privation among the Sioux. The disillusioned leader American Horse, who had signed the agreement, expressed his rage: "The commission made us believe that we would get full sacks if we signed the bill, but instead of that our sacks are empty."[75]

The reduced ration was only the latest tribulation adding to the desperation and anger overwhelming the people at the agencies. The Sioux needed help but were at a loss to find it. Washington had betrayed them. Reformer friends in the East were strangely silent. In council among themselves, the tribesmen turned to their old chiefs. Red Cloud, Young Man Afraid, Little Wound, and Sitting Bull had opposed the agreement and continued to rail against it but offered little in the way of meaningful advice. American Horse, Grass, Gall, Rain in the Face, and even Sitting Bull's stepson One Bull had signed the document but also saw no relief from the mounting troubles, including the provision of basic subsistence. Into this cloud of helplessness and despair in this worst decade in the Lakotas' existence,

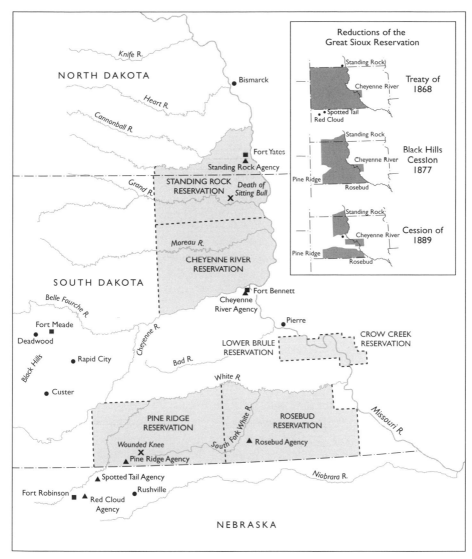

The Teton Sioux Reservations, 1890. Adapted from Robert M. Utley, *The Indian Frontier of the American West, 1846–1890* (Albuquerque: University of New Mexico Press, 1984), 250.

when they were overwhelmed by cultural disintegration, infighting, and starvation, came a ray of hope.[76]

The Paiute prophet Wovoka in Nevada preached a new religion that offered prospects for Indian people and a course not dependent upon white promises. Wovoka saw a land free of white people, inhabited by all generations of Indians that had gone before, bounteous in buffalo and other game and all the riches of the natural world, and free of sickness and want, a land where all people lived in peace. Wovoka's religion combined many of the old spiritual beliefs with teachings drawn from Christian missionaries. He promised an exclusively Indian world, gained by practicing the tenets of this faith and dancing a prescribed Ghost Dance. In a world torn upside down, the promise of the Ghost Dance religion was an elixir warmly welcomed by the Indians of the American West in 1890.[77]

A delegation of Sioux pilgrimaged to Nevada to learn from Wovoka, the new messiah. As conditions worsened back home, especially on the Pine Ridge Reservation, this promising religion easily took hold. In Dakota, however, Wovoka's apostles added unique features to the prophet's teachings. While he taught nonviolence, the Sioux came to believe that the promise of the Ghost Dance religion could be hastened by direct action. The people did not need to fear any consequences from a drastic course because of their embrace of the "sacred shirt," or "ghost shirt" as the whites called it, which would deflect white men's bullets. Among the Oglalas and Brulés, Ghost Dancing grew turbulent and defiant. Pine Ridge agent Daniel F. Royer, a weak and ineffectual patronage appointee new to the job, held no sway among his charges and had earned the contemptuous name "Young Man Afraid of His Indians." Unable to exercise any control at Pine Ridge and with the Ghost Dance fervor taking an overtly threatening turn, Royer called for troops to protect agency personnel and stem the growing fear among settlers living just beyond the reservation's boundaries.[78]

Throughout the summer and fall Ghost Dancing spread from Pine Ridge and Rosebud north to the Cheyenne River and Standing Rock reservations. It ignited much of the same furor and anxiety that blanketed the south, though the intensity never reached the flashpoint as at Pine Ridge. Most of the old chiefs were cautious, but their counsel was invariably ignored. American Horse and Young Man Afraid in the south opposed the new religion, as did Gall and Grass in the north. Red Cloud expressed the same middle-of-the-road ambivalence—respecting the old world while sensing the inevitability of the new—that had characterized his counsel since the time of the Great Sioux War. Those close to him read in this what they wanted or needed. With Sitting Bull, however, Ghost Dancing took hold. A Sun Dance arbor of old was erected near his cabins on the Grand River. Although he was not a dancer himself, he encouraged the participation of his followers and refused all efforts by agency officials, missionaries, and nonbelievers to cast off these new teachings and send the people home.[79]

The arrival of troops at Pine Ridge and Rosebud in November galvanized the Ghost Dancers in the armed defense of their religion. Some three thousand men, women, and children fled their homes for a remote northwestern corner of the Pine Ridge Reservation, an elevated, virtually impenetrable finger of the Cuny Table appropriately known as the Stronghold. Troops continued to concentrate at the agencies and small hamlets just south and west of the reservation's boundaries. Nearly five thousand came from as far away as California, Colorado, and Texas, almost all deploying to this emergency by rail just as Sherman and Sheridan had imagined when they championed the expansion of the nation's railroad grid and the concentration of forces at large posts. Command of this unprecedented response fell to Major General Nelson A. Miles of the Division of the Missouri, another of the old Great Sioux War leaders, who had taken command of the division after Crook's untimely death in March 1890. The army had no wish to assault the Stronghold and wanted only to end the whole affair without bloodshed. But several developments dashed any prospects of a peaceful resolution to this maddening crisis.[80]

The first occurred at Standing Rock, the northernmost of the newly defined Sioux reservations and the principal home of the Hunkpapa Sioux. There Agent McLaughlin ordered the arrest and incarceration of Sitting Bull until the crisis abated. McLaughlin dispatched Indian police to arrest Sitting Bull at daybreak on December 15, supported by cavalry from Fort Yates. But news of the arrest had spread: the policemen were met at Sitting Bull's cabins by growing throngs of his supporters. A melee erupted, and shots rang out. The cavalry had paused on a distant hill to allow this to be an Indian action alone. Before it reached the scene, the aged patriarch and his son Crow Foot, who had tendered the surrender of his father's carbine at Fort Buford in 1881, lay dead, among six other followers. Four policemen also had been killed and four more wounded, two of whom died later. The wails and incantations of Sitting Bull's wives and other family members and supporters, most of whom had witnessed the killings from a cabin near Sitting Bull's, added to the horror of the scene. Sitting Bull's body was carried to Fort Yates and buried in the post cemetery on December 17. As with the tragic death of Crazy Horse in 1877, the nation venerated the tortured memory of Sitting Bull from the start and still does.[81]

But the Ghost Dance crisis took an even more terrible turn. Near the Cheyenne River Reservation south of Standing Rock, Big Foot and his Miniconjou followers also had warmly embraced the Ghost Dance. Big Foot was a nonprogressive, as all who opposed or obstructed the schemes of acculturation were labeled. But he was regarded by Red Cloud and other Pine Ridge centrists as a peacemaker and was invited to travel to Pine Ridge to help end the troubles there. As Big Foot started out, his camp swelled with Hunkpapa refugees from the Sitting Bull melee on the Grand River. The old chief was keenly aware of the precarious situation surrounding him. General Miles was also aware of this movement and feared that Big Foot was headed for the Stronghold instead of the Pine Ridge Agency. Troops combed the frozen White River badlands and plains and on December 28 found and escorted Big Foot and his followers to Wounded Knee Creek, some twenty miles east of Pine Ridge Agency and well south of the Stronghold. Throughout that night Big Foot's camp of some 350 people was surrounded by 500 Seventh cavalrymen, led by Colonel James W. Forsyth. He commanded the deployment from the most prominent hill overlooking the scene, upon which he positioned four Hotchkiss cannon. The irony of this chance discovery of Big Foot's band by the Seventh Cavalry and the presence of survivors of the Little Big Horn Battle of the

Great Sioux War on both sides has clouded this story ever since, though it is largely immaterial.[82]

Neither side anticipated a fight. But on the morning of December 29, when Forsyth's troops attempted to disarm Big Foot's band, shots broke the tension and close-range firing erupted on both sides. For a while the fighting in the tipis and wickiups was desperate and sometimes hand-to-hand. But the troops withdrew to commanding positions and rained down a lethal fire, augmented by Forsyth's artillery, which flattened the mostly canvas lodges and filled the air with deadly shrapnel. The shooting lasted about an hour and left the battlefield strewn with unfathomable carnage. Big Foot was dead. At least one hundred and fifty of his followers lay dead, and fifty more were wounded. The army lost twenty-five dead and thirty-nine wounded. Any hope of putting an end to the Ghost Dance frenzy without bloodshed was dashed at Wounded Knee Creek. The next day Lakota warriors ambushed Seventh Cavalrymen at Drexel Mission, northwest of Pine Ridge Agency on White Clay Creek, and exacted a small measure of revenge before other soldiers arrived and ended that fighting.[83]

Troops carted wounded survivors to makeshift hospitals at Pine Ridge Agency and then abandoned the field. An Indian-led rescue party from Pine Ridge scoured the grounds on January 1 and located several additional survivors. Relic hunters also combed the field, collecting moccasins and other souvenirs of value and interest. In hindsight, perhaps the most important visitors to the Wounded Knee Massacre grounds were two itinerant photographers from Nebraska. They took a gallery of images showing the carnage, the litter of the decimated camp, and the burial work that ensued in early January. All the Indian dead, frozen in grossly contorted shapes, were interred in a common grave on the same hilltop where the Hotchkiss guns had rained down such lethal fire on December 29. The pictures are horrific.[84]

Within weeks the Ghost Dance crisis ended. The army tightened its cordon around the Stronghold as Indian and white negotiators worked to restore confidence and induce the surrender of the dancers. Miles issued food and offered assurances that no more bloodshed would occur. As the Sioux faced the inevitable, yet again, a mass surrender occurred at Pine Ridge Agency in mid-January.[85]

Wounded Knee was an enormous blunder that has skewed the legacy of the Lakotas and Indian-white relations in the American West since 1890. This legacy included the extraordinary ascendancy of the Sioux and their allies at the Little Big Horn in 1876, rallying heroically in a successful defense of a way of life, the downhearted surrenders of 1877 and 1880–81, the fitful adjustments to reservation life in the 1880s, the incessant push for farming, education, and Christianity at the expense of the traditional ways, and the great land theft of 1889. But nothing compared to the horrendous physical and emotional devastation that occurred at Wounded Knee Creek on December 29, 1890. The Wounded Knee Massacre was another day of infamy in American history that has lingered in memory, side by side with Little Big Horn, as the bloody price paid to settle Sioux Country in the nineteenth century.

Among the venerable Hunkpapa war chiefs whose legacies were linked directly to the Great Sioux War, Gall took no role in the Ghost Dancing and lived out his life on the Standing Rock Reservation. He had taken up farming there and was reasonably successful. He was also committed to the causes of education and assimilation, believing that cooperation with the authorities at Standing Rock was the best way to advance the interests of his people. In his younger years Gall had been a formidable warrior and had fought valiantly in the 1860s and 1870s in many northern plains battles with whites, including Killdeer Mountain and Little Big Horn. On the reservation he struggled against weight problems and other health maladies that contributed to his death on December 4 or 8, 1894, at the age of fifty-four. Gall had adjusted to reservation life and ended his years as a thoughtful culture broker in a time of extraordinary transition and stress.[86]

The dominant Lakota and Northern Cheyenne chiefs whose lives were connected to the Great Sioux War included immortal war, spiritual, and political leaders such as Crazy Horse, Little Wolf, Morning Star, Spotted Tail, Sitting Bull, and Gall. But Red Cloud outlived them all, surviving into the twentieth century with a reputation equal to that of the greatest of all the Lakotas and Cheyennes. This accomplished warrior, renowned for his fighting prowess from the 1840s forward, was the principal architect of Indian resistance on the Bozeman Trail in the 1860s in a protracted conflict that came to bear his name. Almost from the earliest times, Red Cloud demonstrated political skills equal to his fighting abilities, ably setting conditions that ended the 1860s war and providing the model for all manner of negotiations thereafter on matters related to agency affairs, the Black Hills, and the Great Sioux War. While Red Cloud was not a war leader against Crook, Terry, or Custer in 1876, his age and wisdom dictated that he would play a crucial role in bringing about the best resolutions possible in a situation with conditions and demands well beyond the control of his people. He was a shrewd advocate in the agency relocation crisis in the late 1870s and in the Ghost Dancing and its aftermath and lived for nearly nineteen long, hard years after that. Wrinkled, stooped, and blind, Red Cloud died on December 10, 1909, at the age of eighty-eight. While the glories of his past were long gone and the future of his people was still clouded, Red Cloud's actions and memory ennobled Indians and whites then and to this day still.[87]

8

SACRED GROUND

As Lieutenant General Philip Henry Sheridan gazed across Custer Battlefield on July 21, 1877, an important destination on his month-long survey of Sioux Country, his concerns were evident. On those high swales above the Little Big Horn River, with hundreds of Seventh Cavalry burials barely sheathed beneath loose Montana soil, Sheridan struggled to understand the demise of his dear friend, George Armstrong Custer. He had nurtured the friendship and devotion of this spirited if conflicted comrade since the days of the Civil War. Their bonds had deepened in a cycle of postwar campaigns and adventures in the West. Even when Custer incurred President Grant's wrath in the spring of 1876 for having cast aspersions on the administration during the investigations of army post traderships, Sheridan came to his protégé's aid. He helped rescue Custer from deep political trouble because he was needed in the coming campaign against the Sioux. More than merely understanding the Little Big Horn Battle, Sheridan saw that this "holy ground" needed careful attention. A friend and a heralded army regiment were both destroyed there. Proper attention to the immediate care and long-term preservation of this place would be a tribute to both Custer and the U.S. Army that waged this fateful Indian war. Within months Sheridan wrote Sherman that he wanted the site set aside as a national cemetery and thereby triggered a vigorous campaign for a cause he saw as both deserving and right.[1]

The battlefield explored by Sheridan in 1877 was still a wretched mess and had evolved very little since June 28, 1876, when the battle's survivors first buried their dead. At that time the field was strewn with the mutilated, bloated, fetid bodies of soldiers and horses after three days of baking sun and flies. The site included the Indian village, the river crossings, Reno's entrenchment area, and the hillsides and deep swales where Custer and his men perished. In the immediate wake of the battle, surviving Seventh Cavalry companies were dispersed across the ground to tend the dead, but a dearth of picks and shovels in the command left men armed only with knives, hatchets, and tin cups and plates. Enlisted casualties received a few scoops of thin soil or branches of sage. The bodies of officers received somewhat more attention. Despite widespread mutilations and decomposition, most officers were identified by tattoos, names on shreds of clothing, or physical attributes. Among them, George Custer's remains were unique: he was found sitting as if resting or asleep between the bodies of two fallen soldiers, stripped naked and with two wounds plainly visible, but not grossly mutilated like the others. As with the enlisted men, the officers were mostly buried where they fell, in shallow but carefully dug graves. The officers' burials were marked with stakes driven into the ground. Each name was written on a scrap of paper and placed into a cartridge case, which was driven into the top of the stake. Custer and his brother Tom were wrapped in canvas shrouds and blankets and buried side by side in the same grave, about eighteen inches deep and ringed with stones. It was "the best burial of any of the bodies on the field," recalled First Sergeant John M. Ryan of M Company, who was among Custer's gravediggers.[2]

A Second Cavalryman who was present remembered that the burials were cursory, amounting to mere "respectful gestures." The decomposition of the remains allowed for little more. General Terry, arriving with Colonel Gibbon and the Montana troops on June 27, showered foremost care on the fifty-two wounded men among the survivors. While the burials occurred on June 28, other soldiers worked in the valley fashioning litters and travois to carry those wounded to the steamboat *Far West,* moored at the mouth of the Little Big Horn River and poised to evacuate these needy troopers to medical care downriver. The psychological toll of the Little Big Horn disaster played heavily in Terry's haste; for a second time these northern Indians had routed Sheridan's Army, here terribly. (He was not yet aware of the bold Indian demonstration against Crook's troops at the mouth of Prairie Dog Creek on June 9 and Crook's lamentable withdrawal from Rosebud Creek on June 17 after the phenomenal battle there, of course. These clashes amounted to four Indian-dominated engagements during the remarkable ascendancy of the Northern Nation.) If the soldiers encamped there could take any comfort on June 28, it lay in their ability to get away from what one officer called the "pestilence-laden atmosphere" of the Little Big Horn Battlefield.[3]

In the months between Terry's departure from the battlefield in late June 1876 and Lieutenant Colonel Michael Sheridan's arrival one year later, scavenging animals and northern plains weather had thoroughly scattered the field's exposed human and equine remains and pests had attacked the visceral shreds. These native elements mostly neutralized the fetid odors associated with decomposition but also rendered the field ghoulish, with human and horse bones scattered nearly everywhere. The notion of commonsense burial on American battlefields had already challenged the nation when it confronted the staggering casualties of the Civil War. Civil War Americans were eager to provide dead comrades and kin with the privilege of more sensitive treatment, including full ritual burials in designated cemeteries as well as embalming and shipment home. These concepts helped shape General Sheridan's vision of a cemetery at the Little Big Horn. So did the Seventh Cavalry's grieving widows, families, and friends, who variously advocated removals to some national cemetery or at least reburials of their dead in "some less lonely spot."[4]

More than any other senior officer, Sheridan engaged in an expansive correspondence with survivors and families. "I have been much pressed by the friends of the officers who fell with Custer . . . to bring in their bodies. I have assured them that we would do all we could to accomplish this purpose," he wrote General Terry in late March 1877.[5] Sheridan asked Sherman whether the secretary of war would authorize sufficient funding for this purpose. Although the War Department vacillated at first, contingency money was found and allocated.[6]

Sheridan assigned the delicate task of disinterment and reburial to his brother Michael, long detached from line service with the Seventh Cavalry and serving in division headquarters as an aide-de-camp with the rank of lieutenant colonel. From Major Reno came preliminary information on the original burials at Little Big Horn. Generally, those officers who died with Custer were interred by order of rank, Reno reported, but Captain Miles Keogh and Lieutenants John Crittenden, James Calhoun, and Donald McIntosh and contract surgeon James DeWolf were buried separately. First Lieutenant Henry Nowlan, in 1876 the Seventh Cavalry's quartermaster and detailed to the headquarters component of Terry's column, had marked the graves and would be able to point them out, but Reno predicted that "it will be a labor to recover the bodies."[7]

News of the proposed 1877 Little Big Horn Battlefield expedition spread quickly, and correspondence with families intensified. Some expressed wishes for private burials in hometown plots, and George Custer's remains were destined for the Military Academy cemetery at West Point, but most families were content with suggested reinterments in the national cemetery at Fort Leavenworth, Kansas. Only Colonel Thomas Crittenden of the Seventeenth Infantry expressed the desire that his son John be left on the field where he fell.[8]

Michael Sheridan departed Chicago by rail on May 21, bound initially for Bismarck. There he took passage on the steamer *John G. Fletcher* and arrived at Tongue River Cantonment on June 20. He met Captain Nowlan and Company I, Seventh Cavalry, detailed from the large Seventh Cavalry complement then patrolling the north bank of the lower Yellowstone River in one of the final deployments of the Great Sioux War. Nowlan's involvement was critical, because he was familiar with the Little Big Horn burials and carried a sketch map confirming several important locations. His company would provide security in this time of lingering anxiety in Sioux Country at the close of the war and also wield shovels for the recovery of officers' remains and the reburial of the others.[9]

With Sheridan continuing upriver by boat and then on horseback up the Big Horn River and Nowlan's company traveling overland, the two reached the fledgling Big Horn Post on June 28. There Sheridan made arrangements with Lieutenant Colonel George Buell, commander of the new fort, for the construction of pine boxes to carry exhumed remains from the battlefield and four oxen-drawn wagons for conveyance to and from the site. After these matters had been dealt with on June 30 the party continued to the battlefield, arriving on the morning of July 2. The remainder of that day was spent examining the rolling hillsides east of the river. The men of Company I were deployed in dismounted skirmish line intervals (typically a fifteen-foot separation) and fanned the field for several miles around, marking graves or exposed remains with slender willow stakes to aid the reburial work the next day. That evening in camp the soldiers converted cedar boughs into three-foot-long stakes intended to mark individual gravesites more formally.[10]

The reburial work commenced on July 3 under the general supervision of Second Lieutenant Hugh L. Scott, Nowlan's subaltern. The shallow graves and exposed remains were interred on the same sites or in the same trenches as before but covered over with a good measure of soil, "tastefully heaped and packed with spades and mallets." Each set of remains was marked with a cedar stake. Sheridan's official report and subsequent newspaper accounts expressed satisfaction with the work, but privately Scott was less optimistic, later recalling that "the soil was like sugar and I have no doubt the first rain liquefied it and exposed the bones later." Time would prove him right.[11]

Meanwhile, Sheridan, Nowlan, and a squad from Company I concentrated their efforts on the battlefield landmark already known as Last Stand Hill. There the remains of George and Thomas Custer, George Yates, William Cooke, Algernon Smith, and William Reily were located and exhumed. The bones and occasional pieces of bodily substance were carefully placed in the pine boxes. Sheridan noted that identifications were unmistakable, because Nowlan and some of the enlisted men now present had buried these men initially, and numbers on cedar stakes at the head of each grave corresponded with numbers on Nowlan's map. Still, animals had uncovered and scattered many burials.[12]

The precise identification of Custer's remains in particular was questioned later. One of the soldiers involved, Sergeant Michael C. Caddle, recounted how a body, supposedly Custer's, was removed from the ground and placed in a box. But then a blouse upon which that body had been lying was picked up. An examination of the blouse revealed the name of the wearer: Corporal William Teeman of Company F. Supposing that the retrieved remains belonged to Teeman and not that this blouse merely served as a burial pillow for Custer, the soldiers carefully examined the ground again, uncovered another body, and placed it in the box. "I think we got the right body the second time," Caddle recalled with a cackle. Dismayed by any possible uncertainty, Sheridan allegedly remarked: "Nail the box up; it is alright as long as the people think so." Confusion was certainly possible, despite the stakes and the map, because these officers' remains were crowded by the bones of some thirty other soldiers who had perished on that hillside.[13]

Sheridan and Nowlan exhumed and boxed the remains of Myles Keogh and James Calhoun. They dug a three-foot-deep grave for John Crittenden, burying his remains on the spot where he fell, in obedience to his father's wishes. The next day, July 4, the burial detail advanced to Reno's entrenchment area and exhumed the remains of Donald McIntosh, Benjamin Hodgson, and James DeWolf. By noon the work was largely finished. The small box coffins were loaded into the wagons, and the train departed for Big Horn Post. The remains of officers James G. Sturgis, James Porter, Henry Harrington, and George Lord were not located and had not been discovered a year earlier. While awaiting river transportation, the eleven pine boxes were placed under guard in the first and only building standing at the new post. At Fort Abraham Lincoln the remains were transferred to metallic burial caskets and consigned to the Northern Pacific Railroad. In due course, George Custer was buried in the United States Military Academy cemetery; Hodgson in the Laurel Hill Cemetery in Philadelphia; Tom Custer, Yates, Smith, Calhoun, and McIntosh in the Fort Leavenworth National Cemetery; Keogh in the Fort Hill Cemetery, Auburn, New York; Reily in the Mount Olivet Cemetery, Washington, D.C.; Cooke in the Hamilton Cemetery, Ontario, Canada; and DeWolf in the Woodlawn Cemetery in Norwalk, Ohio.[14]

Michael Sheridan expressed satisfaction with his work. He had no lumber to recover all the graves but marked them so that they might be collected later and "buried in a cemetery, if one be declared there, or else removed to the cemetery at Post No. 2." Already the notion of permanent protection for the site and graves, probably in the manner of a national cemetery, was being discussed by those in the headquarters of the Division of the Missouri.[15]

When General Sheridan came to the battlefield three weeks later, young Lieutenant Scott's fear that seasonal rains would reexpose the graves proved to be justified. In any case, perhaps one day's work was insufficient to pay proper attention to so many burials scattered over such a vast landscape. Many of the other members of Sheridan's party who explored the ground commented on its unsightly condition. First Lieutenant John Bourke, Crook's aide-de-camp, recalled: "As we made our way along the ravine [downward from Last Stand Hill], we stumbled upon four skulls in one collection, a lone one in another place, another under a little bush and still another, picked up by my orderly." Elsewhere, he said, "it was hard to go ten yards in any direction without stepping on portions of the human anatomy and skeletons of horses, singly or mingled together." Bourke noted that seventeen skeletons were found in all, ten of which had never been buried.[16] Young Homer W. Wheeler, a second lieutenant in Sheridan's Fifth Cavalry escort, confirmed that a recent severe hailstorm had washed out several bodies buried near a ravine. A Fifth Cavalry enlisted man in the escort recalled seeing "the skeletons of six men, and a seventh showing fragments of chevrons, on the ground a short distance from where we forded the creek." Second Lieutenant Eben Swift of the Fifth Cavalry noted unburied bodies, rags of uniforms, and broken bits of equipment scattered about.[17]

The deplorable condition of the field was so unsettling that Sheridan ordered another policing. This one was organized by Lieutenant Colonel George A. Forsyth, Sheridan's military secretary.

Forsyth and Major Verling K. Hart, commanding the Fifth Cavalry escort, detailed sixty enlisted men and three commissioned officers from the companies, equipped them with every spade, shovel, and pick in the command, and again carefully surveyed the battlefield. They topped the graves tended by Michael Sheridan's crew and buried everything else they discovered. Forsyth called his search thorough and exhaustive and believed that no human bone had been left unburied. But he also warned that at times in the spring or after the rains portions of skeletons would be exposed because the soil was so thin.[18]

General Sheridan was immensely pleased with Forsyth's work, reporting to Sherman that he left the field with "all the graves nicely raised as in cemeteries inside of civilization, and most, if not all, marked with head-boards or stakes." But he also candidly added that he was "half inclined to think, strange as it may appear, that nearly all the desecration of graves at the Custer battle-field has been done by curiosity hunters in the shape of human coyotes. I myself have known of one or two cases where bones were exhibited as relics from the . . . field."[19] Providing for the battlefield's long-term care and preservation became a solemn concern for the army's most senior officers.

Sheridan rightly worried about episodes of trophy hunting, thieving, and desecration occurring on the battlefield. Barely a month after his visit, a party of miners making their way north from the Big Horn Mountains paused to explore the vast graveyard and village. One of them, Herman Bischoff, was fascinated by the litter in the Indian village and collected tin plates and canteens as souvenirs. Across the river, however, he saw a "terrible sight," with exposed bones scattered widely, several skulls visible (including one in an army cap), and a frightful smell from still decomposing horses. Another member of this party commented on the thousands of cartridge shells lying seemingly everywhere and noted the graves, each with a small amount of earth thrown over it. In one instance a head protruded from one end and feet from the other.[20]

Later in September 1877 Second Lieutenant Harry L. Bailey, Twenty-first Infantry, traveling with companies of the Second Cavalry Regiment during their transfer to the Big Horn Post from the

Department of the Platte, explored Custer Battlefield as they passed by. Mostly the graves were in good order, Bailey wrote, but twelve skulls and assorted human bones were found aboveground, and in two or three instances skulls were stuck upon grave stakes. The commander leading the transfer, Lieutenant Colonel Albert G. Brackett, had the remains collected and interred. This was a struggle, according to Bailey, considering the few implements at hand. Another in the command, Sergeant Major Alvarado M. Fuller, remembered using horse thigh bones.[21]

One of the more egregious instances of grave robbing in these early years came to the attention of Lieutenant Colonel Buell at Fort Custer in August 1878. He received word that the keeper of the Rock Creek stage station located opposite the battlefield possessed a "trophy" skull taken from the field and evidently intended for Al or Matt Patrick, the proprietors of the stage line. The post adjutant, First Lieutenant William C. Rawolle, dispatched a sergeant to the station keeper bearing a letter of admonishment from Buell and a demand that the skull be surrendered to the sergeant.[22]

Already Custer Battlefield was welcoming prominent visitors, some from local military posts and others traveling on Yellowstone River steamboats to Terry's Landing and then overland to Fort Custer and the battlefield. One of the more notable early explorers was Jerusha Sturgis, wife of Seventh Cavalry Colonel Samuel D. Sturgis, and their daughters, Ella M. Lawler and Nina L. Dousman, who visited the battlefield on August 19, 1878. They were seeking information and evidence pertaining to their son and brother, Second Lieutenant James Sturgis, Seventh Cavalry, who was recorded as missing after the battle. Sturgis's remains were not identified in 1876. Headless bodies were noted on the field, however, and bloodstained clothing bearing Sturgis's name was found in the village, along with severed and fire-blackened human heads. According to one enlisted survivor, one head seemed to be that of Lieutenant Sturgis. Apparently such details were kept from the Sturgis family, and by 1878 a spurious grave had been erected for the fallen officer near Last Stand Hill and viewed by his mother and sisters. What the family knew of the ruse is unrecorded. Members of the party did comment on the continuing dreadful condition of the field, with bleaching horse bones and human skulls everywhere.[23]

The matter of bleaching bones and occasionally observed skulls proved to be a continuing embarrassment to the army, especially when publicized, as in the case of the Sturgis family. That fall General Sherman instructed Terry to tend the field again. On October 29, 1878, Terry directed Buell to make a careful examination of the grounds for human bones and bury them at some one point on the field and also to erect a high cone or pyramid of loose stones to protect those remains from any future depredations by wild animals. Terry suggested that the most suitable location for that grave was the highest point on the ridge just to the rear of the place where Custer's body was located. "Let this be done by an adequate force and in a thorough manner," he admonished.[24]

The oncoming winter delayed prompt compliance. But in early April 1879 Buell's successor, Lieutenant Colonel Brackett, detailed Captain George K. Sanderson and Company C, Eleventh Infantry, to the battlefield to undertake the recurrent delicate work. Sanderson's men carefully scoured all parts of the field and collected all observable human bones, which he thought amounted to the remains of four or five different bodies. They interred the bones on the highest point to the rear of Custer's original burial place. Sanderson could find no cobblestones within five miles of the battlefield, so instead he erected a cordwood pyramid atop the central grave. Believing that horse bones were the cause of the continuing uproar, he had them collected as well and placed within the cordwood monument. Sanderson's men carefully remounded all the graves. "The whole field now presents a perfectly clean appearance, each grave remounded and all animal bones removed," he reported at the conclusion of his work. Sanderson appended to his report photographs taken by Stanley J. Morrow of Yankton, Dakota. A traveling photographer with seasonal studios at Forts Keogh and Custer, Morrow took nearly two dozen photographs of the cleanup, including piled horse bones, cleansed vistas, the cordwood monument under construction and in its finished state, the spurious Sturgis grave, and other markers and headboards that had found their way to the field since the time of the battle. The Morrow photographs, while not the first taken of Custer Battlefield, provide an evocative sense of this isolated and revered place while still in its rawest, unprotected, undeveloped state.[25]

In the intervening years since the battle, a campaign of compassion had run its course for the benefit of the widows and orphans of the Little Big Horn. In her memoir recounting life in Dakota with her husband, Elizabeth Custer wrote that the Little Big Horn Battle had "wrecked the lives of twenty-six women at Fort Lincoln, and orphaned children of officers and soldiers joined their cry to that of their bereaved mothers." Certainly wives and children at other Seventh Cavalry posts were comparably devastated. Nearly all of these dependents were almost wholly reliant upon their husbands for their financial security, day-to-day subsistence, and even the quarters they occupied. While they might eventually expect a small pension, these families were now destitute, with nowhere to turn.[26]

Barely weeks after the battle, the *Army and Navy Journal,* an independent weekly newspaper devoted to the interests of America's armed forces, observed the national cry for a monument to those who fell with Custer at the Little Big Horn. The newspaper dared to suggest instead the creation of a fund for the widows and little children rendered helpless by the deaths of their soldier husbands and fathers. Encouraged by a good response, the *Journal* announced the initiation of this movement in its July 29, 1876, issue. "The time has undoubtedly arrived when relief should be extended. Such sudden and unexpected bereavement never before fell to the lot of one regiment, and we are sure that every officer and soldier who reads [this] will gladly alleviate to the extent of his ability the deep distress of these helpless ones."[27]

The Widows' Relief Fund campaign was championed by William Conant Church, the founder, publisher, and editor of the *Army and Navy Journal.* Church, a second-generation newspaperman from New York and a Civil War veteran, also founded *Galaxy Magazine.* He was instrumental in the establishment of the National Rifle Association and served as its second president. His foremost interest, however, was the nation's military establishment. He delighted in causes like this and in the confidential relationship between his *Journal* and its correspondents, many of whom were front-line officers of the army, navy, and national guard. The newspaper was filled with comprehensive, reliable news, including official appointments, promotions, changes of station, resignations, court-martial proceedings, reports on foreign wars, essays on weapons and tactics, and much more. The *Journal* was essential reading at every military installation in America and of course thus perfect for the campaign that Church launched.[28]

Responses from the field to Church's pleading were prompt and generous. Nearly every weekly issue of the *Journal* from July 29, 1876, into April 1877 carried news of the fund-raising campaign and specific acknowledgment of contributors. Some donations came singly and many more in the collective names of regiments and posts. A generous contribution of $500 at the onset was promptly forwarded to General Sheridan for immediate distribution in instances of pressing need. By the end of August more than $3,000 had been received; and by the end of the year the sum exceeded $12,000, of which $9,000 had already been distributed to bereaved widows and orphans. The outpouring was astonishing. "We are commencing to hear from the Military Posts," the *Journal* noted in August. "The Inmates of the Soldiers' Home at Washington, the veterans of every war in which the Regular Army has been engaged, have given substantial evidence of their sympathy. The oldest of the donors is nearly 90 years of age, and remembers the early days when he carried a rifle in the Black Hawk War."[29]

The *Journal* worked to ensure the equitable distribution of the monies received, establishing a trust fund and overseer and routinely publishing accountings of receipts and distributions. The allotments generally conformed to the rates accorded to ranks by existing pension laws, and the *Journal* deemed that monies raised from enlisted men should go to wives and families of enlisted men. The Seventh Cavalry counted fourteen such widows and twenty-five children, who had received checks varying from $193 to $365 by January. The monthly enlisted pension rate was $8, so these sums were significant. In its September 16 issue the *Journal* acknowledged receiving a letter from an officer's widow, speaking for three bereaved ladies and expressing appreciation for the "remembrance of us, but we particularly desire that our share of the fund so generously raised be given to the widows and children of the enlisted men." The writer is thought to be Maggie Calhoun, wife of the Seventh Cavalry's First Lieutenant James Calhoun and George Custer's sister, writing on behalf of Elizabeth Custer and Annie Yates, wife of Captain George Yates.[30]

In its November 17, 1877, issue the *Journal* provided its readers with a final report on the Widows' Relief Fund. In all, $14,068.35 was received: $7,476.50 was distributed to wives and dependents of officers, $5,722.43 given to the widows and orphans of enlisted men, $810 provided to General Sheridan for early cash distributions, and $9.42 spent on sundry expenses. The *Journal* noted that "the whole course of the Widows' Relief Fund and the large proportion contributed by the enlisted men are an honor to the Services, and show that the American Army is in its truest sense a band of brothers." It was William Conant Church's and the *Army and Navy Journal*'s finest hour.[31]

The army grappled with one other matter in the years immediately following the Little Big Horn Battle, a festering unpleasantness not of its own instigation. Except for the courts-martial in April 1876 and January 1877 of Captains Henry Noyes and Alexander Moore and Colonel Joseph J. Reynolds in the wake of the Powder River debacle of March 17, 1876, the army demonstrated little enthusiasm for assessing blame for its defeat in Montana or any other failing of the Great Sioux War. After all, in the long run Sheridan's Army had prevailed in this war despite its lamentable start in the spring and summer of 1876.[32]

But the public charges brought by Frederick Whittaker, particularly against Major Marcus A. Reno, ultimately could not be ignored. Whittaker was a staff reporter for the *Army and Navy Journal* and the author of a fawning biography of Custer, *A Complete Life of General George A. Custer*, published in early December 1876 and the first such biography written. He blamed Custer's death not on any actions of his own but on the failings of Grant, for his mean-spiritedness in first withholding Custer's participation in the campaign and then subordinating him to Terry. Whittaker also blamed Captain Frederick Benteen for outright disobedience of Custer's direct order "Come on. Big village. Be quick. Bring packs." Most of all he blamed Reno, charging him with cowardice for his unsoldierly and costly retreat from the valley and his questionable conduct and indecision on the bluffs, especially when gunfire, most certainly Custer's, could be heard downriver. Grant ignored the charges, and Benteen's reputation only grew as friends within the regiment and beyond came to see him as the battle's hero. But Reno, with few allies and a reputation in shambles for other character flaws, of which he had many, withered under the increasingly relentless and poisonous assault.[33]

As the tone against Reno grew harsher and increasingly public, Whittaker's charges could no longer be ignored. Despite the War Department's reluctance to investigate Little Big Horn and Reno, the major made his own plea for an examination into his conduct in the battle so that he might have an opportunity to vindicate his character. Finally, Sherman approved Reno's request on June 25, 1878, and on the same day the secretary of war ordered a court of inquiry.

Unlike courts-martial, courts of inquiry were solely investigative in nature. Their limited purpose was to "examine into the nature of any transaction of, or accusation or imputation against, any officer or soldier upon a demand by the officer or soldier." They were legally constituted courts of the military service, presided over by one, two, or three officers and a judge-advocate, had subpoena authority, and examined witnesses under oath. But courts of inquiry could not mete out punishments, that being the business of a court-martial proceeding.[34]

Reno's court of inquiry convened at the stately Palmer House in Chicago on Monday, January 13, 1879. This elite hotel was the temporary headquarters of the Military Division of the Missouri after a fire destroyed Sheridan's office building a few blocks away. Three officers presided, including Colonel John H. King, Ninth Infantry, senior officer and president of the court; Colonel Wesley Merritt, Fifth Cavalry; and Lieutenant Colonel William B. Royall, Third Cavalry. First Lieutenant Jesse M. Lee, regimental adjutant of the Ninth Infantry, was appointed recorder of the court. All but King had served in the Great Sioux War. Merritt and Royall participated in Crook's grueling Big Horn and Yellowstone Expedition and infamous Starvation March in the summer and fall of 1876, and Lee marched with Crook on the Powder River Expedition later that fall. Lee, functioning as the agent at Spotted Tail Agency in Nebraska in 1877, also figured in the arrest and killing of Crazy Horse. Reno retained the legal services of Lyman D. Gilbert, a talented young attorney and family friend from Harrisburg, Pennsylvania. Lee hired a stenographer from Leavenworth, Kansas, H. C. Hollister, to maintain the official account of the proceedings.[35]

Over the course of four and a half weeks in daily sessions except on Sundays, and open to the press and public, twenty-three witnesses were called and testified on all aspects of the famous battle. Most were officers of the Seventh Cavalry who had served alongside Reno at Little Big Horn, plus Doctor Henry Porter, the only medical officer to survive the battle; a handful of enlisted men and citizens who had participated in the battle; several other officers, including Colonel John Gibbon of the Seventh Infantry, who provided information pertinent to the topography of the battlefield; and Major Reno himself. Although it was not a prosecutorial exercise, Lee, as recorder (the equivalent of a judge-advocate), examined the witnesses carefully and sometimes tenaciously. He sought "to elicit all the facts in the case, whether they are for or against Major Reno." The presiding officers rarely asked questions, but Gilbert, Reno's counsel, mounted a spirited defense. He stressed the positive in testimony and even invariably elicited something useful from witnesses disposed against his client or, when necessary, successfully discredited the testimony.[36]

Despite personal feelings for or against Reno, who did not have a large circle of friends in the regiment, the Seventh Cavalry's officers largely stood together and defended the honor of the unit by avoiding blame and refusing to brand the major a coward. The officers' responses were calculated, because they were fully aware that complete openness about the battle could well expose their own fallible conduct at Little Big Horn. Moreover, regimental pride was at stake: a stain on the Seventh Cavalry and any of its own would never completely disappear. Merritt, author of the court's findings and opinion, evidently also saw it that way and wrote an exoneration of Reno at the conclusion of the proceedings: "The conduct of the officers throughout was excellent, and while subordinates in some instances did more for the safety of the command by brilliant displays of courage than did Major Reno, there was nothing in his conduct which requires the animadversion from this Court. No further proceedings are necessary." From the army's perspective, the case for culpability at the Little Big Horn was properly and publicly investigated and officially closed.[37]

Whittaker was furious, labeling the Reno court of inquiry a mockery of justice and a whitewash, but then went silent on the matter. Merritt was later alleged to have said to his adjutant that "the officers wouldn't tell us anything and we could do nothing more than damn Reno with faint praise." Indeed, through the course of the well-reported proceedings, the public, like Whittaker, saw an officer whose flight from the valley was unsoldierly and costly. His leadership on the bluffs seemed marked with confusion and vacillation. Even the partially deaf Lieutenant Edward Godfrey had heard gunfire downriver in Custer's direction, so what explained Reno's supposed deafness on that critical issue? Merritt's faint praise, in fact, stained Reno for the short remainder of his career and life. The major was dismissed from the service on April 1, 1880, by sentence of a court-martial in yet another matter coloring his sordid existence. He went to his grave on March 30, 1889, guilty in the public's mind of bringing death to George Armstrong Custer. Meanwhile, Custer's reputation lived on in the consciousness of America and the world, enhanced by the adulation and visibility of his widow, Elizabeth, and actions still unfolding at his Montana battlefield.[38]

When Captain George Sanderson and Company C of the Eleventh Infantry cleansed the Little Big Horn Battlefield of bones in April 1879, he suggested gathering all human remains from throughout the field and placing them in a common grave. He further recommended that a stone mound be built over it or that headstones be placed at each grave. "Either would be an enduring monument," he wrote. By then Sanderson's commendations merely buttressed movements afoot within the War Department to erect a formal monument at Little Big Horn and see to its designation as a national cemetery, precisely as General Sheridan had recommended for several years.[39]

The system of national cemeteries had evolved considerably since it was authorized by Congress in 1862. An act that year empowered the president to purchase and enclose cemetery grounds for the burial of soldiers who died in the service of the country. The issue was driven by the Herculean need to bury the dead of the Civil War. Almost immediately fourteen national cemeteries were established at troop concentration and training camps. Forts Leavenworth and Scott in Kansas had their post cemeteries incorporated into the system because of their importance as military operations centers. Two battlefields, Antietam, Maryland, and Mill Springs, Kentucky, became national cemeteries, these being the first instances where battlefield dead were buried almost where they fell. By 1870 the number of national cemeteries had grown to seventy-three, including other Civil War battlefield areas, several general hospital cemeteries, and additional post cemeteries that were enlarged and redesignated. Efforts were also underway to relocate the remains of Civil War Union dead from the war's scattered battlefields, isolated churchyards, farms, plantations, railroad sidings, and every other place where Northern casualties might repose in temporary graves, resulting in the interment of some 300,000 remains in national cemeteries.[40]

These actions in the East to secure places for Civil War dead played directly into Sheridan's sense of obligation and commendation for establishing a national cemetery at Custer Battlefield or relocating those dead to the nearby Fort Custer post cemetery. The only alternatives, both less satisfying and unduly expensive, were reburials in the Fort McPherson National Cemetery in central Nebraska (established in 1873 and at the time the national cemetery closest to Montana Territory) or in Fort Leavenworth National Cemetery (an even greater distance away but at least more directly linked by the shipment prospects on the Yellowstone and Missouri rivers).[41]

Even before Sanderson's battlefield cleanup was undertaken in April 1879 and perhaps unknown to the captain at the time, the War Department signaled its intent to create a national cemetery at Custer's Battlefield when the secretary of war authorized its establishment on January 29, 1879. Sheridan's relentless campaigning had certainly played a role in the action, as did occasional reports from Montana on the lingering deplorable conditions of the field, most recently from the Sturgis family. The establishment of the cemetery was formalized by the Headquarters of the Army in General Orders No. 78, on August 1, 1879, announcing that the ground known as the "Custer Battle-field," on the Little Big Horn River, Montana Territory, was henceforth a national cemetery of the fourth class.[42]

The War Department also embraced the creation of a substantial granite monument for the battlefield, a prospect occasionally discussed since the time of the battle, in addition to the monument initiative that ultimately honored Custer at West Point in 1879. Under the direction of Brigadier General Montgomery C. Meigs, the army's quartermaster general, plans evolved for a memorial of sufficient size to hold the names of all the officers and men who fell in the fight and "massive and heavy enough to remain for ages where placed—a landmark of the conflict between civilization and barbarism," in Meigs's words.[43]

The army awarded a contract for the monument on February 21, 1879, to the Mount Auburn Marble and Granite Works of Cambridge, Massachusetts, source of remarkable light gray stone already widely employed in cemetery memorials and substantial buildings throughout the East. The contract specified an obelisk measuring six feet wide at the base, three feet six inches across the top, and eleven feet six inches high. Alexander McDonald, a Scottish stone cutter who founded the company in 1856, prepared the monument in three sections weighing 38,547 pounds in all. It bore the names of 261 officers, enlisted men, Indian scouts, and civilians killed in the battle engraved onto its four faces and the inscription:

IN MEMORY OF
OFFICERS AND SOLDIERS WHO FELL NEAR THIS PLACE
FIGHTING WITH THE 7TH UNITED STATES CAVALRY
AGAINST SIOUX INDIANS,
ON THE 25TH AND 26TH OF JUNE,
A.D. 1876.[44]

McDonald shipped the Custer monument in three crated sections on July 21, 1879. The stones took a cumbersome, slow route by way of the army post at Governor's Island in New York Harbor, by ship on the St. Lawrence River and Great Lakes to Duluth, Minnesota, by a Northern Pacific freight train to Bismarck, and by steamboat on the Missouri and Yellowstone rivers to the mouth of the Big Horn River, arriving there before the boating season closed in 1880. First Lieutenant and Adjutant Charles F. Roe of the Second Cavalry at Fort Custer supervised moving the stones from the mouth of the Big Horn to Last Stand Hill on the battlefield in February 1881, employing a specially constructed sledge pulled by twenty-four mules.[45]

Later that July Roe and Company C, Second Cavalry, temporarily commanded by Second Lieutenant Alfred M. Fuller of Company F, raised the monument on Last Stand Hill. The stones were set on a substantial masonry foundation bound with iron tie rods and plate washers set six feet into the ground, maneuvered by using a special derrick crane fashioned from ash poles cut along the river and mule power. The stones were positioned with comparative ease, Roe reported, despite weighing many tons each.[46]

After placing the monument, Roe then directed the digging of a trench ten feet from the base on all four sides to receive the battlefield's remains. The men of Company C took great pains, he noted, in gathering together the remains from the Custer sector, Reno's Hill, and the valley, placing them at the base of the monument, and covering them with more stone and then earth. It was impractical, Roe reported, to place the remains in a crypt or tomb beneath the monument, because the local stone available was only useful in making a solid, not hollowed, foundation.[47]

Roe noted that a stake was planted wherever remains were found, "so that future visitors can see where the men actually fell." In 1890 these temporary markers were replaced with marble headstones of the sort authorized for national cemeteries, but uniquely inscribed: for enlisted men, "U.S. soldier 7th Cavalry fell here June 25 1876"; and for officers, individual name, rank, and unit and the words "fell here June 25 1876." "I feel confident that all the remains are gathered together and placed at [the] base of the monument," Roe reported.

The lone exception was Lieutenant Crittenden, whose remains were preserved where he fell beneath a headstone provided by his father.[48]

By the early 1880s Custer's Battlefield, as it was long known, and Custer National Cemetery had emerged as a place of reverence, as all battlefields and national cemeteries had become in nineteenth-century America.[49] Custer Battlefield featured a striking stone monument set high on the most imposing hill on the field, aptly revered as Last Stand Hill. And the battlefield was receiving the judicious care of the War Department, befitting a designated national cemetery. It offered the continual intrigue of a timeless landscape, spotted with markers showing where men actually fell in one of America's most enigmatic Indian battles. For decades this distant, hallowed place paid tribute to both George Armstrong Custer and the U.S. Army. In future years Custer Battlefield National Monument, or rather Little Bighorn Battlefield National Monument, would be recognized as a memorial to *all* who fought there. But in Sheridan's day this captivating place in lonely southeastern Montana served only to remind the nation of the price paid by the U.S. Army in transforming Sioux Country on the northern Great Plains.

While Little Bighorn Battlefield has long served its purpose and has a devoted audience, other captivating places in Sioux Country beckon and speak to the price of change on the northern plains in the transforming decades of the late nineteenth century. The Wounded Knee Massacre site in the midst of the Pine Ridge Indian Reservation in southwestern South Dakota is a bloodied field of another sort and quite a counterpoint to Little Bighorn. As at Little Bighorn, a solitary granite monument erected in 1902 atop a mass grave marks the site where 144 of the Lakotas killed there in 1890 were buried on the hilltop overlooking the field. But the likeness ends there. Attempts through the years, especially in the late twentieth century, to preserve and interpret the Wounded Knee Massacre site more substantially have never succeeded. Where Little Bighorn is dominated by the trappings common at a modern national park historic site visited by hundreds of thousands of people annually, Wounded Knee remains a forlorn, hallowed, undeveloped, almost unwelcoming place, with no conveniences, comforts, or visitor amenities. Barely a few hundred people visit the field annually. But the opportunity remains to stand on the site's prominent hilltop, gaze upon an open landscape, and fully sense the makings of a tragic day. Wounded Knee is sacred ground too, in many respects equal to Little Bighorn, begging reflection on the blood shed by Lakotas in the transformation of Sioux Country on the northern Great Plains.

Glimpses of the natural majesty of Sioux Country abound, even as roads, rails, contrails, power lines, pipelines, and towns and cities remind us that we live in twenty-first-century America. An appreciation of untrammeled Sioux Country is worth seeking. Virtually every corner of the northern plains has places where breezes stir the cottonwoods lining the banks of quiet prairie streams, native grasslands sweep to the distant horizon, and distant views of the Black Hills from South Dakota, Nebraska, and Wyoming still hold a mysterious grip. But the small scale is magnified at places such as Theodore Roosevelt National Park in western North Dakota and other parks and preserves like it. While that prairie park's gateway community, Medora, evokes memories of the Marquis de Morès, Theodore Roosevelt, and the Northern Pacific Railroad, the real lure is the undulating native prairie and Little Missouri River bottomlands just beyond the town. The timeless attributes of a grassland world virtually unchanged from the days before cattle, when great herds of buffalo and elk dominated the countryside, are almost overwhelming. In larger measure it offers a glimpse of Sioux Country in its primordial state.

One more place in Sioux Country captures the majesty of the land and legacy of a people. After Sitting Bull was killed by tribal policemen in 1890, his remains were interred in the Fort Yates post cemetery, where they reposed for sixty-three years in a marked but largely forgotten grave. From time to time some family members expressed the desire that he be buried along the Grand River nearer his reservation-era home. When attempts to achieve such a reburial failed, Sitting Bull's remains were exhumed under cover of darkness in April 1953 and placed in a hilltop grave overlooking the Missouri River just below the confluence of the Grand, near Mobridge, South Dakota. To ensure the permanency of the effort, the burial plot was covered with twenty tons of steel rails and concrete and topped with a bust sculpted from granite by Korczak Ziolkowski, who later conceived the Crazy Horse mountain sculpture near Custer, South Dakota. Since then a small battle has raged over the righteousness of the reburial, but perhaps the result is apt. Sitting Bull's gravesite sits alone at the end of a quiet one-way lane miles from the nearest highway. The place is desolate and forlorn. Sitting Bull's granite bust is almost ghostlike. The wind incessantly whistles. There may be no better burial place in America for Sitting Bull's mortal remains, and no better spot for Americans to contemplate the transforming and costly legacy of the Great Sioux War than this lonely hillside on the banks of the Missouri River.

Notes

PREFACE

1. Brown, "A New Focus on the Sioux War"; Anderson, "A Challenge to Brown's Indian Wars Thesis"; Brown, "Rebuttal to a 'Challenge'"; Anderson, "Silence Not Acquiescence"; Anderson, "Two Slips Corrected"; Utley, "Origins of the Great Sioux War."

2. See Ostler, *The Plains Sioux and U.S. Colonialism from Lewis and Clark to Wounded Knee*, 2–6; Nugent, "The American Habit of Empire," 5–7; and Nugent, *Habits of Empire*, 234–36.

CHAPTER 1. A GOOD YEAR TO DIE?

1. For perspectives on the Great Sioux War, see Hedren, *Great Sioux War Orders of Battle*; Robinson, *A Good Year to Die*; Utley, *The Lance and the Shield*, chapters 9–15; and Bray, *Crazy Horse*, chapters 16–20.

2. The earliest known use of the name "Great Sioux War" is in a headline in the *Cheyenne Daily Leader*, August 7, 1876. Some other early uses are in the title of Joseph A. Altsheler's book *Last of the Chiefs: A Story of the Great Sioux War* (1909) and in Jesse M. Lee's 1914 account of Crazy Horse's death, "The Capture and Death of an Indian Chieftain," 323. I am grateful to Jerry Greene and Marc Abrams for these observations.

3. McDermott, *Red Cloud's War*; Madsen and Madsen, *North to Montana*.

4. Barbour, *Fort Union and the Upper Missouri Fur Trade*, 26–28; Bray, "Teton Sioux Population History"; White, "The Winning of the

West"; Ewers, "Intertribal Warfare as the Precursor of Indian-White Warfare on the Northern Great Plains."

5. Denig, *Five Indian Tribes of the Upper Missouri*, 16–28.

6. Utley, *The Lance and the Shield*, 31, 88.

7. The complete treaty is presented in Kappler, ed., *Indian Affairs*. For an interpretation of salient articles, see Hedren, *Fort Laramie in 1876*, 2–7.

8. These hunting lands are defined in articles 11 and 16. See Hedren, *Fort Laramie in 1876*, 4–5; and Brown, "A New Focus on the Sioux War," in Hedren, ed., *The Great Sioux War*, 28–30.

9. Edgar I. Stewart, "Major Brisbin's Relief of Fort Pease," in Hedren, ed., *The Great Sioux War*, 115–21; Kelly, *Fort Buford*, 5–24.

10. Froiland, *Natural History of the Black Hills*, 11; Sundstrom, "The Sacred Black Hills."

11. In 1874 Custer posed with perhaps the last grizzly bear shot in the Black Hills. See Jackson, *Custer's Gold*, photo section.

12. Sundstrom, *Cultural History of the Black Hills*; Calloway, *One Vast Winter Count* chapter 6.

13. Parker, *Gold in the Black Hills*, 11–14.

14. Malone and Rauch, *Crisis of the Union*, 302–304.

15. Jackson, *Custer's Gold*; Hedren, *Fort Laramie in 1876*, 12–15.

16. Anderson, "Indian Peace-Talkers," 250–51; Powell, *Sweet Medicine*, 192–93.

17. Anderson, "Indian Peace-Talkers," 250–51; Hyde, *Spotted Tail's Folk*, 269.

18. Greene, *Yellowstone Command*, 197–98.

19. Anderson, "Indian Peace-Talkers," 252–53; Buecker, *Fort Robinson and the American West*, 94–95; Buecker and Paul, eds., *The Crazy Horse Surrender Ledger*, 10, 14.

20. Utley, *The Lance and the Shield*, 179–80.

21. Ibid., 180–82.

22. Hedren, *Great Sioux War Orders of Battle*, 149–52; Greene, *Yellowstone Command*, 201–202.

23. Greene, *Yellowstone Command*, 208–209; Greene, ed., *Lakota and Cheyenne*, 134–47.

24. Greene, *Yellowstone Command*, 209–13.

25. Hedren, *Great Sioux War Orders of Battle*, 71–73.

26. Buecker, "'Can You Send Us Immediate Relief'?" 111–13.

27. Hedren, *Great Sioux War Orders of Battle*, 154–55; *Cheyenne Daily Leader*, May 22, 1877; Hedren, *Fort Laramie in 1876*, 202.

28. Greene, "Out with a Whimper"; Hedren, *Great Sioux War Orders of Battle*, 152–54.

29. Greene, *Yellowstone Command,* 221–23; Greene, ed., *Frontier Soldier,* 62–65, 77.

30. Hedren, *Great Sioux War Orders of Battle,* 170–72; Russell, "How Many Indians Were Killed?" 47.

31. Powell, *Sweet Medicine,* 167.

CHAPTER 2. SHERIDAN AND SHERMAN EXPLORE SIOUX COUNTRY

1. Hutton, *Phil Sheridan and His Army,* chapters 13–14; Hedren, *Fort Laramie in 1876,* 17–18, 111–12, 116–18, 166, 170–72.

2. "Lieutenant-General Sheridan's Report of a Reconnaissance of the Bighorn Mountains and the Valleys of the Bighorn and Yellowstone under His Personal Supervision during the Month of July, 1877," in *Reports of Inspection,* 11 (hereafter Sheridan's Report); Sheridan, *Personal Memoirs of Philip Henry Sheridan,* 526.

3. Robert M. Utley, "War Houses in the Sioux Country," in Hedren, ed., *The Great Sioux War,* 252–63.

4. Sheridan to Sherman, June 15, 1877, William Tecumseh Sherman Papers, Library of Congress (hereafter Sherman Papers); Special Orders No. 136, Headquarters of the Army, June 22, 1877 (quotation), RG 393, National Archives.

5. Sheridan's Report, 12; *Cheyenne Daily Leader,* June 17, 1877.

6. Robinson, ed., *The Diaries of John Gregory Bourke,* 311–12; Wheeler, *Buffalo Days,* 154.

7. Sheridan's Report, 12; Delos B. Sacket, "An Itinerary of the Route Marched over on a Reconnaissance along and through the Bighorn Mountains, from Camp Brown, Wyoming, to the New Post on Bighorn River, Montana," in *Reports of Inspection,* 15–16 (hereafter Sacket, "An Itinerary"); Robinson, ed., *The Diaries of John Gregory Bourke,* 313–14. On the phenomenon of Crook's hunting expeditions, see Hedren, *Fort Laramie in 1876,* 172, 180–81, 223; and Fusco, "The Last Hunt of Gen. George A. Crook."

8. Sheridan's Report, 112–13; Sacket, "An Itinerary," 16.

9. "Journal of Major Geo. A. Forsyth on General Sheridan's Trip to the Big Horn Mountains," July 4, 1877, Natalie Beaumont Forsyth Collection, Arizona Historical Society; Robinson, ed., *The Diaries of John Gregory Bourke,* 317–18; Wheeler, *Buffalo Days,* 160.

10. Robinson, ed., *The Diaries of John Gregory Bourke,* 319–21; Wheeler, *Buffalo Days,* 162–64.

11. Robinson, ed., *The Diaries of John Gregory Bourke,* 322–25.

12. Sacket, "An Itinerary," 18; "Journal of Major Geo. A. Forsyth," July 11, 15, 1877; Robinson, ed., *The Diaries of John Gregory Bourke,* 326–28; Sheridan's Report, 13.

13. Robinson, ed., *The Diaries of John Gregory Bourke*, 328–29. For stories of Big Horn gold, see *Cheyenne Daily Leader*, March 27, June 10, 22, and 28, and July 8 and 17, 1877.

14. Sibley's purpose had been to reconnoiter the country north of Crook's Goose Creek camp and secure assistance from the Crow Indian Agency. For an overview, see Willert, "The Sibley Scout."

15. Sacket, "An Itinerary," 19; Robinson, ed., *The Diaries of John Gregory Bourke*, 333–34.

16. Hedren, *Great Sioux War Orders of Battle*, 154–55; Robinson, ed., *The Diaries of John Gregory Bourke*, 335–36.

17. Robinson, ed., *The Diaries of John Gregory Bourke*, 336–37; Sheridan's Report, 13–14.

18. Robinson, ed., *The Diaries of John Gregory Bourke*, 336–38.

19. Ibid., 338–42. For a retrospective on this village, see Richard A. Fox, Jr., "West River History: The Indian Village on Little Bighorn River, June 25–26, 1876," in Rankin, ed., *Legacy*.

20. Paul L. Hedren, "'Holy Ground': The United States Army Embraces Custer's Battlefield," in Rankin, ed., *Legacy*, 193–95; Hutton, *Phil Sheridan and His Army*, 329.

21. Robinson, ed., *The Diaries of John Gregory Bourke*, 340–41; Hedren, ed., "Eben Swift's Army Service on the Plains," 148; "Journal of Major Geo. A. Forsyth," July 21, 1877; Wheeler, *Buffalo Days*, 184.

22. Robinson, ed., *The Diaries of John Gregory Bourke*, 342.

23. George P. Buell Appointments, Commissions, Personal File 1102 ACP 1883, RG 94, National Archives; Leckie, "Buell's Campaign."

24. Robinson, ed., *The Diaries of John Gregory Bourke*, 342–43.

25. Ibid., 342–43, 345.

26. Ibid., 343–44; "Journal of Major Geo. A. Forsyth," July 23, 1877.

27. Robinson, ed., *The Diaries of John Gregory Bourke*, 344–45.

28. Sherman to Geo. W. McCrary, July 17, 1877, in *Reports of Inspection*; "Copy of Memoranda Made by O. M. Poe, Colonel, A.D.C., Etc., While Accompanying General W. T. Sherman on a Trip from the Mississippi River to the Pacific Ocean, during the Months of July, August, September, and October, 1877," in *Reports of Inspection* (hereafter "Copy of Memoranda Made by O. M. Poe").

29. Sherman to McCrary, July 17, 1877; "Copy of Memoranda Made by O. M. Poe," July 8–9, 1877; Hanson, *The Conquest of the Missouri*, 369–70.

30. "Copy of Memoranda Made by O. M. Poe," July 9–12, 1877; Hedren, "'Holy Ground,'" 194.

31. The standard source on Upper Missouri steamboating is Lass, *A History of Steamboating on the Upper Missouri River*; chapters 8–9 are

particularly relevant here. Lass is also the sole authority on Yellowstone River steamboating. See William E. Lass, "Steamboats on the Yellowstone," in Hedren, ed., *The Great Sioux War*, 206–29.

32. Kroeker, *Great Plains Command*, 120–42; Hutton, *Phil Sheridan and His Army*, 170–71. The debate on the worth of the northern plains is treated exhaustively by Stewart, ed., *Penny-an-Acre Empire in the West*; his conclusions in chapter 15 are sound. Hazen was wrong in his indictment, Stewart asserts, and failed to grasp the infinite variety of landscapes on the northern plains, with barren and arid tracts well balanced by areas of great fertility and potential. Hazen was also wrong in believing that the types of agriculture existing east of the Missouri River could be transferred without modification to territories west of the river. But Stewart suggests that Custer, the effervescent optimist, was wrong too and allowed his enthusiasm to cloud his judgment. In any case, neither Hazen nor Custer foresaw the development of agricultural and exploitive industries like cattle, cereal grains, and coal that reaped the inherent bounty of a supposed barren land.

33. "Copy of Memoranda Made by O. M. Poe," July 13, 1877; McClernand, *On Time for Disaster*, 101–102.

34. Department of Dakota Special Orders No. 83, June 23, 1877, RG 393, National Archives.

35. "Copy of Memoranda Made by O. M. Poe," July 14, 16, 1877.

36. Ibid., July 17, 1877; Hanson, *The Conquest of the Missouri*, 372; Hedren, *Great Sioux War Orders of Battle*, 123–27.

37. Sherman to McCrary, July 17, 1877.

38. Ibid.

39. Hanson, *The Conquest of the Missouri*, 373–74; "Copy of Memoranda Made by O. M. Poe," July 18, 1877; Greene, *Yellowstone Command*, 223. The Fifth Infantry Medal of Honor recipients are identified in the *Army and Navy Journal*, August 11, 1877. In all, eighty-two Medals of Honor were awarded for heroism in thirteen different Great Sioux War actions. In that regard, see Hedren, "'Three cool, determined men.'"

40. "Copy of Memoranda Made by O. M. Poe," July 18–21, 1877; "Captain Gilbreath's Story," in Upton, ed., *Fort Custer on the Big Horn*, 35; Edgar I. Stewart, "Major Brisbin's Relief of Fort Pease," in Hedren, ed., *The Great Sioux War*, 115–21.

41. "Copy of Memoranda Made by O. M. Poe," July 21–22, 1877; West, *Capitalism on the Frontier*, 46.

42. Upton, ed., *Fort Custer on the Big Horn*, 35 (Gilbreath quotation); Robinson, ed., *The Diaries of John Gregory Bourke*, 345; Sherman to McCrary, July 25, 1877, in *Reports of Inspection*.

43. Sherman to McCrary, July 25, 1877; Sheridan's Report, 13–14.

44. "Copy of Memoranda Made by O. M. Poe," July 23–24, 1877.

45. Ibid., July 24, 1877; Hanson, *The Conquest of the Missouri*, 375. I argued otherwise in "'Holy Ground,'" 197.

46. Sherman to McCrary, July 25, 1877; "Copy of Memoranda Made by O. M. Poe," July 25, 1877; Upton, ed., *Fort Custer on the Big Horn 1877–1898*, 35–37.

47. Sherman to McCrary, July 25, 1877; "Copy of Memoranda Made by O. M. Poe," July 25, 1877.

48. Sherman to McCrary, July 25, August 3, 1877; "Copy of Memoranda Made by O. M. Poe," July 26–August 1, 1877.

49. Sherman to McCrary, July 25, 1877; "Copy of Memoranda Made by O. M. Poe," July 24, 1877.

50. For the story of the Battle of the Big Hole, see Haines, *An Elusive Victory*; and Greene, *Nez Perce Summer*, 128–40. The remainder of Sherman's western adventure is detailed in his continuing letters to McCrary and in "Copy of Memoranda Made by O. M. Poe," both in *Reports of Inspection*.

51. Robinson, ed., *The Diaries of John Gregory Bourke*, 346–48; "Journal of Major Geo. A. Forsyth," July 24, 1877; "Report of Brigadier-General Terry," in U.S. War Department, *Report of the Secretary of War, 1877*, 545.

52. Robinson, ed., *The Diaries of John Gregory Bourke*, 348. On the Starvation March, see Greene, *Slim Buttes*; and King, *Campaigning with Crook and Stories of Army Life*, chapters 13–14.

53. Robinson, ed., *The Diaries of John Gregory Bourke*, 348–49.

54. "Journal of Major Geo. A. Forsyth," July 25, 1877; Robinson, ed., *The Diaries of John Gregory Bourke*, 349; Fort Buford Medical History, July 1877, transcribed in Fort Buford Records, vol. 5, Fort Union Trading Post National Historic Site.

55. Robinson, ed., *The Diaries of John Gregory Bourke*, 351–54. For an overview of the army and 1877 labor riots, see Hutton, *Phil Sheridan and His Army*, 175–77.

Chapter 3. New Forts and a New Mission

1. Fort Laramie's role in the Great Sioux War is closely detailed in Hedren, *Fort Laramie in 1876*, with critical context provided in chapters 1 and 2. Fort Laramie's long and eventful military history is eloquently told in McChristian, *Fort Laramie*.

2. Lindmier, *Drybone*, chapter 5.

3. Bray, "Teton Sioux Population History," 175; Buecker, *Fort Robinson and the American West*, 101.

4. Hedren, "Camp Sheridan, Nebraska."

5. Omaha Barracks (1868), Fort Hartsuff (1874), Fort McPherson (1863), and North Platte Station (1867), Nebraska; Camp Stambaugh (1870), Camp Brown (1869), and Fort Bridger (1858), Wyoming; Camp Douglas (1862) and Fort Cameron (1872), Utah; Fort Hall (1870), Idaho.

6. Forts Wadsworth (1864), Abercrombie (1858), Seward (1872), Totten (1867), and Pembina (1870), Dakota; and Forts Ripley (1849) and Snelling (1819), Minnesota.

7. Hedren, *Great Sioux War Orders of Battle*, 77–78.

8. Hedren, *Fort Laramie in 1876*, 229–30; Hedren, "Garrisoning the Black Hills Road."

9. Hedren, *Great Sioux War Orders of Battle*, 128–30.

10. Ibid., 123–27.

11. *Saint Paul and Minneapolis Pioneer Press*, March 17 and April 2, 1877.

12. *Saint Paul and Minneapolis Pioneer Press*, May 11, 1877; "Died— Poor," *Sioux City Journal*, December 25, 1891. According to Poor's obituary, he also superintended the construction of Fort Assinniboine.

13. *Saint Paul and Minneapolis Pioneer Press*, May 11, 15, and 19, 1877; Department of Dakota Special Orders No. 57, May 10, 1877, RG 393, National Archives; Geo. P. Buell, "Bighorn Post, Mont.," in U.S. War Department, *Report of the Secretary of War, 1877*, 550–51. The civilian workforce was named in the May 11 *Saint Paul and Minneapolis Pioneer Press*.

14. *Saint Paul and Minneapolis Pioneer Press*, May 25, 1877 (this issue names the Post Number One construction crew); Lass, "Steamboats on the Yellowstone," 217.

15. *Saint Paul and Minneapolis Pioneer Press*, July 18, 1877.

16. *Saint Paul and Minneapolis Pioneer Press*, August 24, 1877.

17. *Saint Paul and Minneapolis Pioneer Press*, August 29, 1877; Headquarters of the Army General Order No. 101, November 8, 1877, RG 393, National Archives.

18. Frazer, *Forts of the West*, 79–80, 82; Upton, ed., *Fort Custer on the Big Horn*, 273–91; Greene, *Yellowstone Command*, 233; Sherman to McCrary, July 25, 1877, 44 (quotation).

19. Wm. W. Belknap, "Report of the Secretary of War," in U.S. War Department, *Report of the Secretary of War, 1875*, 21; "Report of Brigadier-General John Pope," in U.S. War Department, *Report of the Secretary of War, 1877*, 63–64. Pope's crusade had gained considerable momentum by the early 1880s. In 1882 Sherman unveiled his own plan for a "radical change in our whole system of piecemeal work in quartering troops of the United States." He outlined several strategic frontiers (including on

the northern plains) and acknowledged that obsolete interior posts, which had "grown up in the progress of the settlement of the Continent, were absolutely demanded by the necessities of the country at the time, [but] . . . having fulfilled their purpose should be allowed to die out." U.S. War Department, *Report of the Secretary of War, 1882,* 10, 12, 16.

20. "Report of Brigadier-General Terry," in U.S. War Department, *Report of the Secretary of War, 1877,* 519.

21. "Report of the Commanding General of the Department of Dakota, General Gibbon Commanding," in U.S. War Department, *Report of the Secretary of War, 1878,* 68–69; "Report of Brig. Gen. Alfred H. Terry," in U.S. War Department, *Report of the Secretary of War, 1879,* 51, 64; Lee, *Fort Meade and the Black Hills,* 22–23, 25–26, 41.

22. Lee, *Fort Meade and the Black Hills,* 44–45.

23. "Report of Brigadier-General Terry," in U.S. War Department, *Report of the Secretary of War, 1877,* 519; "Report of the Commanding General of the Department of Dakota, General Gibbon Commanding," in U.S. War Department, *Report of the Secretary of War, 1878,* 66–68.

24. Hardeman, "Brick Stronghold of the Border"; Johnson, "The Gilded Age & the Frontier Military."

25. U.S. War Department, *Report of the Secretary of War, 1879,* 5, 65.

26. Ibid., 65.

27. U.S. War Department, *Report of the Secretary of War, 1880,* 60; Frazer, *Forts of the West,* 83.

28. Frazer, *Forts of the West,* 83; Koury, *Military Posts of Montana,* 69–72.

29. U.S. War Department, *Report of the Secretary of War, 1878,* 66.

30. Murray, *Military Posts in the Powder River Country,* 111, 115, 117; U.S. War Department, *Report of the Secretary of War, 1878,* 382.

31. Murray, *Military Posts in the Powder River Country,* 139; Bollinger, *Fort McKinney 1877 to 1894,* 43–45; Davis, *Wyoming Range War,* 174–80; "Report of Lieutenant-General Sheridan," in U.S. War Department, *Report of the Secretary of War, 1881,* 82–83 (quotation).

32. Buecker, *Fort Robinson and the American West,* 118–22.

33. Ibid., 122–23.

34. Ibid., 123, 149, 196–97.

35. U.S. War Department, *Report of the Secretary of War, 1879,* 227, and *Report of the Secretary of War, 1880,* 55; Buecker, *Fort Niobrara,* 2–3, 6.

36. U.S. War Department, *Report of the Secretary of War, 1884,* 116.

37. Buecker, "Fort Niobrara."

38. Fort Randall (1856–92), Whetstone Agency (1870–72), Fort Hale (1870–84), Fort Thompson (1864–71), Fort Sully (1866–94), Fort Bennett (1870–91), and Grand River Agency (1870–75).

39. Frazer, *Forts of the West*, 137–38. See also Schuler, *Fort Sully.*

40. *Outline Descriptions of the Posts in the Military Division of the Missouri*, 62, 66; Daniel, "Dismounting the Sioux."

41. Hedren, "Sitting Bull's Surrender at Fort Buford"; Frazer, *Forts of the West*, 116.

42. Kelly, *Fort Buford*, 81–85; Frazer, *Forts of the West*, 112–13.

43. Adams, *The Post near Cheyenne.*

44. Buecker, *Fort Robinson and the American Century.*

CHAPTER 4. THE ARMY AND THE NORTHERN PACIFIC RAILROAD

1. Robert G. Athearn, "The Firewagon Road," in Hedren, ed., *The Great Sioux War*, 65–84 (Crook quotation, 76); General Orders No. 69, September 30, 1880, Headquarters of the Army, Adjutant General's Office, in Department of Dakota General Orders, 1880–81, RG 393, National Archives; U.S. War Department, *Report of the Secretary of War, 1880*, 4 (Sherman quotation).

2. Frazer, *Forts of the West*, 111, 114.

3. Lubetkin, "The Forgotten Yellowstone Surveying Expeditions of 1871," 34–35; Lubetkin, *Jay Cooke's Gamble*, 93–113; Renz, *The History of the Northern Pacific Railroad*, 37.

4. Lubetkin, "The Forgotten Yellowstone Surveying Expeditions of 1871," 40–42, 46; Lubetkin, *Jay Cooke's Gamble*, 80–92.

5. Robertson, "'We Are Going to Have a Big Sioux War,'" 9, 11; Lubetkin, *Jay Cooke's Gamble*, 131–47.

6. Robertson, "'We Are Going to Have a Big Sioux War,'" 10–15; Lubetkin, *Jay Cooke's Gamble*, 148–61.

7. Rolston, "The Yellowstone Expedition of 1873," 22–29; Lubetkin, *Jay Cooke's Gamble*, 242–67; Harry H. Anderson, "A Challenge to Brown's Sioux Indian Wars Thesis," in Hedren, ed., *The Great Sioux War*, 44; Hutton, *Phil Sheridan and His Army*, 286.

8. Smalley, *History of the Northern Pacific Railroad*, 390–96; Murphy, "The Northern Pacific Railway Bridge at Bismarck." This bridge was a signature feature for the railroad and the city of Bismarck; portions remain in use to this day.

9. Winther, *The Transportation Frontier*, 100. The Northern Pacific Railroad land grant was double that of the central line, amounting to a 400-foot right-of-way and alternate sections of land within forty miles of each side of the track.

10. Smalley, *History of the Northern Pacific Railroad*, 395–96; Renz, *The History of the Northern Pacific Railroad*, 65.

11. Renz, *The History of the Northern Pacific Railroad*, 65; Galloway, *The First Transcontinental Railroad*, 276–77. Galloway's work, though focused on the first transcontinental railroad, offers a vivid interpretive overview of the mechanics of constructing railroads on the Great Plains in the nineteenth century.

12. Galloway, *The First Transcontinental Railroad*, 139, 279; Smalley, *History of the Northern Pacific Railroad*, 395, 400.

13. Galloway, *The First Transcontinental Railroad*, 158, 279–81; Renz, *The History of the Northern Pacific Railroad*, 39; Hagen and Mattison, "Pyramid Park," 227. The record of ten miles of track laid in one day has never been surpassed.

14. Fort Abraham Lincoln Post Return, August 1878, Microcopy 617, Roll 628, National Archives.

15. Ibid., April–September 1879; Department of Dakota Special Orders No. 73, July 9, 1879, RG 393, National Archives; Renz, *The History of the Northern Pacific Railroad*, 65. The Seventeenth Infantry company returned to Fort Abraham Lincoln in August and was succeeded by another from the Sixth Infantry.

16. Cantonment Bad Lands Order Books, Orders No. 1, November 16, 1879, and Letter Sent, January 1, 1880 (quotation), RG 393, National Archives; Renz, *The History of the Northern Pacific Railroad*, 65.

17. Department of Dakota Special Orders No. 114, October 16, 1879, RG 393, National Archives; Hagen and Mattison, "Pyramid Park," 223–25; Renz, *The History of the Northern Pacific Railroad*, 69.

18. Hagen and Mattison, "Pyramid Park," 226–27; Renz, *The History of the Northern Pacific Railroad*, 69.

19. Department of Dakota Letters and Endorsements, Northern Pacific Railroad Escort, June 1, 1880, RG 393, National Archives.

20. *Records of Living Officers of the United States Army*, 166–67; Williams, *Military Register of Custer's Last Command*, 216; Hedren, *Great Sioux War Orders of Battle*, 152–54; Department of Dakota Letters and Endorsements, Northern Pacific Railroad Escort, June 1, 1880.

21. Department of Dakota Letters and Endorsements, Northern Pacific Railroad Escort, November 25, 1880, RG 393, National Archives.

22. Department of Dakota Letters and Endorsements, Northern Pacific Railroad Escort, August 3 and August 5, 1880; Department of Dakota General Orders No. 5, Northern Pacific Railroad Escort, August 31, 1880; Department of Dakota Special Orders No. 82, July 10, 1880, RG 393, National Archives.

23. Cantonment Bad Lands Order Books, Special Order No. 23, June 9, 1880; Cantonment Bad Lands Post Return, July 1880, Microcopy 617, Roll 64, National Archives.

24. Department of Dakota Letters and Endorsements, Northern Pacific Railroad Escort, November 25, 1880; Renz, *The History of the Northern Pacific Railroad*, 69–70.

25. Renz, *The History of the Northern Pacific Railroad*, 70, 86; U.S. War Department, *Report of the Secretary of War, 1880*, 63.

26. Department of Dakota Letters and Endorsements, Northern Pacific Railroad Escort, October 12, 1880; Department of Dakota Special Orders No. 143, November 8, 1880, No. 159, November 29, 1880, and No. 54, March 31, 1881; Department of Dakota Telegrams Received, Northern Pacific Railroad Escort, October 8, 1880, RG 393, National Archives.

27. Terry's report to General Sheridan in 1881 documenting the deployment of troops in commands large and small in conjunction with the return of Sioux Indians from Canada spanned eight published pages in U.S. War Department, *Report of the Secretary of War, 1881*, 92–99.

28. Department of Dakota Special Orders No. 124, July 12, 1881; Department of Dakota Orders Issued, Northern Pacific Railroad Escort, No. 1, July 25, 1881, No. 5, August 16, 1881, RG 393, National Archives.

29. West, *Capitalism on the Frontier*, 95; Smalley, *History of the Northern Pacific Railroad*, 398–99.

30. Smalley, *History of the Northern Pacific Railroad*, 400–401; Renz, *The History of the Northern Pacific Railroad*, 86; Hoopes, *This Last West*, 269; West, *Capitalism on the Frontier*, 95, 96 (quotation).

31. Department of Dakota Special Orders No. 178, September 28, 1881, No. 180, October 17, 1881, No. 191, October 20, 1881, No. 195, October 26, 1881, No. 215, November 19, 1881; "Report of Brigadier-General Terry," in U.S. War Department, *Report of the Secretary of War, 1881*, 109 (quotation).

32. Smalley, *History of the Northern Pacific Railroad*, 401; Renz, *The History of the Northern Pacific Railroad*, 86.

33. Department of Dakota Special Orders No. 43, March 20, 1882, and No. 79, May 15, 1882; U.S. War Department, *Report of the Secretary of War, 1882*, 89.

34. Department of Dakota Special Orders No. 100, June 21, 1882; Department of Dakota Orders Issued, Northern Pacific Railroad Escort, No. 1, July 14, 1882, RG 393, National Archives; U.S. War Department, *Report of the Secretary of War, 1882*, 89.

35. West, *Capitalism on the Frontier*, 112–14, 121 (quotation), 128, 139; Smalley, *History of the Northern Pacific Railroad*, 401; Renz, *The History of the Northern Pacific Railroad*, 86.

36. Renz, *The History of the Northern Pacific Railroad*, 86; Smalley, *History of the Northern Pacific Railroad*, 402–407.

37. Department of Dakota Special Orders No. 197, November 24, 1882; Department of Dakota Orders Issued, Northern Pacific Railroad Escort, No. 32, September 15, 1882.

38. Comba to Adjutant General, Department of Dakota, September 5, 1882, Cantonment Bad Lands Order Books, RG 393 (Comba quotation); Department of Dakota Special Orders No. 39, February 26, 1883, RG 393; Cantonment Bad Lands Post Returns, November 1882, March 1883, Microcopy 617, National Archives (Sage quotation).

39. Smalley, *History of the Northern Pacific Railroad*, 417–20.

40. Nolan, "'Not without Labor and Expense,'" 2, 4.

41. Ibid., 4–9; Nolan, *Northern Pacific Views*, 71, 76.

42. Smalley, *History of the Northern Pacific Railroad*, 431.

43. Lass, *A History of Steamboating on the Upper Missouri River*, 142–43; U.S. War Department, *Report of the Secretary of War, 1881*, 99.

44. Brown, *The Plainsmen of the Yellowstone*, 361, quoting an unnamed "pioneer."

Chapter 5. "The Buffaloes Are Gone"

1. The chapter title is a line from the poem "Buffalo Dusk" by Carl Sandburg (1954).

2. Hornaday, *The Extermination of the American Bison*, 437–38; Utley, *The Lance and the Shield*, 7–8; McHugh, *The Time of the Buffalo*, 6–7; Calloway, *One Vast Winter Count*, 274.

3. Lame Deer and Erdoes, *Lame Deer*, 255.

4. Kappler, ed., *Indian Affairs*, 1001–1002; Hedren, *Fort Laramie in 1876*, 155–56. The 1876 agreement was ratified by Congress on February 28, 1877.

5. McHugh, *The Time of the Buffalo*, 286.

6. West, *The Way to the West*, quoting plainsman Henry Dodge, 56, and preacher Joseph Williams, 57.

7. Quoted in Isenberg, *The Destruction of the Bison*, 23.

8. Quoted in Hanson, *The Conquest of the Missouri*, 96–98.

9. Bourke, *On the Border with Crook*, 266; Finerty, *War-Path and Bivouac*, 117–18; Bowen, "The Passing of the Buffalo," 14.

10. Lott, *American Bison*, 69–76; West, *The Way to the West*, 53, 73–76.

11. The terms "robe" and "hide" warrant an explanation. Buffalo robes were fully and naturally tanned by Indian women before entering the trading stream and required no further processing. Hides, the typical product derived from white hunters, were untanned raw skins that went to market in a dried, unprocessed state and were subsequently commercially tanned with chemical products.

12. McHugh, *The Time of the Buffalo*, 253; Hornaday, *The Extermination of the American Bison*, 440.

13. Briggs, *Frontiers of the Northwest*, 156–61; Flores, "Bison Ecology and Plains Diplomacy," 465.

14. Dan Flores, "The Great Contraction," in Rankin, ed., *Legacy*, 17–18.

15. Renz, *The History of the Northern Pacific Railroad*, 65, 70.

16. Brown and Felton, *The Frontier Years*, 68.

17. Hornaday, *The Extermination of the American Bison*, 467.

18. Ibid., 469.

19. Ibid., 469–70, 510; Hoopes, *This Last West*, 386; Smith, *The Champion Buffalo Hunter*, 98. Zahl's biographer asserts that he also killed 107 buffalo, in a single stand occupying a great circle about the size of a single city block. See Burdick, *Tales from Buffalo Land*, 205–206.

20. Brown and Felton, *The Frontier Years*, 73.

21. Hornaday, *The Extermination of the American Bison*, 440, 442–43; Stuart, *Pioneering in Montana*, 104.

22. Hornaday, *The Extermination of the American Bison*, 443.

23. Ibid., 506; Briggs, *Frontiers of the Northwest*, 164.

24. Hanna, *An Old-Timer's Story of the Old Wild West*, 67; Spring, *Seventy Years*, 75 (quotation).

25. Hornaday, *The Extermination of the American Bison*, 509.

26. Bowen, "The Passing of the Buffalo," 15.

27. Quoted in Hornaday, *The Extermination of the American Bison*, 509.

28. Ibid., 467, 512.

29. Ibid., 509–10.

30. Ibid., 512.

31. Isenberg, *The Destruction of the Bison*, 140–41; Roosevelt, *Hunting Trips of a Ranchman*, 237 (quotation).

32. Scott, *Some Memories of a Soldier*, 124.

33. Quoted in Hornaday, *The Extermination of the American Bison*, 513.

34. Quoted in ibid., 439–40.

35. Ibid., 512; Dobak, "Killing the Canadian Buffalo."

36. Quoted in Hornaday, *The Extermination of the American Bison*, 512.

37. Ibid., 530; Hornaday, "The Passing of the Buffalo," 85–86.

38. Hornaday, *The Extermination of the American Bison*, 531; Fort Keogh Post Return, May 1886, Microcopy 617, Roll 572, National Archives.

39. Hornaday, *The Extermination of the American Bison*, 532.

40. Ibid., 532–34. The young buffalo calf, named Sandy, was taken to Washington, where it charmed Smithsonian visitors in the summer of 1886. The calf died that fall, perhaps from eating too much damp clover. Hornaday mounted the animal and incorporated it into his well-known

six-specimen "Buffalo Group," a featured Smithsonian exhibit until 1957. See Shell, "Last of the Wild Buffalo." Sandy and the Buffalo Group are now exhibited in Fort Benton, Montana. See note 45 below.

41. Peterson, ed., "Buffalo Hunting in Montana in 1886," 4–7; Hornaday, *The Extermination of the American Bison*, 534–36.

42. Hornaday, *The Extermination of the American Bison*, 536–37; Peterson, ed., "Buffalo Hunting in Montana in 1886," 7–8.

43. Hornaday, *The Extermination of the American Bison*, 538–40.

44. Ibid., 540–43.

45. Peterson, ed., "Buffalo Hunting in Montana in 1886," 9–11. Hornaday's collection of skins, skeletons, and skulls formed a National Museum exhibit that enthralled visitors for generations. The Buffalo Group noted in note 40 above included the calf captured by Hornaday and shipped east alive in May 1886 and the enormous old bull. The buffalo were mounted and prominently displayed at the Smithsonian in Washington from 1888 to 1957, when the collection was inexplicably disassembled and dispersed to several institutions in Montana. At the instigation of John Lepley of Fort Benton, Montana, in 1992 this group of six was reassembled from storage, restored, and returned to public display in Fort Benton's Montana Agricultural Center and Museum. It reposes there today as a remarkable testimonial to the once magnificent northern herd. Shell, "Last of the Wild Buffalo," 30. Hornaday tallied his collection in *The Extermination of the American Bison*, 545. The disposition of other Hornaday specimens is discussed in Peterson, ed., "Buffalo Hunting in Montana in 1886," 12–13.

46. McHugh, *The Time of the Buffalo*, 293–94.

47. Hornaday, *The Extermination of the American Bison*, 522; Roe, *The North American Buffalo*, 463–65.

48. McHugh, *The Time of the Buffalo*, 294. Russell, *The Lives and Legends of Buffalo Bill*, 343–47.

49. McHugh, *The Time of the Buffalo*, 294–95; Jacoby, *Crimes against Nature*, 123, 126–27; Hampton, *How the U.S. Cavalry Saved Our National Parks*, 109–10; Meagher, *The Bison of Yellowstone National Park*, 23, 121. See also Punke, *Last Stand*, reporting eloquently on naturalist George Bird Grinnell's advocacy of buffalo conservation in the popular magazine *Field and Stream*, with special reference to the travails of the buffalo of Yellowstone. The Yellowstone buffalo story is carried to the present day by Franke, *To Save the Wild Bison*.

50. Fleharty, *Wild Animals and Settlers on the Great Plains*, 61–66.

51. For interesting specifics on buffalo bone picking in one Dakota locale, see Hoffbeck, "Sully Springs," 22.

52. Barnett, "The Buffalo Bone Commerce on the Northern Plains"; Barnett, "Ghastly Harvest"; Briggs, *Frontiers of the Northwest*, 178–79; Isenberg, *The Destruction of the Bison*, 159–60.

53. Topping, *Chronicles of the Yellowstone*, 238.

54. DeMallie, "The Sioux in Dakota and Montana Territories," 55, citing Robert McDonald to Fort Keogh Post Adjutant, September 26, 1881, with Terry endorsement, October 7, and Sheridan endorsement, October 13, in Letters Received by the Commissioner of Indian Affairs, No. 1881-18715, RG 75, National Archives and Records Service, Washington, D.C.; Hutton, *Phil Sheridan and His Army*, 246.

55. Farr, "Going to Buffalo," 42–43 (quotation). The debate over the army's role in the destruction of the American buffalo was waged most recently by Smits, "The Frontier Army and the Destruction of the Buffalo"; and Dobak, "The Army and the Buffalo," with Dobak's thoughtful case prevailing handily. See also Flores, *The Natural West*, 52.

56. Lame Deer and Erdoes, *Lame Deer*, 255.

CHAPTER 6. THE BEEF BONANZA

1. Briggs, *Frontiers of the Northwest*, 306.

2. Ibid., 188–89, 206; Osgood, *The Day of the Cattleman*, 45; Latham, *Trans-Missouri Stock Raising*, 41. For a useful biography of Iliff, see Agnes Wright Spring, "A 'Genius for Handling Cattle': John W. Iliff," in Frink, Jackson, and Spring, *When Grass Was King*, 333–450.

3. Latham, *Trans-Missouri Stock Raising*, 42–43; Kuykendall, "The First Cattle North of the Union Pacific Railroad," 70–72.

4. Briggs, *Frontiers of the Northwest*, 199.

5. Ibid., 197–99; Osgood, *The Day of the Cattleman*, 27–30, 32.

6. Rollinson, *Wyoming Cattle Trails*, 317, citing the *Cheyenne Daily Sun*, January 14, 1879; Kuykendall, "The First Cattle North of the Union Pacific Railroad," 71–73; Dunlay, "James Hervey Pratt"; Hedren, *Fort Laramie in 1876*, 113, 140, 184.

7. Hanna, *An Old-Timer's Story of the Old Wild West*, 57.

8. Osgood, *The Day of the Cattleman*, 83.

9. Rollinson, *Wyoming Cattle Trails*, 326–27; Osgood, *The Day of the Cattleman*, 86–87.

10. Jordan, *North American Cattle-Ranching Frontiers*, 210, 225–27; Spring, *Seventy Years*, 24.

11. Osgood, *The Day of the Cattleman*, 88, 117–19; Dale, *The Range Cattle Industry*, 84–89; Yost, *The Call of the Range*, 219; Briggs, *Frontiers of the Northwest*, 214; Hagen and Mattison, "Pyramid Park," 237.

12. Briggs, *Frontiers of the Northwest*, 253–59; Richardson, "Moreton Frewen." The British and Scottish role in the American cattle industry is well told by W. Turrentine Jackson, "British Interests in the Range Cattle Industry," in Frink, Jackson, and Spring, *When Grass Was King*, 133–330. With specific regard to the Swan Land and Cattle Company, see also Woods, *Alex Swan and the Swan Companies.*

13. Osgood, *The Day of the Cattleman*, 91–94; Rollinson, *Wyoming Cattle Trails*, 26–27.

14. Briggs, *Frontiers of the Northwest*, 227; Frink, Jackson, and Spring, *When Grass Was King*, 77; Osgood, *The Day of the Cattleman*, 50–51, 106–108.

15. Malone and Roeder, "The Centennial Year in Montana," 29, 33.

16. Ibid., 33–35; Fletcher, *Free Grass to Fences*, 48.

17. Fletcher, *Free Grass to Fences*, 49.

18. Frink, Jackson, and Spring, *When Grass Was King*, 68.

19. Stewart, "Major Brisbin's Relief of Fort Pease," in Hedren, ed., *The Great Sioux War*, 115–21; Brisbin, *The Beef Bonanza*, xi–xii, 83–84, 158.

20. Fletcher, *Free Grass to Fences*, 52.

21. Rollinson, *Wyoming Cattle Trails*, 340; Brown, *The Plainsmen of the Yellowstone*, 377.

22. Rollinson, *Wyoming Cattle Trails*, 339–40; Brown, *The Plainsmen of the Yellowstone*, 377.

23. Briggs, *Frontiers of the Northwest*, 225–26; Hoopes, *This Last West*, 266, 312; Stuart, *Pioneering in Montana*, 188.

24. Mattison, "Ranching in the Dakota Badlands, Part 1," 97, quoting the *Bismarck Weekly Tribune*, February 13, 1880.

25. Hedren, *Fort Laramie in 1876*, 155–56; "Report of the Commission Appointed to Obtain Certain Concessions from the Sioux," in U.S. Department of the Interior, *Report of the Commissioner of Indian Affairs, 1876*, 330–56.

26. Mattison, "Ranching in the Dakota Badlands, Part 1," 97; Pelzer, *The Cattlemen's Frontier*, 195–201.

27. Quoted in Mattison, "Ranching in the Dakota Badlands, Part 1," 99.

28. Mattison, "Ranching in the Dakota Badlands, Part 2," 184–87; Huidekoper, *My Experiences and Investment in the Bad Lands of Dakota and Some of the Men I Met There*, 22–23.

29. Mattison, "Ranching in the Dakota Badlands, Part 2," 191, 198–201; Tweton, *The Marquis de Morès*, 21.

30. Pelzer, *The Cattlemen's Frontier*, 201–202.

31. Hagen and Mattison, "Pyramid Park," 221–22, 230–31.

32. Mattison, "Ranching in the Dakota Badlands, Part 1," 110–12.

33. Briggs, *Frontiers of the Northwest*, 228; Tweton, *The Marquis de Morès*, 20–21.

34. Tweton, *The Marquis de Morès*, 25, 27–29.

35. Ibid., 30–31; Briggs, *Frontiers of the Northwest*, 229–30.

36. Tweton, *The Marquis de Morès*, 33–40; Briggs, *Frontiers of the Northwest*, 231.

37. Tweton, *The Marquis de Morès*, 40 (quotation), 42, 45, 50; Briggs, *Frontiers of the Northwest*, 231.

38. Briggs, *Frontiers of the Northwest*, 232.

39. Ibid., 116; Morris, *The Rise of Theodore Roosevelt*, 218–24.

40. Mattison, *Roosevelt's Dakota Ranches*, 3–5.

41. Mattison, "Ranching in the Dakota Badlands, Part 2," 183, 191, 193; Briggs, *Frontiers of the Northwest*, 222–23; Morris, *The Rise of Theodore Roosevelt*, 240–44; Hagedorn, *Roosevelt in the Bad Lands*, 465–68 (quotation on 466).

42. Crawford, *Ranching Days in Dakota and Custer's Black Hills Expedition of 1874*, 22–25; Hoopes, *This Last West*, 156–57, 181, 199–200.

43. Yost, *The Call of the Range*, 170–86; Aeschbacher, "Development of Cattle Raising in the Sandhills"; McIntosh, *The Nebraska Sand Hills*, 103–106.

44. Woods, *Wyoming's Big Horn Basin to 1901*, 72–77; Briggs, *Frontiers of the Northwest*, 219.

45. Frink, Jackson, and Spring, *When Grass Was King*, 26; Briggs, *Frontiers of the Northwest*, 220; Morris, *The Rise of Theodore Roosevelt*, 339.

46. Briggs, *Frontiers of the Northwest*, 236–38.

47. Ibid., 238–41; Rackley, "The Hard Winter of 1886–1887"; Stuart, "The Winter of 1886–1887," 32–38.

48. Briggs, *Frontiers of the Northwest*, 241–42, quoting either the *Bismarck Daily Tribune* or *Mandan Daily Pioneer*; Frink, Jackson, and Spring, *When Grass Was King*, 98–100.

49. Stuart, *Pioneering in Montana*, 237.

50. Ibid., 243–44; Mattison, "Ranching in the Dakota Badlands, Part 2," 171; Hagedorn, *Roosevelt in the Bad Lands*, 440–41; Mattison, "Ranching in the Dakota Badlands, Part 1," 123–24; Mattison, "The Hard Winter and the Range Cattle Business"; Fletcher, *Free Grass to Fences*, 90; Jordan, *North American Cattle-Ranching Frontiers*, 238. Some scholars have tended to downplay the claims of extravagant losses in the winter of 1886–87. T. A. Larson of the University of Wyoming labeled the reported losses in Wyoming of eighty and ninety percent "fantastic." While isolated herds may have suffered at extreme rates, Larson estimated that the losses for the whole of Wyoming Territory were not far above fifteen percent. Frink,

Cow Country Cavalcade, 59–60. Jordan, the most recent scholar to examine the saga of cattle on the American frontier, accepts the larger numbers, as I do.

51. Briggs, *Frontiers of the Northwest*, 244–46; Osgood, *The Day of the Cattleman*, 224–29; Dale, *The Range Cattle Industry*, 98; Stuart, "The Winter of 1886–1887," 39–41; Davis, *Wyoming Range War*, 282–83.

Chapter 7. Cycles of Despair and Death

1. Brininstool, *Troopers with Custer*, 145; Graham, *The Reno Court of Inquiry*, 34, 85, 99, 197.

2. Gray, *Centennial Campaign*, 194, 339–40; Bray, *Crazy Horse*, 162, 234–35.

3. Willert, "The Sibley Scout"; Bray, *Crazy Horse*, 240; Gray, *Centennial Campaign*, 341–44. Regarding the "Rule of 1876," see the communication between Brigadier General Alfred Terry and the Military Division of the Missouri, March 24, 1881, in "Sioux Campaign," Special Files of Headquarters, Military Division of the Missouri, Microfilm Publication 1495, National Archives.

4. The surrenders and general disposition of the Northern Nation at war's end are well treated in Powell, *People of the Sacred Mountain*, 2:1141–51; Hyde, *Spotted Tail's Folk*, 266–70; Buecker, *Fort Robinson and the American West*, 92–95. See also the report of J[esse] M. Lee, Spotted Tail Agency, August 10, 1877, in U.S. Department of the Interior, *Report of the Secretary of the Interior, 1877*, 462; and Anderson, "A History of the Cheyenne River Indian Agency and Its Military Post," 472.

5. Buecker and Paul, eds., *The Crazy Horse Surrender Ledger*, 7–16; Bray, *Crazy Horse*, 80, 273–84; Paul, "An Early Reference to Crazy Horse," 189; Utley, *The Lance and the Shield*, 180–82.

6. Svingen, *The Northern Cheyenne Indian Reservation*, 2–6; West, *The Contested Plains*, 68–71; Kappler, ed., *Indian Affairs*, 984–89.

7. Kappler, ed., *Indian Affairs*, 1012–15; Svingen, *The Northern Cheyenne Indian Reservation*, 7, 13; Buecker, *Fort Robinson and the American West*, 125; U.S. Department of the Interior, *Report of the Secretary of the Interior, 1877*, 415 (quotation).

8. Svingen, *The Northern Cheyenne Indian Reservation*, 13, 17–19; Buecker, *Fort Robinson and the American West*, 125–26.

9. Svingen, *The Northern Cheyenne Indian Reservation*, 18–19; Buecker, *Fort Robinson and the American West*, 126–27; Utley, *Frontier Regulars*, 282–83; Grinnell, *The Fighting Cheyennes*, 400.

10. Buecker, *Fort Robinson and the American West*, 127; Grinnell, *The Fighting Cheyennes*, 401–403 (quotation on 403).

11. Powell, *People of the Sacred Mountain*, 1420; Monnett, *Tell Them We Are Going Home*, 16–17; Greene, *Morning Star Dawn*, 50–51.

12. Powell, *People of the Sacred Mountain*, 1419; Monnett, *Tell Them We Are Going Home*, 10–11; Greene, *Morning Star Dawn*, 50–51; Roberts, "The Shame of Little Wolf," 38–39.

13. Buecker, *Fort Robinson and the American West*, 128–29; Utley, *Frontier Regulars*, 283. The Punished Woman's Fork battle is treated exhaustively by Hoig, *Perilous Pursuit*, chapter 13; and Monnett, *Tell Them We Are Going Home*, chapter 4.

14. Buecker, *Fort Robinson and the American West*, 131–33; Monnett, *Tell Them We Are Going Home*, 109–10.

15. Buecker, *Fort Robinson and the American West*, 136–38; Utley, *Frontier Regulars*, 283.

16. Grinnell, *The Fighting Cheyennes*, 418–22 (quotation on 418); Buecker, *Fort Robinson and the American West*, 138–41.

17. Buecker, *Fort Robinson and the American West*, 142–46 (quotation on 146, citing the *Army and Navy Journal*, February 1, 1879).

18. Buecker, *Fort Robinson and the American West*, 147; Grinnell, *The Fighting Cheyennes*, 426.

19. Monnett, *Tell Them We Are Going Home*, 162–69; Roberts, "The Shame of Little Wolf," 41–42.

20. Svingen, *The Northern Cheyenne Indian Reservation*, 21–23, 44; Monnett, *Tell Them We Are Going Home*, 191.

21. Starita, *The Dull Knifes of Pine Ridge*, 69; Monnett, *Tell Them We Are Going Home*, 192, 194.

22. Stands in Timber and Liberty, *Cheyenne Memories*, 47; Svingen, *The Northern Cheyenne Indian Reservation*, 45; Monnett, *Tell Them We Are Going Home*, 195–99; Roberts, "The Shame of Little Wolf," 43–47.

23. Buecker, *Fort Robinson and the American West*, 104–10; Buecker, "Uncertain Surrender," 35–38; Pearson, "Tragedy at Red Cloud Agency," 16–20.

24. Pearson, "Tragedy at Red Cloud Agency," 20–21.

25. Ibid., 21–22.

26. Bray, *Crazy Horse*, 362–72; Pearson, "Tragedy at Red Cloud Agency," 22–23; "Gen. Jesse M. Lee's Account of the Killing of Chief Crazy Horse at Fort Robinson, Nebr.," in Brininstool, ed., *Crazy Horse*, 28–30.

27. Bray, *Crazy Horse*, 380; Buecker, *Fort Robinson and the American West*, 114–15; Pearson, "Tragedy at Red Cloud Agency," 24–25.

28. Buecker, *Fort Robinson and the American West*, 115; Pearson, "Tragedy at Red Cloud Agency," 24–25. The commonplace use of Fort Marion, Florida, as a prison for Plains Indian leaders in the 1870s is detailed by Lookingbill, *War Dance at Fort Marion*.

29. Hardorff, ed., *The Surrender and Death of Crazy Horse*, 147.

30. Buecker, *Fort Robinson and the American West*, 116; Pearson, "Tragedy at Red Cloud Agency," 25–26; Bray, *Crazy Horse*, 383–85; "Louis Bordeaux Interview," in Hardorff, ed., *The Surrender and Death of Crazy Horse*, 110 (quotation). On Gentles, a disputed but critical figure in this story, see Clark, ed., *The Killing of Chief Crazy Horse*, 143–44; John M. Carroll, foreword to Hardorff, *The Oglala Lakota Crazy Horse*, 9–17; Dickson, "Crazy Horse"; and Hardorff, ed., *The Surrender and Death of Crazy Horse*, 147–48.

31. Pearson, "Tragedy at Red Cloud Agency," 26–27; Bray, *Crazy Horse*, 386–87; Hardorff, ed., *The Surrender and Death of Crazy Horse*, 147–48, 184 (quotation).

32. Kadlecek and Kadlecek, *To Kill an Eagle*, 58; Bray, *Crazy Horse*, 391–94.

33. Pearson, "Tragedy at Red Cloud Agency," 27 (Clark quotation); Brininstool, ed., *Crazy Horse*, 39 (Lee quotation); Hardorff, ed., *The Surrender and Death of Crazy Horse*, 238–60; *Cheyenne Daily Leader*, September 9, 12, 1877; *Omaha Daily Bee*, September 6, 1877.

34. Buecker, *Fort Robinson and the American West*, 118–19; Hedren, *Fort Laramie in 1876*, 6. The agency provision appears in article 4 of the 1868 Treaty. Kappler, ed., *Indian Affairs*, 999 (quotation).

35. Buecker, *Fort Robinson and the American West*, 119–20; Olson, *Red Cloud and the Sioux Problem*, 254–55; Bray, "'We Belong to the North,'" 34.

36. Bray, "'We Belong to the North,'" 34.

37. Ibid., 33–35.

38. Ibid., 38–41.

39. Ibid., 39, 42.

40. Olson, *Red Cloud and the Sioux Problem*, 255–57.

41. Ibid., 258–59, 262–63; "Report of the Commissioner of Indian Affairs, November 1, 1878," and "Report of Wm. J. Pollock, Rosebud Agency, October 1, 1878," in U.S. Department of the Interior, *Report of the Secretary of the Interior, 1878*, 460–62, 534–35, respectively.

42. "Report of V. T. McGillycuddy, Pine Ridge Agency, October 15, 1879," in U.S. Department of the Interior, *Report of the Secretary of the Interior, 1879*, 143.

43. Nugent, *Habits of Empire*, 74; LaDow, *The Medicine Line*, 6–7; Barbour, *Fort Union and the Upper Missouri Fur Trade*, 24–25. LaDow narrowly defines the Medicine Line, suggesting that it was "scarcely more than one hundred miles long," encompassing the border more or less north of Harlem and Havre in north-central Montana (3). Most certainly, however,

this powerful, even mystical line spanned the entire prairie region of Dakota and Montana from the Red River of the North to the Rocky Mountains.

44. Rees, *Arc of the Medicine Line*, 5; LaDow, *The Medicine Line*, 10–11; McGrady, *Living with Strangers*, 30–31; Greene, *Beyond Bear's Paw*, 15–16.

45. Utley, *The Lance and the Shield*, 183–84, 189–90.

46. Ibid., 186–89; McGrady, *Living with Strangers*, 70–73 (quotation on 73).

47. Utley, *The Lance and the Shield*, 191; Joyner, "The Hegira of Sitting Bull to Canada," 8–9.

48. Utley, *The Lance and the Shield*, 191–92; *Report of the Sitting Bull Indian Commission*, 4–6; *Records of Living Officers of the United States Army*, 12–13; Diehl, *The Staff Correspondent*, 118; "Papers relating to the Sioux Indians of the United States who have taken refuge in Canadian Territory," Public Archives of Canada, 77, RG 7, Governor General's Office Numbered Files; Seventh Cavalry Regimental Return, October 1877, Microcopy 744, National Archives; Seventh Infantry Regimental Return, October 1877, Microcopy 665, National Archives.

49. *Report of the Sitting Bull Indian Commission*, 6; Zimmer, *Frontier Soldier*, 134–35; Second Cavalry Regimental Return, October 1877, Microcopy 744, National Archives; Diehl, *The Staff Correspondent*, 124–25; *Benton Record*, October 26, 1877.

50. Utley, *The Lance and the Shield*, 192–93; Greene, *Beyond Bear's Paw*, 36–39.

51. This admonishment appeared in the *New York Herald*, October 22, 1877, and a slightly different version in the *Chicago Times*, October 23, 1877. See also Manzione, *"I Am Looking to the North for My Life,"* 100; and Greene, *Beyond Bear's Paw*, 38.

52. *Report of the Sitting Bull Indian Commission*, 6; Joyner, "The Hegira of Sitting Bull to Canada," 12; Greene, *Beyond Bear's Paw*, 41.

53. Utley, *The Lance and the Shield*, 194–95; *Report of the Sitting Bull Indian Commission*, 6; Greene, *Beyond Bear's Paw*, 40. Rain in the Face was specifically noted among Indian dancers the evening before. Contemporary sources do not record him among the chiefs and headmen present at the meeting with the commission on October 17, but his presence seems logical.

54. The president's entire address, word for word, is found in *Report of the Sitting Bull Indian Commission*, 6–8 (Terry quotations), and was also reprinted in full in the *New York Herald*, October 22 and 23, 1877, and *Army and Navy Journal*, October 27, 1877; see respectively Abrams, *Newspaper Chronicle of the Indian Wars*, 148–67; and Hutchins, The Army and Navy Journal *on the Battle of the Little Bighorn and Related Matters*, 158–59. For a useful recap, see Utley, *The Lance and the Shield*, 195–96.

55. Sitting Bull's responses, word for word, are recorded in *Report of the Sitting Bull Indian Commission*, 8–9. See also Utley, *The Lance and the Shield*, 196.

56. Utley, *The Lance and the Shield*, 197–98; *Report of the Sitting Bull Indian Commission*, 11 (first quotation); Joyner, "The Hegira of Sitting Bull to Canada," 13–14 (second quotation on 14).

57. McGrady, *Living with Strangers*, 73–74. McGrady's estimates are well justified and appear definitive. Utley, *The Lance and the Shield*, 200, suggests upward of eight hundred lodges and five thousand people, including the Nez Perces; Greene, *Beyond Bear's Paw*, 27, proposes a range of four thousand to five thousand Sioux.

58. Utley, *The Lance and the Shield*, 201–202; McGrady, *Living with Strangers*, 90–91; DeMallie, "The Sioux in Dakota and Montana Territories," 46; Dobak, "Killing the Canadian Buffalo."

59. Utley, *The Lance and the Shield*, 208–209; Larson, *Gall*, 165–66; Greene, *Yellowstone Command*, 227–28.

60. Manzione, *"I Am Looking to the North for My Life,"* 132, 138; Larson, *Gall*, 166–67; Joyner, "The Hegira of Sitting Bull to Canada," 15–16.

61. DeMallie, "The Sioux in Dakota and Montana Territories," 46–54; Larson, *Gall*, 170–71; Utley, *The Lance and the Shield*, 218, noting Spotted Eagle's quiet disappearance from Fort Keogh and his being among those surrendering at Fort Buford on July 19. See "List of Indian Prisoners of War, Sitting Bull's Band," 1881, appendix C, in Greene, *Fort Randall on the Missouri*, with Spotted Eagle and his family noted on 187.

62. The story of Sitting Bull's surrender is told in full by Hedren, *Sitting Bull's Surrender at Fort Buford*, with Sitting Bull's statement on 29.

63. Ibid., 33, 35.

64. Greene, *Fort Randall on the Missouri*, 140–47.

65. Utley, *The Lance and the Shield*, 241.

66. Papandrea, *They Never Surrendered*, 1, 6–7, 26–27.

67. These matters of transitional change are thoughtfully explored by Utley, *The Indian Frontier of the American West*, 227–30; and Larson, *Red Cloud*, 217–18.

68. Utley, *The Indian Frontier of the American West*, 236 (quotation), 239–41.

69. Ibid., 241–45.

70. Hyde, *Spotted Tail's Folk*, 298–301; Hyde, *A Sioux Chronicle*, 63–65; Clow, "The Anatomy of a Shooting"; Robinson, ed., *The Diaries of John Gregory Bourke*, 146 (Crook quotation).

71. Utley, *The Indian Frontier of the American West*, 246; Greene, "The Sioux Land Commission of 1889," 41–42.

72. Greene, "The Sioux Land Commission of 1889," 43; Olson, *Red Cloud and the Sioux Problem*, 309.

73. Utley, *The Indian Frontier of the American West*, 247; Utley, *The Lance and the Shield*, 272; Greene, "The Sioux Land Commission of 1889," 44–45.

74. Utley, *The Indian Frontier of the American West*, 247–49, 251 (quotation); Robinson, *General Crook and the Western Frontier*, 299.

75. Utley, *The Indian Frontier of the American West*, 249; Olson, *Red Cloud and the Sioux Problem*, 321 (quotation).

76. Olson, *Red Cloud and the Sioux Problem*, 321; Utley, *The Indian Frontier of the American West*, 251; Utley, *The Lance and the Shield*, 278–79; Larson, *Gall*, 208.

77. This description is drawn closely from Utley, *The Indian Frontier of the American West*, 251–52; but see also Andersson, *The Lakota Ghost Dance of 1890*, 24–29.

78. Utley, *The Indian Frontier of the American West*, 253–54; Andersson, *The Lakota Ghost Dance of 1890*, 46, 67–68, 105.

79. Olson, *Red Cloud and the Sioux Problem*, 322–23; Larson, *Gall*, 212–13; Utley, *The Lance and the Shield*, 284–85.

80. Utley, *The Indian Frontier of the American West*, 254–55.

81. Ibid., 255; Utley, *The Lance and the Shield*, 296–307.

82. Utley, *The Indian Frontier of the American West*, 255–56.

83. Ibid., 257; Utley, *Frontier Regulars*, 406–409.

84. Jensen, Paul, and Carter, *Eyewitness at Wounded Knee*, 100–117.

85. Andersson, *The Lakota Ghost Dance of* 1890, 158–61.

86. Larson, *Gall*, 230–38.

87. In addition to the histories of Red Cloud and his times cited repeatedly in this chapter, see also Hyde, *Red Cloud's Folk*; Paul, ed., *Autobiography of Red Cloud*; and Goodyear, *Red Cloud*.

Chapter 8. Sacred Ground

1. On Sheridan and Custer, see Hutton, *Phil Sheridan and His Army*, 32, 305–11. The reverential "holy ground where our poor men died like sheep in the shambles" was penned on July 21, 1877, by First Lieutenant John G. Bourke, Third Cavalry, who accompanied Sheridan to the Little Big Horn Battlefield. Robinson, ed., *The Diaries of John Gregory Bourke*, 339. The Sheridan-Sherman communication regarding a national cemetery, dated April 8, 1878, appears in Philip H. Sheridan Papers, MSS 19,308, Reel 9, Library of Congress (hereafter Sheridan Papers).

2. Hardorff, *The Custer Battle Casualties*, 23–31; Greene, *Stricken Field*, 19–20; Barnard, *Ten Years with Custer*, 304 (quotation).

3. Marquis, *Custer, Cavalry & Crows*, 82 (first quotation); Paul L. Hedren, "'Holy Ground': The United States Army Embraces Custer's Battlefield," in Rankin, ed., *Legacy*, 189–90; Gray, "Captain Clifford's Story— Part II," 83 (second quotation).

4. Hardorff, *The Custer Battle Casualties*, 53–54; Faust, *This Republic Is Suffering*, 61, 80; "Custer's Braves," *Saint Paul and Minneapolis Pioneer Press*, May 24, 1877 (quotation).

5. Sheridan to Terry, March 26, 1877, Reel 8, Sheridan Papers.

6. Sheridan to Sherman, April 4, 1877, Edward D. Townsend to Sheridan, April 18, 1877, Townsend to Sheridan, April 28, 1877, Reel 8, Sheridan Papers; Hedren, "'Holy Ground,'" 193.

7. Military Division of the Missouri Special Orders No. 40, May 16, 1877, copy at Little Bighorn Battlefield National Monument; Reno to George A. Forsyth, April 29, 1877, P. H. Sheridan to M. V. Sheridan, May 16, 1877, Reel 8, Sheridan Papers; Hedren, "'Holy Ground,'" 193.

8. P. H. Sheridan to M. V. Sheridan, May 16, 1877, Thomas L. Crittenden to P. H. Sheridan, May 10, 1877, Reel 8, Sheridan Papers; Hedren, "'Holy Ground,'" 193.

9. Hardorff, *The Custer Battle Casualties*, 37; "Colonel Sheridan's Report," in Graham, ed., *The Custer Myth*, 373; Department of Dakota Special Orders No. 63, May 22, 1877, Record Group 393, Entry 1191, National Archives; Hedren, *Great Sioux War Orders of Battle*, 152–54.

10. Hardorff, *The Custer Battle Casualties*, 38–39; "Colonel Sheridan's Report," 374–75.

11. Hardorff, *The Custer Battle Casualties*, 39 (first quotation); Scott, *Some Memories of a Soldier*, 48 (second quotation).

12. "Colonel Sheridan's Report," 374–75.

13. Ibid.; Hardorff, *The Custer Battle Casualties*, 39–40, 45, 46 (quotations).

14. "Colonel Sheridan's Report," 374–75; Hardorff, *The Custer Battle Casualties*, 40–42.

15. "Colonel Sheridan's Report," 375.

16. Robinson, ed., *The Diaries of John Gregory Bourke*, 339–41.

17. Wheeler, *Buffalo Days*, 169; Greene, *Stricken Field*, 25, quoting A. W. Shannehan in *Winners of the West*, August 30, 1932; Hedren, ed., "Eben Swift's Army Service on the Plains," 148.

18. Forsyth to Sheridan, April 8, 1878, Reel 9, Sheridan Papers.

19. Sheridan to Sherman, April 8, 1878, Reel 9, Sheridan Papers.

20. Bischoff, "Deadwood to the Big Horns, 1877," 27; Allen, *Adventures with Indians and Game*, 68–69.

21. Harry Lee Bailey, Twenty-first U.S. Infantry, "On the Custer Field," Papers of the Order of Indian Wars, U.S. Army Military History Institute; Hardorff, *The Custer Battle Casualties*, 65.

22. Fort Custer Letter Sent, August 30, 1878, copy at Little Bighorn Battlefield National Monument; Spring, *The Cheyenne and Black Hills Stage and Express Routes*, 291–92.

23. Greene, *Stricken Field*, 28–29; Brust, Pohanka, and Barnard, *Where Custer Fell*, 112, 115–17.

24. Hardorff, *The Custer Battle Casualties*, 66; Greene, *Stricken Field*, 28, quoting Department of Dakota AAG to Buell, October 29, 1878, copy at Little Bighorn Battlefield National Monument.

25. Sanderson to Post Adjutant, Fort Custer, April 7, 1879, copy at Little Bighorn Battlefield National Monument; Greene, *Stricken Field*, 29; Hardorff, *The Custer Battle Casualties*, 67 68; Brust, "Stanley J. Morrow's 1879 Photographs of the Little Big Horn Battlefield," 47–78. The earliest surviving photograph of the Custer Battlefield was taken by John H. Fouch on July 7, 1877, just after Michael Sheridan's departure. See Brust, "John H. Fouch"; and Brust, Pohanka, and Barnard, *Where Custer Fell*, 130–32.

26. Custer, *Boots and Saddles*, 268 (quotation); Stewart, "The Custer Battle and Widow's Weeds," 53.

27. Hutchins, ed., The Army and Navy Journal *on the Battle of the Little Bighorn and Related Matters*, citing "The Widows and Orphans," July 15, 1876, 32, and "A Widows' Relief Fund," July 29, 1876, 60 (quotation), 61.

28. Hutchins, "Introduction," in The Army and Navy Journal *on the Battle of the Little Bighorn and Related Matters*, 11; Bigelow, *William Conant Church & The Army and Navy Journal*, 204.

29. Hutchins, The Army and Navy Journal *on the Battle of the Little Bighorn and Related Matters*, 63, 85 (quotations), 238–40, 252. Subscriptions to the Widows' Relief Fund are reported in full on 238–53.

30. Ibid., 89–90, 98 (quotation), 109–10; Stewart, "The Custer Battle and Widow's Weeds," 54–57; Hedren, "'Holy Ground,'" 192. The widows and children of enlisted men were enumerated in the *Army and Navy Journal*, October 28, 1876 (Hutchins, The Army and Navy Journal *on the Battle of the Little Bighorn and Related Matters*, 110), copying the "List of Widows of Enlisted Men, 7th U.S. Cavalry" provided by the army; see also Reel 9, Sheridan Papers. Stewart's list is improperly transcribed.

31. Hutchins, The Army and Navy Journal *on the Battle of the Little Bighorn and Related Matters*, 14, 163 (quotation).

32. On the Noyes, Moore, and Reynolds courts-martial, see Vaughn, *The Reynolds Campaign on Powder River*, 166–90; Hedren, *Fort Laramie in 1876*, 80–82, 216–17; and Barnett, "Powder River."

33. On Reno during these postwar years, see Donovan, *A Terrible Glory*, 349–52; and Nichols, *In Custer's Shadow*, 239–61.

34. Wilhelm, *A Military Dictionary and Gazetteer*, 119.

35. Donovan, *A Terrible Glory*, 353–56. Donovan's synopsis of the Reno court is the finest in the literature, but see also Bookwalter, *Honor Tarnished;* Johnson, "'Operation Whitewash'? A Reconsideration of the Reno Court of Inquiry," in Taunton, ed., *"No Pride in the Little Big Horn,"* 42–51; and Graham, preface to *Abstract of the Official Record of Proceedings of the Reno Court of Inquiry,* iii–xiv.

36. Donovan, *A Terrible Glory*, 366–70, 371 (quotation); Nichols, comp. and ed., *Reno Court of Inquiry,* x–xii; Johnson, "'Operation Whitewash'?" 49.

37. Donovan, *A Terrible Glory*, 378–80; Johnson, "'Operation Whitewash'?"; General Orders No. 17, March 11, 1879, Headquarters of the Army, Adjutant General's Office, RG 393, National Archives; Nichols, comp. and ed., *Reno Court of Inquiry,* 627–28, 629 (quotation). The official record of the Reno Court of Inquiry ran some thirteen hundred foolscap pages; although kept from the public for some three-quarters of a century, it is easily accessed today. The Nichols edition, *Reno Court of Inquiry,* is complete and is the most useful. Several newspaper versions are available, including the important *Chicago Times* account (*Reno Court of Inquiry*); and *Saint Paul and Minneapolis Pioneer Press* version (*Reno Court of Inquiry*). Also useful is the careful reporting in *The Army and Navy Journal* (Hutchins, ed., The Army and Navy Journal *on the Battle of the Little Bighorn and Related Matters*). Graham's *Abstract of the Official Record of Proceedings of the Reno Court of Inquiry* is useful both for its succinctness and clarity and for the author's important additions and interpretations of military jurisprudence.

38. Donovan, *A Terrible Glory*, 377, 378 (quotation), 379–82; Johnson, "'Operation Whitewash'?" 49–50.

39. Greene, *Stricken Field,* 29; Gray, "Nightmares to Daydreams," 37, reprinting in full Sanderson's report of April 7, 1879.

40. Holt, *American Military Cemeteries,* 2–3. The emphasis throughout this era was on the careful burial of Union dead. The burial and reburial of Confederate dead and the marking of Confederate graves were largely undertaken through the initiatives of Southern communities and Confederate veterans' organizations and not systematized in the National Cemetery movement.

41. Ibid., 143.

42. General Orders No. 78, August 1, 1879, Headquarters of the Army, Adjutant General's Office, RG 393, National Archives. The classification system was based on the relative size of the cemetery (this one considered small) and the pay of the superintendent, which varied from $75 per month for first-class cemeteries to $60 per month for fourth-class. See General Orders No. 51, June 22, 1872, Headquarters of the Army, Adjutant General's Office, RG 393, National Archives.

43. "Report of the Quartermaster-General," October 10, 1879, in U.S. War Department, *Report of the Secretary of War, 1879,* 229, 230 (quotation). On the West Point monument, see Minnie Dubbs Millbrook, "A Monument to Custer," in Hedren, ed., *The Great Sioux War 1876–1877;* and Hutchins, ed., The Army and Navy Journal *on the Battle of the Little Bighorn and Related Matters,* 199, 201.

44. Greene, *Stricken Field,* 31; Roe to Assistant Adjutant General, Department of the Dakota, August 6, 1881, copy at Little Bighorn Battlefield National Monument (hereafter Roe Report); Hutchins, ed., The Army and Navy Journal *on the Battle of the Little Bighorn and Related Matters,* 211 (inscription).

45. Greene, *Stricken Field,* 31–32; Hardorff, *The Custer Battle Casualties,* 69; Roe Report.

46. Fort Custer Orders No. 81, July 5, 1881, Record Group 393, Fort Custer, Mont. (111), Entry 12, National Archives; Roe Report; Davidson to Assistant Adjutant General, Department of the Dakota, February 25, 1881, copy at Little Bighorn Battlefield National Monument. The notion of gathering all the remains at Little Big Horn Battlefield and placing them in a vault beneath the granite monument was noted as early as August 1879 in the "Report of Capt. A. F. Rockwell, in Charge of National Cemeteries," in U.S. War Department, *Report of the Secretary of War, 1879,* 364. Roe included sketches showing the derrick crane, foundation, and monument (reproduced in Greene, *Stricken Field,* 109).

47. Roe Report.

48. Ibid.; Greene, *Stricken Field,* 40.

49. Sellars, "Vigil of Silence."

Bibliography

MANUSCRIPT COLLECTIONS

Arizona Historical Society, Tucson
  Natalie Beaumont Forsyth Collection.
Fort Union Trading Post National Historic Site, Williston, North Dakota
  Fort Buford Records.
Library of Congress, Washington, D.C.
  Philip H. Sheridan Papers.
  William Tecumseh Sherman Papers.
Little Bighorn Battlefield National Monument, Crow Agency, Montana
  Archival Collections.
National Archives and Records Service, Washington, D.C.
  Microcopy 617, Cantonment Bad Lands Post Returns, 1880, 1882–83; Fort Abraham Lincoln Post Returns, 1878–79; Fort Keogh Post Returns, 1886.
  Microcopy 665, Seventh Infantry Regimental Returns, 1877.
  Microcopy 744, Second Cavalry Regimental Returns, 1877; Seventh Cavalry Regimental Returns, 1877.
  Microfilm Publication 1495, "Sioux Campaign." Special Files of Headquarters, Military Division of the Missouri.
  Record Group 94, Records of the Office of the Adjutant General. George P. Buell Appointment, Commission, Personal File.
  Record Group 393, Records of United States Army Continental Commands Cantonment Bad Lands Letters Sent, 1880; Cantonment Bad Lands Order Books, 1879, 1880, 1882; Department of Dakota General Orders, 1880–81; Department of Dakota General Orders,

Northern Pacific Railroad Escort, 1880; Department of Dakota Letters and Endorsements, Northern Pacific Railroad Escort, 1880; Department of Dakota Orders Issued, Northern Pacific Railroad Escort, 1881–82; Department of Dakota Special Orders, 1877, 1879–83; Department of Dakota Telegrams Received, Northern Pacific Railroad Escort, 1880; Fort Custer Orders, 1881; Headquarters of the Army General Orders, 1872, 1877, 1879; Headquarters of the Army Special Orders, 1877.

Public Archives of Canada, Ottawa
Record Group 7, Governor General's Office Numbered Files, "Papers relating to the Sioux Indians of the United States who have taken refuge in Canadian Territory" [ca. 1879].

U.S. Army Military History Institute, Carlisle Barracks, Pennsylvania Order of Indian Wars Collection.

Government Documents

Report of the Sitting Bull Indian Commission. Washington, D.C.: Government Printing Office, 1877.

U.S. Department of the Interior. *Report of the Commissioner of Indian Affairs, 1876.* Washington, D.C.: Government Printing Office, 1876.

———. *Report of the Secretary of the Interior, 1878.* Washington, D.C.: Government Printing Office, 1879.

———. *Report of the Secretary of the Interior, 1879.* Washington, D.C.: Government Printing Office, 1880.

U.S. War Department. *Report of the Secretary of War, 1875.* Washington, D.C.: Government Printing Office, 1875.

———. *Report of the Secretary of War, 1877.* Washington, D.C.: Government Printing Office, 1877.

———. *Report of the Secretary of War, 1878.* Washington, D.C.: Government Printing Office, 1878.

———. *Report of the Secretary of War, 1879.* Washington, D.C.: Government Printing Office, 1879.

———. *Report of the Secretary of War, 1880.* Washington, D.C.: Government Printing Office, 1880.

———. *Report of the Secretary of War, 1881.* Washington, D.C.: Government Printing Office, 1881.

———. *Report of the Secretary of War, 1882.* Washington, D.C.: Government Printing Office, 1882.

———. *Report of the Secretary of War, 1884.* Washington, D.C.: Government Printing Office, 1884.

Books and Articles

Abrams, Marc H. *Newspaper Chronicle of the Indian Wars.* Vol. 9. Brooklyn: privately printed, 2010.

Adams, Gerald M. *The Post near Cheyenne: A History of Fort D. A. Russell, 1867–1930.* Boulder, Colo.: Pruett Publishing Co., 1989.

Aeschbacher, W. D. "Development of Cattle Raising in the Sandhills." *Nebraska History* 28 (January–March 1947): 41–64.

Allen, William A. *Adventures with Indians and Game, or Twenty Years in the Rocky Mountains.* Chicago: A. W. Bowen and Co., 1903.

Altsheler, Joseph A. *The Last of the Chiefs: A Story of the Great Sioux War.* New York: D. Appleton and Co., 1909.

Anderson, Harry H. "A Challenge to Brown's Indian Wars Thesis." *Montana The Magazine of Western History* 12 (January 1962): 40–49.

———. "A History of the Cheyenne River Indian Agency and Its Military Post, Fort Bennett, 1868–1891." In *South Dakota Report and Historical Collections,* vol. 28, 390–551. Pierre: South Dakota Historical Society, 1957.

———. "Indian Peace-Talkers and the Conclusion of the Sioux War of 1876." *Nebraska History* 44 (December 1963): 233–55.

———. "Silence Not Acquiescence." *Montana The Magazine of Western History* 12 (Summer 1962): 80.

———. "Two Slips Corrected." *Montana The Magazine of Western History* 13 (Winter 1963): 87.

Andersson, Rani-Henrik. *The Lakota Ghost Dance of 1890.* Lincoln: University of Nebraska Press, 2008.

Barbour, Barton H. *Fort Union and the Upper Missouri Fur Trade.* Norman: University of Oklahoma Press, 2001.

Barnard, Sandy. *Ten Years with Custer: A 7th Cavalryman's Memoirs.* Terre Haute, Ind.: AST Press, 2001.

Barnett, LeRoy. "The Buffalo Bone Commerce on the Northern Plains." *North Dakota History* 39 (Winter 1972): 23–42.

———. "Ghastly Harvest: Montana's Trade in Buffalo Bones." *Montana The Magazine of Western History* 25 (Summer 1975): 2–13.

Barnett, Louise. "Powder River." *Greasy Grass* 16 (May 2000): 2–9, 11–12.

Bigelow, Donald N. *William Conant Church & The Army and Navy Journal.* New York: Columbia University Press, 1952.

Bischoff, Herman. "Deadwood to the Big Horns, 1877" (translated by Edna L. Waldo). *Annals of Wyoming* 9 (April 1933–January 1935): 19–34.

Bollinger, Gil. *Fort McKinney 1877 to 1894: A Wyoming Frontier Post.* Buffalo, Wyo.: Jim Gatchell Memorial Museum Press, 2006.

Bookwalter, Thomas E. *Honor Tarnished: The Reno Court of Inquiry.* West Carrollton, Ohio: Little Horn Press, 1979.

Bourke, John G. *On the Border with Crook.* New York: Charles Scribner's Sons, 1891.

Bowen, William H. O. [*sic:* C.]. "The Passing of the Buffalo." *Oregon Sportsman* 2 (November 1925): 14–15.

Bray, Kingsley M. *Crazy Horse: A Lakota Life.* Norman: University of Oklahoma Press, 2006.

———. "Teton Sioux Population History, 1655–1881." *Nebraska History* 75 (Summer 1994): 165–88.

———. "'We Belong to the North': The Flights of the Northern Indians from the White River Agencies, 1877–1878." *Montana The Magazine of Western History* 55 (Summer 2005): 28–47.

Briggs, Harold E. *Frontiers of the Northwest: A History of the Upper Missouri Valley.* New York: D. Appleton-Century Co., 1940.

Brininstool, E. A., ed. *Crazy Horse: The Invincible Ogalalla Sioux Chief.* Los Angeles: Wetzel Publishing, Co., 1949.

———. *Troopers with Custer: Historic Incidents of the Battle of the Little Big Horn.* Harrisburg, Pa.: Stackpole Co., 1952.

Brisbin, James S. *The Beef Bonanza; or, How to Get Rich on the Plains.* Philadelphia: J. B. Lippincott and Co., 1881; reprint Norman: University of Oklahoma Press, 1959.

Brown, Mark H. "A New Focus on the Sioux War." *Montana The Magazine of Western History* 11 (October 1961): 76–85. Reprinted in Paul L. Hedren, ed., *The Great Sioux War 1876–77: The Best from* Montana The Magazine of Western History, 25–37. Helena: Montana Historical Society Press, 1991.

———. *The Plainsmen of the Yellowstone: A History of the Yellowstone Basin.* New York: G. P. Putnam's Sons, 1961.

———. "Rebuttal to a 'Challenge.'" *Montana The Magazine of Western History* 12 (April 1962): 93–95.

Brown, Mark H., and W. R. Felton. *The Frontier Years: L. A. Huffman, Photographer of the Plains.* New York: Bramhill House, 1955.

Brust, James S. "John H. Fouch, First Post Photographer at Fort Keogh." *Montana The Magazine of Western History* 44 (Spring 1994): 2–17.

———. "Stanley J. Morrow's 1879 Photographs of the Little Big Horn Battlefield." In *9th Annual Symposium Custer Battlefield Historical & Museum Association, June 23, 1995,* 47–78. Hardin, Mont.: CBHMA, 1996.

Brust, James S., Brian C. Pohanka, and Sandy Barnard. *Where Custer Fell: Photographs of the Little Bighorn Battlefield Then and Now.* Norman: University of Oklahoma Press, 2005.

Buecker, Thomas R. "'Can You Send Us Immediate Relief'?: Army Expeditions to the Northern Black Hills, 1876–1878." *South Dakota History* 25 (Summer 1995): 95–115.

———. "Fort Niobrara, 1880–1906." *Nebraska History* 65 (Fall 1984): 300–325.

———. *Fort Robinson and the American Century, 1900–1948.* Lincoln: Nebraska State Historical Society, 2002.

———. *Fort Robinson and the American West, 1874–1899.* Lincoln: Nebraska State Historical Society, 1999.

———. "Uncertain Surrender: Crazy Horse at Red Cloud Agency 1877." In *12th Annual Symposium, Custer Battlefield Historical & Museum Assn., Inc., Held at Hardin, Montana on June 26, 1998,* 35–50. Hardin, Mont.: Custer Battlefield Historical and Museum Association, 1998.

Buecker, Thomas R., and R. Eli Paul, eds. *The Crazy Horse Surrender Ledger.* Lincoln: Nebraska State Historical Society, 1994.

Burdick, Usher L. *Tales from Buffalo Land: The Story of Fort Buford.* Baltimore: Wirth Brothers, 1940.

Calloway, Colin G. *One Vast Winter Count: The Native American West before Lewis and Clark.* Lincoln: University of Nebraska Press, 2003.

Clark, Robert A., ed. *The Killing of Chief Crazy Horse.* Lincoln: University of Nebraska Press, 1988.

Clow, Richmond L. "The Anatomy of a Shooting: Crow Dog and Spotted Tail, 1879–1881." *South Dakota History* 28 (Winter 1998): 209–27.

Crawford, Lewis F. *Ranching Days in Dakota and Custer's Black Hills Expedition of 1874.* Baltimore: Wirth Brothers, 1950.

Custer, Elizabeth B. *Boots and Saddles; or, Life in Dakota with General Custer.* New York: Harper and Brothers, 1885.

Dale, Edward E. *The Range Cattle Industry: Ranching on the Great Plains from 1865 to 1925.* Norman: University of Oklahoma Press, 1960.

Daniel, Forrest W. "Dismounting the Sioux." *North Dakota History* 41 (Summer 1974): 8–13.

Davis, John W. *Wyoming Range War: The Infamous Invasion of Johnson County.* Norman: University of Oklahoma Press, 2010.

DeMallie, Raymond J. "The Sioux in Dakota and Montana Territories: Cultural and Historical Background of the Ogden B. Read Collection." In Glenn E. Markoe, ed., *Vestiges of a Proud Nation: The Ogden B. Read Northern Plains Indian Collection,* 18–69. Burlington, Vt.: Robert Hull Fleming Museum, 1986.

Denig, Edwin T. *Five Indian Tribes of the Upper Missouri.* Norman: University of Oklahoma Press, 1961.

Dickson, Ephriam D., III. "Crazy Horse: Who Really Wielded the Bayonet That Killed the Oglala Leader?" *Greasy Grass* 12 (May 1996): 2–10.

Diehl, Charles S. *The Staff Correspondent.* San Antonio: Clegg Co., 1931.

Dobak, William A. "The Army and the Buffalo: A Demur." *Western Historical Quarterly* 26 (Summer 1995): 197–202.

———. "Killing the Canadian Buffalo, 1821–1881." *Western Historical Quarterly* 27 (Spring 1996): 33–52.

Donovan, James. *A Terrible Glory: Custer and the Little Bighorn, The Last Great Battle of the American West.* New York: Little, Brown and Co., 2008.

Dunlay, Thomas W. "James Hervey Pratt: Frontier Entrepreneur." *Nebraska History* 59 (Summer 1978): 210–30.

Ewers, John C. "Intertribal Warfare as the Precursor of Indian-White Warfare on the Northern Great Plains." *Western Historical Quarterly* 6 (October 1975): 397–410.

Farr, William E. "Going to Buffalo: Indian Hunting Migrations across the Rocky Mountains, Part 2, Civilian Permits, Army Escorts." *Montana The Magazine of Western History* 54 (Spring 2004): 26–43.

Faust, Drew Gilpin. *This Republic Is Suffering: Death and the American Civil War.* New York: Alfred A. Knopf, 2008.

Finerty, John F. *War-Path and Bivouac; or, The Conquest of the Sioux.* Chicago: Donohue and Henneberry, 1890.

Fleharty, Eugene D. *Wild Animals and Settlers on the Great Plains.* Norman: University of Oklahoma Press, 1995.

Fletcher, Robert H. *Free Grass to Fences: The Montana Cattle Range Story.* New York: University Publishers, 1960.

Flores, Dan. "Bison Ecology and Plains Diplomacy: The Southern Plains from 1800 to 1850." *Journal of American History* 78 (September 1991): 465–85.

———. *The Natural West: Environmental History in the Great Plains and Rocky Mountains.* Norman: University of Oklahoma Press, 2001.

Franke, Mary Ann. *To Save the Wild Bison: Life on the Edge in Yellowstone.* Norman: University of Oklahoma Press, 2005.

Frazer, Robert W. *Forts of the West: Military Forts and Presidios and Posts Commonly Called Forts West of the Mississippi River to 1898.* Norman: University of Oklahoma Press, 1965.

Frink, Maurice. *Cow Country Cavalcade: Eighty Years of the Wyoming Stock Growers Association.* Denver: Old West Publishing Co., 1954.

Frink, Maurice, W. Turrentine Jackson, and Agnes Wright Spring. *When Grass Was King: Contributions to the Western Range Cattle Industry Study.* Boulder: University of Colorado Press, 1956.

Froiland, Sven G. *Natural History of the Black Hills.* Sioux Falls: Center for Western Studies, Augustana College, 1978.

Fusco, Eugene M. "The Last Hunt of Gen. George A. Crook." *Montana The Magazine of Western History* 12 (Autumn 1962): 36–46.

Galloway, John D. *The First Transcontinental Railroad: Central Pacific, Union Pacific.* New York: Simmons-Boardman, 1950.

Goodyear, Frank H., III. *Red Cloud: Photographs of a Lakota Chief.* Lincoln: University of Nebraska Press, 2003.

Graham, William A. *Abstract of the Official Record of Proceedings of the Reno Court of Inquiry:.* Harrisburg, Pa.: Stackpole Co., 1954.

—————, ed. *The Custer Myth: A Source Book of Custeriana.* Harrisburg, Pa.: Stackpole Co., 1953.

Gray, John S. "Captain Clifford's Story—Part II." *Westerners Brand Book* (Chicago) 26 (January 1970): 81–83, 86–88.

—————. *Centennial Campaign: The Sioux War of 1876.* Fort Collins, Colo.: Old Army Press, 1976.

—————. "Nightmares to Daydreams." *By Valor & Arms: The Journal of American Military History* 1 (Summer 1975): 30–39.

Greene, Jerome A. *Beyond Bear's Paw: The Nez Perce Indians in Canada.* Norman: University of Oklahoma Press, 2010.

—————. *Fort Randall on the Missouri, 1856–1892.* Pierre: South Dakota State Historical Society Press, 2005.

—————, ed. *Lakota and Cheyenne: Indian Views of the Great Sioux War, 1876–1877.* Norman: University of Oklahoma Press, 1994.

—————. *Morning Star Dawn: The Powder River Expedition and the Northern Cheyennes, 1876.* Norman: University of Oklahoma Press, 2003.

—————. *Nez Perce Summer, 1877: The U.S. Army and the Nee-Me-Poo Crisis.* Helena: Montana Historical Society Press, 2000.

—————. "Out with a Whimper: The Little Missouri Expedition and the Close of the Great Sioux War." *South Dakota History* 35 (Spring 2005): 1–39.

—————. "The Sioux Land Commission of 1889: Prelude to Wounded Knee." *South Dakota History* 1 (Winter 1970): 41–72.

—————. *Slim Buttes, 1876: An Episode of the Great Sioux War.* Norman: University of Oklahoma Press, 1982.

—————. *Stricken Field: The Little Bighorn since 1876.* Norman: University of Oklahoma Press, 2008.

—————. *Yellowstone Command: Colonel Nelson A. Miles and the Great Sioux War, 1876–1877.* Lincoln: University of Nebraska Press, 1991.

Grinnell, George B. *The Fighting Cheyennes.* Norman: University of Oklahoma Press, 1956.

Hagedorn, Hermann. *Roosevelt in the Bad Lands.* Boston and New York: Houghton Mifflin Co., 1921.

Hagen, Olaf T., and Ray H. Mattison. "Pyramid Park—Where Roosevelt Came to Hunt." *North Dakota History* 19 October 1952): 215–39.

Haines, Aubrey L. *An Elusive Victory: The Battle of the Big Hole*. West Glacier, Mont.: Glacier Natural History Association, 1991.

Hampton, H. Duane. *How the U.S. Cavalry Saved Our National Parks*. Bloomington: Indiana University Press, 1971.

Hanna, Oliver Perry. *An Old-Timer's Story of the Old Wild West*. Casper, Wyo.: Hawks Book Co., 1984.

Hanson, Joseph M. *The Conquest of the Missouri, Being the Story of the Life and Exploits of Captain Grant Marsh*. Chicago: A. C. McClurg and Co., 1909.

Hardeman, Nicholas P. "Brick Stronghold of the Border: Fort Assinniboine, 1879–1911." *Montana The Magazine of Western History* 29 (April 1979): 54–67.

Hardorff, Richard G. *The Custer Battle Casualties: Burials, Exhumations, and Reinterments*. El Segundo, Calif.: Upton and Sons, Publishers, 1989.

———. *The Oglala Lakota Crazy Horse*. Mattituck, N.Y.: J. M. Carroll and Co., 1985.

———, ed. *The Surrender and Death of Crazy Horse: A Source Book about a Tragic Episode in Lakota History*. Spokane: Arthur H. Clark Co., 1998.

Hedren, Paul L. "Camp Sheridan, Nebraska: The Uncommonly Quiet Post on Beaver Creek." *Nebraska History* 91 (Summer 2010): 80–93.

———, ed. "Eben Swift's Army Service on the Plains, 1876–1879." *Annals of Wyoming* 50 (Spring 1978): 141–55.

———. *Fort Laramie in 1876: Chronicle of a Frontier Post at War*. Lincoln: University of Nebraska Press, 1988.

———. "Garrisoning the Black Hills Road: The United States Army's Camps on Sage Creek and Mouth of Red Canyon, 1876–1877." *South Dakota History* 37 (Spring 2007): 1–45.

———. *Great Sioux War Orders of Battle: How the United States Army Waged War on the Northern Plains, 1876–1877*. Norman: Arthur H. Clark Co., 2011.

———, ed. *The Great Sioux War 1876–77: The Best from* Montana The Magazine of Western History. Helena: Montana Historical Society Press, 1991.

———. "Sitting Bull's Surrender at Fort Buford: An Episode in American History." *North Dakota History* 62 (Fall 1995): 2–15.

———. *Sitting Bull's Surrender at Fort Buford: An Episode in American History*. Williston, N.Dak.: Fort Union Association, 1997.

———. "'Three cool, determined men': The Sioux War Heroism of Privates Evans, Stewart, and Bell." *Montana The Magazine of Western History* 41 (Winter 1991): 14–27.

Hoffbeck, Steven R. "Sully Springs: Saga of a Badlands Railroad Community." *North Dakota History* 58 (Summer 1991): 16–61.

Hoig, Stan. *Perilous Pursuit: The U.S. Cavalry and the Northern Cheyennes.* Boulder: University Press of Colorado, 2002.

Holt, Dean W. *American Military Cemeteries: A Comprehensive Illustrated Guide to the Hallowed Grounds of the United States, Including Cemeteries Overseas.* Jefferson, N.C.: McFarland and Co., 1992.

Hoopes, Lorman L. *This Last West: Miles City, Montana Territory, and Environs, 1876–1886—The People, the Geography, the Incredible History.* Miles City: the author, 1990.

Hornaday, William T. *The Extermination of the American Bison.* Washington, D.C.: Government Printing Office, 1889.

———. "The Passing of the Buffalo." *Cosmopolitan* (October 1887): 85–98 and (November 1887): 231–43.

Huidekoper, A. C. *My Experiences and Investment in the Bad Lands of Dakota and Some of the Men I Met There.* Baltimore: Wirth Brothers, 1947.

Hutchins, James S., ed. The Army and Navy Journal *on the Battle of the Little Bighorn and Related Matters, 1876–1881.* El Segundo, Calif.: Upton and Sons, Publishers, 2003.

Hutton, Paul A. *Phil Sheridan and His Army.* Lincoln: University of Nebraska Press, 1985.

Hyde, George E. *Red Cloud's Folk: A History of the Oglala Sioux Indians.* Norman: University of Oklahoma Press, 1937.

———. *A Sioux Chronicle.* Norman: University of Oklahoma Press, 1980.

———. *Spotted Tail's Folk: A History of the Brulé Sioux.* Norman: University of Oklahoma Press, 1961.

Isenberg, Andrew C. *The Destruction of the Bison.* New York: Cambridge University Press, 2000.

Jackson, Donald. *Custer's Gold: The United States Cavalry Expedition of 1874.* New Haven, Conn.: Yale University Press, 1966.

Jacoby, Karl. *Crimes against Nature: Squatters, Poachers, Thieves, and the Hidden History of American Conservation.* Berkeley: University of California Press, 2001.

Jensen, Richard E., R. Eli Paul, and John E. Carter. *Eyewitness at Wounded Knee.* Lincoln: University of Nebraska Press, 1991.

Johnson, Jeffrey A. "The Gilded Age & the Frontier Military: Society and Culture at Fort Assiniboine, Montana Territory, 1879–1905." *Journal of the West* 45 (Summer 2006): 65–71.

Jordan, Terry G. *North American Cattle-Ranching Frontiers: Origins, Diffusion, and Differentiation.* Albuquerque: University of New Mexico Press, 1993.

Joyner, Christopher C. "The Hegira of Sitting Bull to Canada: Diplomatic Realpolitik, 1876–1881." *Journal of the West* 13 (April 1974): 6–18.

Kadlecek, Edward, and Mabell Kadlecek. *To Kill an Eagle: Indian Views on the Last Days of Crazy Horse.* Boulder, Colo.: Johnson Books, 1981.

Kappler, Charles J., ed. *Indian Affairs: Laws and Treaties.* Washington, D.C.: Government Printing Office, 1903; reprint, *Indian Treaties, 1778–1883.* Mattituck, N.Y.: Amereon House, 1972.

Kelly, Carla. *Fort Buford, Sentinel at the Confluence.* Williston, N.Dak.: Fort Union Association, 2009.

King, Charles. *Campaigning with Crook and Stories of Army Life.* New York: Harper and Brothers, 1890.

Koury, Michael J. *Military Posts of Montana.* Bellevue, Nebr.: Old Army Press, 1970.

Kroeker, Marvin E. *Great Plains Command: William B. Hazen in the Frontier West.* Norman: University of Oklahoma Press, 1976.

Kuykendall, John M. "The First Cattle North of the Union Pacific Railroad." *Colorado Magazine* 7 (March 1930): 69–74.

LaDow, Beth. *The Medicine Line: Life and Death on the Northern American Borderland.* New York: Routledge, 2001.

Lame Deer, John Fire, and Richard Erdoes. *Lame Deer, Seeker of Visions.* New York: Simon and Schuster, 1972.

Larson, Robert W. *Gall, Lakota War Chief.* Norman: University of Oklahoma Press, 2007.

———. *Red Cloud, Warrior-Statesman of the Lakota Sioux.* Norman: University of Oklahoma Press, 1997.

Lass, William E. *A History of Steamboating on the Upper Missouri River.* Lincoln: University of Nebraska Press, 1962.

Latham, Hiram. *Trans-Missouri Stock Raising.* Denver: Old West Publishing Company, 1962.

Leckie, William H. "Buell's Campaign." *Red River Valley Historical Review* 3 (Spring 1978): 186–95.

Lee, Jessie M. "The Capture and Death of an American Chieftain." *Journal of the Military Service Institution* 54 (1914): 323–40.

Lee, Robert. *Fort Meade and the Black Hills.* Lincoln: University of Nebraska Press, 1991.

Lindmier, Tom. *Drybone: A History of Fort Fetterman, Wyoming.* Glendo, Wyo.: High Plains Press, 2002.

Lookingbill, Brad D. *War Dance at Fort Marion: Plains Indian Prisoners.* Norman: University of Oklahoma, 2006.

Lott, Dale F. *American Bison: A Natural History.* Berkeley: University of California Press, 2002.

Lubetkin, M. John. "The Forgotten Yellowstone Surveying Expeditions of 1871: W. Milnor Roberts and the Northern Pacific Railroad in

Montana." *Montana The Magazine of Western History* 52 (Winter 2002): 32–47.

———. *Jay Cooke's Gamble: The Northern Pacific Railroad, the Sioux, and the Panic of 1873.* Norman: University of Oklahoma Press, 2006.

Madsen, Betty M., and Brigham D. Madsen. *North to Montana: Jehus, Bullwhackers, and Mule Skinners on the Montana Trail.* Salt Lake City: University of Utah Press, 1980.

Malone, Dumas, and Basil Rauch. *Crisis of the Union, 1841–1877.* New York: Appleton-Century-Crofts, 1960.

Malone, Michael P., and Richard B. Roeder. "The Centennial Year in Montana: In the Field and Pasture—Agriculture." *Montana The Magazine of Western History* 25 (Spring 1975): 20–35.

Manzione, Joseph. *"I Am Looking to the North for My Life": Sitting Bull, 1876–1881.* Salt Lake City: University of Utah Press, 1991.

Marquis, Thomas. *Custer, Cavalry & Crows: The Story of William White.* Fort Collins, Colo.: Old Army Press, 1975.

Mattison, Ray H. "The Hard Winter and the Range Cattle Business." *The Montana Magazine of History* 1 (October 1951): 5–21.

———. "Ranching in the Dakota Badlands: A Study of Roosevelt's Contemporaries, Part 1." *North Dakota History* 19 (April 1952): 93–128.

———. "Ranching in the Dakota Badlands: A Study of Roosevelt's Contemporaries, Part 2." *North Dakota History* 19 (July 1952): 167–206.

———. *Roosevelt's Dakota Ranches.* Bismarck: [State Historical Society of North Dakota], n.d.

McChristian, Douglas C. *Fort Laramie: Military Bastion of the High Plains.* Norman: Arthur H. Clark Co., 2009.

McClernand, Edward J. *On Time for Disaster.* Lincoln: University of Nebraska Press, 1989.

McDermott, John D. *Red Cloud's War: The Bozeman Trail, 1866–1868.* Norman: Arthur H. Clark Co., 2010.

McGrady, David G. *Living with Strangers: The Nineteenth-Century Sioux and the Canadian-American Borderlands.* Lincoln: University of Nebraska Press, 2006.

McHugh, Tom. *The Time of the Buffalo.* New York: Alfred A. Knopf, 1972.

McIntosh, Charles B. *The Nebraska Sand Hills: The Human Landscape.* Lincoln: University of Nebraska Press, 1996.

Meagher, Margaret M. *The Bison of Yellowstone National Park.* Washington, D.C.: National Park Service, 1973.

Monnett, John H. *Tell Them We Are Going Home: The Odyssey of the Northern Cheyennes.* Norman: University of Oklahoma Press, 2001.

Morris, Edmund. *The Rise of Theodore Roosevelt.* New York: Coward, McCann and Geoghegan, 1979.

Murphy, Edward C. "The Northern Pacific Railway Bridge at Bismarck." *North Dakota History* 62 (Spring 1995): 2–19.

Murray, Robert A. *Military Posts in the Powder River Country of Wyoming, 1865–1894.* Lincoln: University of Nebraska Press, 1968.

Nichols, Ronald H. *In Custer's Shadow: Major Marcus Reno.* Fort Collins, Colo.: Old Army Press, 1999.

———, comp. and ed. *Reno Court of Inquiry: Proceedings of a Court of Inquiry in the Case of Major Marcus A. Reno.* Hardin, Mont.: Custer Battlefield Historical and Museum Association, 2007.

Nolan, Edward W. *Northern Pacific Views: The Railroad Photography of F. Jay Haynes, 1876–1905.* Helena: Montana Historical Society Press, 1983.

———. "'Not without Labor and Expense': The Villard-Northern Pacific Last Spike Excursion, 1883." *Montana The Magazine of Western History* 33 (Summer 1983): 2–11.

Nugent, Walter. "The American Habit of Empire, and the Cases of Polk and Bush." *Western Historical Quarterly* 38 (Spring 2007): 5–24.

———. *Habits of Empire: A History of American Expansion.* New York: Alfred A. Knopf, 2008.

Olson, James C. *Red Cloud and the Sioux Problem.* Lincoln: University of Nebraska Press, 1965.

Osgood, Ernest S. *The Day of the Cattleman.* Minneapolis: University of Minnesota Press, 1929.

Ostler, Jeffrey. *The Plains Sioux and U.S. Colonialism from Lewis and Clark to Wounded Knee.* New York: Cambridge University Press, 2004.

Outline Descriptions of the Posts in the Military Division of the Missouri, Commanded by Lieutenant General P. H. Sheridan. Chicago: Headquarters Military Division of the Missouri, 1876; reprint, Bellevue, Nebr.: Old Army Press, 1969.

Papandrea, Ronald J. *They Never Surrendered: The Lakota Sioux Band That Stayed in Canada.* Warren, Mich.: the author, 2003.

Parker, Watson. *Gold in the Black Hills.* Norman: University of Oklahoma Press, 1966.

Paul, R. Eli, ed. *Autobiography of Red Cloud, War Leader of the Oglalas.* Helena: Montana Historical Society Press, 1997.

———. "An Early Reference to Crazy Horse." *Nebraska History* 75 (Summer 1994): 189–90.

Pearson, Jeffrey V. "Tragedy at Red Cloud Agency: The Surrender, Confinement, and Death of Crazy Horse." *Montana The Magazine of Western History* 55 (Summer 2005): 14–27.

Pelzer, Louis. *The Cattlemen's Frontier: A Record of the Trans-Mississippi Cattle Industry from Oxen Trails to Pooling Companies, 1850–1890.* Glendale, Calif.: Arthur H. Clark Co., 1936.

Peterson, John M., ed. "Buffalo Hunting in Montana in 1886: The Diary of W. Harvey Brown." *Montana The Magazine of Western History* 31 (October 1981): 2–13.

Powell, Peter J. *People of the Sacred Mountain: A History of the Northern Cheyenne Chiefs and Warrior Societies, 1830–1879,* 2 vols. San Francisco: Harper and Row, 1981.

———. *Sweet Medicine: The Continuing Role of the Sacred Arrows, the Sun Dance, and the Sacred Buffalo Hat in Northern Cheyenne History.* 2 vols. Norman: University of Oklahoma Press, 1969.

Punke, Michael. *Last Stand: George Bird Grinnell, the Battle to Save the Buffalo, and the Birth of the New West.* New York: Harper-Collins Publishers, 2007.

Rackley, Barbara F. "The Hard Winter of 1886–1887." *Montana The Magazine of Western History* 21 (January 1971): 50–59.

Rankin, Charles E., ed. *Legacy: New Perspectives on the Battle of the Little Bighorn.* Helena: Montana Historical Society Press, 1996.

Records of Living Officers of the United States Army. Philadelphia: L. R. Hamersly and Co., 1884.

Rees, Tony. *Arc of the Medicine Line: Mapping the World's Longest Undefended Border across the Western Plains.* Lincoln: University of Nebraska Press, 2007.

Reno Court of Inquiry. Ed. *Chicago Times.* Fort Collins, Colo.: Old Army Press, 1972.

Reno Court of Inquiry. Ed. *Saint Paul and Minneapolis Pioneer Press.* Howell, Mich.: Powder River Press, 1993.

Renz, Louis T. *The History of the Northern Pacific Railroad.* Fairfield, Wash.: Ye Galleon Press, 1980.

Reports of Inspection Made in the Summer of 1877 by Generals P. H. Sheridan and W. T. Sherman of Country North of the Union Pacific Railroad. Washington, D.C.: Government Printing Office, 1878; reprint, Fairfield, Wash.: Ye Galleon Press, 1984.

Richardson, Ernest M. "Moreton Frewen: Cattle King with Monocle." *Montana The Magazine of Western History* 11 (Autumn 1961): 38–45.

Roberts, Gary L. "The Shame of Little Wolf." *Montana The Magazine of Western History* 28 (July 1978): 36–47.

Robertson, Francis B. "'We Are Going to Have a Big Sioux War': Colonel David S. Stanley's Yellowstone Expedition, 1872." *Montana The Magazine of Western History* 34 (Autumn 1984): 2–15.

Robinson, Charles M., III, ed. *The Diaries of John Gregory Bourke, Volume Two, July 29, 1876–April 7, 1878.* Denton: University of North Texas Press, 2005.

———. *General Crook and the Western Frontier.* Norman: University of Oklahoma Press, 2001.

————. *A Good Year to Die: The Story of the Great Sioux War.* New York: Random House, 1995.

Roe, Frank G. *The North American Buffalo: A Critical Study of the Species in Its Wild State.* Toronto: University of Toronto Press, 1951.

Rollinson, John K. *Wyoming Cattle Trails.* Caldwell, Idaho: Caxton Printers, 1948.

Rolston, Alan. "The Yellowstone Expedition of 1873." *Montana The Magazine of Western History* 20 (April 1970): 20–29.

Roosevelt, Theodore. *Hunting Trips of a Ranchman & The Wilderness Hunter.* New York: Modern Library, 1996.

Russell, Don. "How Many Indians Were Killed?" *American West* 10 (July 1973): 42–47, 61–63.

————. *The Lives and Legends of Buffalo Bill.* Norman: University of Oklahoma Press, 1960.

Schuler, Harold H. *Fort Sully: Guns at Sunset.* Vermillion: University of South Dakota Press, 1992.

Scott, Hugh Lenox. *Some Memories of a Soldier.* New York: Century Company, 1928.

Sellars, Richard West. "Vigil of Silence: The Civil War Memorials." *History News* (July–August 1986): 19–21.

Shell, Hanna Rose. "Last of the Wild Buffalo." *Smithsonian* (February 2000): 26, 28, 30.

Sheridan, Michael V. *Personal Memoirs of Philip Henry Sheridan.* 2 vols. New York: D. Appleton and Co., 1904.

Smalley, Eugene V. *History of the Northern Pacific Railroad.* New York: G. P. Putnam's Sons, 1883.

Smith, Victor G. *The Champion Buffalo Hunter: The Frontier Memoirs of Yellowstone Vic Smith.* Helena. Mont.: Twodot, 1997.

Smits, David D. "The Frontier Army and the Destruction of the Buffalo: 1865–1883." *Western Historical Quarterly* 25 (Autumn 1994): 312–38.

Spring, Agnes Wright. *The Cheyenne and Black Hills Stage and Express Routes.* Glendale, Calif.: Arthur H. Clark Co., 1949.

————. *Seventy Years: A Panoramic History of the Wyoming Stock Growers Association Interwoven with Data Relative to the Cattle Industry in Wyoming.* N.p.: Wyoming Stock Growers Association, 1942.

Stands in Timber, John, and Margot Liberty. *Cheyenne Memories.* New Haven, Conn.: Yale University Press, 1967.

Starita, Joe. *The Dull Knifes of Pine Ridge: A Lakota Odyssey.* New York: G. P. Putnam's Sons, 1995.

Steltenkamp, Michael F. *Nicholas Black Elk: Medicine Man, Missionary, Mystic.* Norman: University of Oklahoma Press, 2009.

Stewart, Edgar I. "The Custer Battle and Widow's Weeds." *Montana The Magazine of Western History* 22 (January 1972): 52–59.

——, ed. *Penny-an-Acre Empire in the West.* Norman: University of Oklahoma Press, 1968.

Stuart, Granville. *Pioneering in Montana: The Making of a State, 1864–1887.* Lincoln: University of Nebraska Press, 1977.

Stuart, Leland E. "The Winter of 1886–1887: The Last of Whose 5,000?" *Montana The Magazine of Western History* 38 (Winter 1988): 32–41.

Sundstrom, Linea. *Cultural History of the Black Hills with Reference to Adjacent Areas of the Northern Plains.* Reprints in Anthropology, vol. 40. Lincoln, Nebr.: J & L Reprint Co., 1989.

——. "The Sacred Black Hills: An Ethnohistorical Review." *Great Plains Quarterly* 17 (Summer/Fall 1997): 185–212.

Svingen, Orlan J. *The Northern Cheyenne Indian Reservation, 1877–1900.* Niwot: University Press of Colorado, 1993.

Taunton, Francis B., ed. *"No Pride in the Little Big Horn."* London: English Westerners' Society, 1987.

Topping, E. S. *Chronicles of the Yellowstone.* Minneapolis: Ross and Haines, 1968.

Tweton, D. Jerome. *The Marquis de Morès, Dakota Capitalist, French Nationalist.* Fargo: North Dakota Institute for Regional Studies, 1972.

Upton, Richard, ed. *Fort Custer on the Big Horn, 1877–1898.* Glendale, Calif.: Arthur H. Clark Co., 1973.

Utley, Robert M. *Frontier Regulars: The United States Army and the Indian, 1866–1890.* New York: Macmillan Publishing Co., 1973.

——. *The Indian Frontier of the American West, 1846–1890.* Albuquerque: University of New Mexico Press, 1984.

——. *The Lance and the Shield: The Life and Times of Sitting Bull.* New York: Henry Holt and Co., 1993.

——. "Origins of the Great Sioux War: The Brown-Anderson Controversy Revisited." *Montana The Magazine of Western History* 42 (Autumn 1992): 48–52.

Vaughn, J. W. *The Reynolds Campaign on Powder River.* Norman: University of Oklahoma Press, 1961.

West, Carroll Van. *Capitalism on the Frontier: Billings and the Yellowstone Valley in the Nineteenth Century.* Lincoln: University of Nebraska Press, 1993.

West, Elliott. *The Contested Plains: Indians, Goldseekers, and the Rush to Colorado.* Lawrence: University Press of Kansas, 1998.

——. *The Way to the West: Essays on the Central Plains.* Albuquerque: University of New Mexico Press, 1995.

Wheeler, Homer W. *Buffalo Days: Forty Years in the Old West.* New York: A. L. Burt Co., Publishers, 1925.

White, Richard. "The Winning of the West: The Expansion of the Western Sioux in the Eighteenth and Nineteenth Centuries." *Journal of American History* 65 (September 1978): 319–32.

Wilhelm, Thomas. *A Military Dictionary and Gazetteer.* Philadelphia: L. R. Hamersly and Co., 1881.

Willert, James. "The Sibley Scout." *Research Review: Journal of the Little Big Horn Associates* 9 (January 1995): 24–31.

Williams, Roger L. *Military Register of Custer's Last Command.* Norman: Arthur H. Clark Co., 2009.

Winther, Oscar O. *The Transportation Frontier: Trans-Mississippi West, 1865–1890.* New York: Holt, Rinehart and Winston, 1964.

Woods, Lawrence M. *Alex Swan and the Swan Companies.* Norman: Arthur H. Clark Co., 2006.

———. *Wyoming's Big Horn Basin to 1901: A Late Frontier.* Spokane, Wash.: Arthur H. Clark Co., 1997.

Yost, Nellie Snyder. *The Call of the Range: The Story of the Nebraska Stock Growers Association.* Denver: Sage Books, 1966.

Zimmer, William F. *Frontier Soldier: An Enlisted Man's Journal of the Sioux and Nez Perce Campaigns, 1877.* Ed. Jerome A. Greene. Helena: Montana Historical Society Press, 1998.

Newspapers

Army and Navy Journal, 1877, 1879.
Benton Record, 1877.
Cheyenne Daily Leader, 1876, 1877.
Cheyenne Daily Sun, 1879.
Chicago Times, 1877.
Mandan Daily Pioneer, 1887.
New York Herald, 1877.
Omaha Daily Bee, 1877.
Saint Paul and Minneapolis Pioneer Press, 1877.
Sioux City Journal, 1891.

Index